THE MIRROR
ON
STILL WATER

A Journey To the Heart Of love

The Mirror on Still Water
A Journey to the Heart of Love

From our Elder Brother Jesus
Scribed by Joel Wright

ISBN: 978-0-9767485-4-0

Second Edition Published by Project Healing Press

Edited By: Robert Stoelting, Pathways of Light

Cover and Interior Design: Susan Sylvia, Staircase Press Design

Printed in the United States of America

Copyright © 2009 by WLH LLC

First edition © 1997 by Joel Wright
1st Printing November 1997

ISBN: 0-87418-325-1

The Mirror on Still Water
A Journey to the Heart of Love

As given by our Elder Brother Jesus
Scribed By Joel Wright
Presented by: Laszlo and Agnes More, Thornton Mortensen, Ila B. Richter and Saul Steinberg

Project Healing Press
St. Louis, Missouri
www.projecthealingpress.com

PROJECT
HEALING
PRESS

Excerpt from *The Book ON... and Jesus Answers*
© 2009 WLH LLC

On Practicing The Cycle of Healing
Reprinted from *The Book ON... and Jesus Answers*
© 2008, 2009 Mary Gerard

Excerpt from *The Mentor Within – Let Your SELF Be Seen*
© 2006, 2008 Mary Gerard

Excerpt from *Visions of Illumination*
© 2009 Mary Gerard

Excerpt from *The Peace of God is my One Goal*
© 1989 by Sharing Miracles, Houston, TX

THE MIRROR ON STILL WATER

A Journey To the Heart Of Love

From our Elder Brother Jesus

Scribed by Joel Wright

ACKNOWLEDGMENTS

My life and my work come full circle now, in part because of an inclination from one man, Mark Allen Lavin, who in 1982 dropped a package of miracles on my doorstep. Thanks to him I learned that miracles are indeed ours to share.

My thanks to José Hernandez and his "friends" for their help in moving this material closer to its printed form.

Thanks to Ila B. Richter and Thornton K. Mortensen for their long editorial labors over the manuscript of this book.

To Saul Steinberg, I am so very grateful for his being able to answer my deepened prayer to have this material published that all the world may see.

And thanks to my beautiful Lila for her loyal support, gut level honesty and a heart of devotion to God, all of which I received so deeply that now I can truly give.

I love you all…

Joel Wright

December 8, 1997

DEDICATION

To Paula Elaine Wright,
the incredible daughter of my dreams
— my child of God —
who brought and brings to us all
the joyous Light of our real Father's Love …
I love you.

And to each and every other child of God,
who will someday surely
shed the "skin" of being "only human,"
to risk a metamorphosis into
gentleness, innocence and Divine illumination,
to become What you truly are,
God's miracle workers.

TABLE OF CONTENTS

1 THE MIRROR ON STILL WATER

A Journey to the Heart of Love

2 DISCUSSIONS, QUESTIONS AND TEACHINGS

The Relationship of Sickness to Guilt: Obsessions, Abuse, Depression and Recovery

3 EMPLOYMENT AND THE REAL PURPOSE OF THE WORLD

7 LIVING FOR LIGHT AND PEACE

The Mirror On Still Water

A Journey To the Heart Of love

INTRODUCTION

Since this is one of the few places in *The Mirror on Still Water* in which I speak personally to you as the scribe of this material, I would like to take this time to explain to each of you what I think this book is about.

First, let me explain what it means to be a "scribe." Scribing is not as unusual as one may think. We all do it at times in our lives — those times when something slips out of our mouths or onto paper that seems to be the perfect quip, bringing joy and laughter to all it touches. There are many recorded documents that are truly inspired through the work of a scribe. This is one such document, one in which Jesus and the Holy Spirit speaks through me to all. I use the word "Jesus" because it comforts me and because this is how the Voice identifies himself to me. It should be noted, however, that Jesus, the Holy Spirit and God *are* all One. There are many names for the higher Love we all share. *Use what comforts you.*

When I originally began this book, I expected it to be only reflections from the Christ that would come through me about what we are *all* doing here. I had no idea that Jesus had something else in mind for the book's purpose. As it turned out, portions of the book are a general message to all of us that Jesus uses to prepare us for the other portions, which are his direct assistance to a person who has asked for help. It seems also that the entries between each of the personal scribings are more an explanation of what we are all preparing to experience *together*. The personal scribings are based more on real life experiences in which people have truly asked for help and who have received specific, direct guidance through me from Jesus. The core of the book is thus more "real life" because it is a witness to actual communications with him, as well as true life healings that have occurred as a direct result.

As you read the first chapter of introduction to him in the material, bear in mind that Jesus' viewpoint is reversed from typical views of the body and the world we see ourselves in. This stands to reason, since all he wants and has is Heaven, while all we *seem* to have is the potential for Heaven, because what we want is quite wide open to question. We *see* a world based on an experience largely founded in fear with a moment here and there of experiencing truth and real Love, while he lives in only the real experience of Love and of being loved, and thus teaches only Love. That is why he does what he does and indeed he does it with His perfect consistency.

Jesus has a wonderful sense of humor. Throughout the book he teaches us that it is important to laugh at the silliness of our worldly situation. He repeatedly advises us not to take the world, or ourselves, seriously. He does, however, approach each of us with a dialogue for healing that is not serious, but *sincere* in intent. This is because this is our one true need in this world. If we read carefully "between the lines," we can easily see his joyous smile and the happiness he is leading us to.

Lastly, it has been suggested by Jesus that we read this book meditatively. If you read it simply to obtain theoretical ideas or in a hurry as if it were a novel, you will no doubt miss the overall teaching. Jesus is a master in gentleness and true healing. Those who will not take the little time for themselves to be quiet and gentle with themselves may have difficulty or resistance to hearing his messages. However, he reminds us that the rewards will be powerful for those who do take the time to just be still. This is *his* book to help us with *our experience* in the world we live in today. It is not meant to offer a lofty and theoretical approach to living our lives. It is his guidance for active and proper decision making in real life.

I hope you may be able to take them to heart as I have been able to in putting together this inspirational work. May gentle laughter follow you and find you. God bless you in God's Light.

Joel Wright

INTRODUCING
THE VOICE FOR LOVE

The sound of stillness — It is this sacred sound which cannot be heard with the sentient ears. Nor can words express its tones, nor eyes see its hues. It is a sound that is heard in Spirit. The sound of Christ is within the burbling of a summer creek, within the rhythmic wisps blown through leaves that flutter from the windy fall. It is the gentleness within a baby's sigh. It is what you all long to hear, yet often fear to listen for. Your very being contains the Voice for this lovely expression, for deep within you, in your very essence, your Spirit yearns to meet you where the mirror on still water abides.

MANY WORLDS

In each mind there are many worlds, but in Spirit there is One. It appears to each of you that you are experiencing one world together, but I assure you that this is far from the case. Your worlds change from moment to moment and through each of your choices, another world seems to appear. Some of you seem stuck in only one world and from above we view this as somewhat unfortunate, for those who cannot seem to experience a change in their views believe they are in a sort of "hell." For to them a change of view means utter disaster, because it would also mean a loss of all they hold dear. But for those who willingly give up their worlds for another, they will find deepening; they will embrace in their risk a glorious rebirth into an understanding of the depth and power of their own minds. Through this process they will find, in their own heart, the wisdom of a Power unknown in the everyday world they seem to share together.

Yet it is not as easy to simply change your worlds as you may think. It is in fact your very thinking born of habit that seems to keep the world in place, unchanging and stunted in its ability to offer more than mere drab and often painful repetitiveness. Through each world you invent and seek to keep in place, an incredible, and I dare say impossible, process begins. Yet it will not seem impossible, but true to you who made it. It is a process which involves enormous effort on your part and one which goes against the entire purpose you were created for. Yet since it is you who have placed a value on your "creation," absolutely no one, not even God Who created you, would dare to take it away from you. You may indeed ask yourself, "Why would I make such a world that I might value above the flowingness of Creation which God so freely gave me?" And Spirit's gentle answer:

"My child, you must have forgotten from Where you Came. I will remind you, should you ask to remember your holy Name."

Because of the simple fact that you believe you have made such a seemingly separate world, it only stands to reason that you must also cherish it until something else is introduced that seems more becoming. So, as you wallow deeper into your individual mires of seeming self-sacrifice and suffering, it becomes more and more necessary for those of us who have trudged this very same path once before, to offer you assistance from another World that far exceeds the present one in which you seem to "live." This is why I have come today: To remind you that, having been where you are and now being Where I am, I might gently serve as a reminder that might ease and lift you up from a world that often seems painful and "real."

For thousands of years great healers have lived here who have spoken at times about the very same thing I am speaking of now. Imagine what it might be like if thousands of these healers were placed in your world all at the same time. Now imagine millions. What do you think might happen to the world you share with one another? Never in time has this happened. In time it is not necessary or possible for each of you to visibly "see" this happening, but it will and it is happening right now. Where you say? In what you all term as the "silent revolution." Others call it the "second coming." This we find somewhat amusing from our viewpoint, for I assure you that one is quite sufficient indeed! For the coming of Christ will not wait on time. *My return* has *come for you* now.

BREAKING AWAY

Each one of you came into the physical world with two purposes, one which you invented and another which was created for you. Had you kept in mind only the purpose God gave to you, certainly you wouldn't have had the need to experience the present dilemma you see yourself in. The fact that you are here in this world holds only one truly valuable point — that you are now indeed confused. Denying this confusion is possible, but hardly honest. Indeed, this kind of dishonesty is what made the world so poignantly real to you. In a world as dense as you have chosen to be in, is it any wonder that you might so easily equate death with Life and Life with death? Yet every time you succumb to anger, this is exactly what you are doing to yourself. Anger, as justified and as real as it may seem, is perhaps the most dishonest of all the emotions you are capable of. It is confusion that has been denied.

One would think that the mind should be capable of overcoming the confusion that this world brings. Many have spent most of their lives attempting to do just that, only to admit failure in the end. The mind they see as their self becomes, shall we say, a questionable asset. Then somehow, in this failure, they are suddenly lifted from the very confusion they have worked all their lives to rise above. In failure there is no denial.

I will explain something to you now that might at first seem preposterous. Like each of you, I have a Mind. Yet I have no particular body that I must nurture, clothe and feed. As the Christ, I am quite content to be in all of you, just as you are all in me. Once having had a body, I know what your experience in the world can be like. But I do not choose to identify with it because I once realized, not in time but *in* eternity, that I have only *one* purpose, not two. Inventing another purpose at this point would hardly be helpful to you or me.

The difference between my Mind and your earthly mind (ego) is quite simple — yours was invented for the purpose of separation and mine was created *for* and *as* Unity. You may think that I have to think just like you think in order for me to share this expression with you. Appearances are deceptive just *because* they are appearances. Even this message may seem to be a scattering of many different words with many possible interpretations. Yet if you were to quiet your mind and listen very carefully, you would instantly see that my message is only One. It has but one direction and purpose. It is unambiguous though, through your own personal interpretation, it could become easily confused.

The mind you *see* yourself in *is* an interpretation and is *always* open to question. Thus the identity that you have taken is equally open to question. Your own mind was invented *for* the purpose of confusion and forgetting, although it *can* be utilized on behalf of remembering and clarity. Salvation, as you call it, is only this — remembering.

Your own human mind is connected to a tiny thread of Light, which leads to the Divine Mind of our Creator. In no way is it possible that these minds shall ever reunite. You will not take your human mind into eternity with you and this thought is very threatening to you. However I assure you that the shift is indeed quite harmless.

In offering this information to you, it is not as if I must think about what to say to you. In using the Divine Mind, one of the prerequisites is that I must not *think* for my "self." In your world you call this spontaneity or intuition: That is when one suddenly forgets his or her own mind and hears another Voice. Usually this is uplifting to you except when there is a sense of danger. When danger is present, you may hear your guiding angel say, "Get out of the way!" You would likely hear it not in words, but in feelings, as if you were suddenly kicked out of your present awareness into an altered awareness. In times of playfulness, when you are not guarding your thoughts or territory, you may find yourself saying the silliest things to a loved one and wondering where it came from. On the other hand, those of you who are more at home in your intuition may find it very distressing when it seems that you are once again locked into the world's robotic way of thinking. Each of you are experiencing the exact level of spiritual awareness that you are capable of accepting and feeling safe in. It is perfectly fine with God wherever you find yourself.

Not having a body makes it easy for me only in the sense that I am no longer caught up in the physical-sensual world of time. I have a function to fulfill all the same and I cannot fulfill it without your cooperation. I live in the Mind of God, a state of mind which is potential to you, yet completely accessible to you at any given moment in time. Your true function is not to do anything on your own. Rather, it is only to be fully willing to listen to and follow the still small Voice within. This is a Voice you are not likely to be accustomed to hearing, for it is a Voice that speaks not in mere words, a hearing that does not require the body's ears. It is the Voice for joy. It is the Voice for Love. It is the Voice you share with the One Who created you. It is What you will someday soon become, not by change, but through remembrance and awakening.

You have not come to the earth to save it, to fix your sisters and brothers, or to even change one tiny thing. *That is what put you here in the first place.* That is your problem, not your answer. Yet the answer to your every problem only waits on you and will become clearer to your heart as you lay down the "tools" you have thought to utilize on "salvation's" behalf. Do not be so interested in your own thinking, but learn to be aware of what your private thoughts are trying to teach you. No matter how hard you might try, you cannot learn of your Self through them. Nor will one lesson in complete happiness ever come from the thoughts which seem to make your private world yours alone.

THE TRAVEL OUT OF TIME

It is in your joining with one another that you will all agree to travel out of time together. You can no more be happy alone than you could leave the world alone. You are each bound to your world only by the gravity of your unhealed relationships. It is those whom you have put out of your hearts that bind you to hell. Oh yes, hell is right here where you have each put it, *in your unhealed relationships.*

It is in your true nature only to give and receive. However, when you want something of another you do not believe you have, you are not truly giving and receiving, just getting and taking in exchange for something you deem "valuable." Your whole world is set up this way. It is hell, is it not?

I will tell you that you are all at a crucial point in your spiritual evolution. Heed my words. You each need to take healing sincerely. I do not mean that you should be serious in your minds, only sincere in your hearts. As far as your own thinking is concerned, I do not take it at all seriously. Why should you? Regarding the healing of what you think with your mind, this is an affair of only the heart. For it is in your hidden hearts where you store the pain thought by an unhealed mind. In the depth of your mind, where this subconscious "heart" resides, you carry with you all the memories unforgiven. The memories are a "key." For behind your heart is the Heart of Hearts — the Heart of Love in Which *you truly live.*

It is reasonable for you each to ask, "What makes it so difficult for all of us here to live in true peace?" If you all knew the answer to this question and could readily accept the answer to it as well, there would be no world as you see it. Yet the memories of all of your suffering together prevent you from recognizing it. If I were to simply give you the answer, you would scoff and laugh; you would not be able to accept the answer in its simplicity. Yours is a world of complication designed by each of you to prevent yourselves from seeing with the Vision of Christ by focusing on fear through the "sight" of the body's eyes.

As we go on in our quest for this answer within the material I am offering you, we will attempt to answer this question together. It is our relationship that will heal the world. That is, you asking your many different questions and me offering the *one Solution* that will heal the world. I have the total willingness to listen to your questions carefully and provide you with meaningful answers. All I now need is your total willingness to listen and receive what you have asked for. If you can do this, you will soon understand the importance of your relationships with everyone, God and your Self. There are many questions that you have each asked me to answer. There are many of you who have not had the opportunity to directly ask me your specific questions within this material. I will tell you that this does not really matter. All of the questions you are asking are the same. So is the answer. As we progress, you will realize that this is so. You will clearly understand the answer to the question, "What makes it so difficult for all of us here to live in true peace?" When enough of you are able *together* to accept the gift this answer offers, I say to you now with all my heart in God's, your suffering here *will* end here.

How is it you think you will leave time? Do you think your body must be laid to rest for you to accomplish this? Of course you do! Why else would you each be so busy testing new techniques for your body's destruction? How is one who uses a needle to inject himself with a fluid, sending himself to temporary oblivion, different from that of the one who avoids his family by becoming a "workaholic?" There is no difference at all. In fact, the one who is "legally" destroying himself slowly makes it all the more difficult for you to understand that it *is* the same. This is what I meant when I said, "Let he who has not sinned cast the first stone." There is not one of you, no matter how spiritually accomplished or successful, who at some time has not acted destructively. Even in your euphoric hour of momentary lapse from this kind of thinking, there is not one of you who did not stand back and point your finger and say, "He's the one with the problem!" Humorous, don't you think?

Herein lies your dilemma together. You each *think* the problem is outside you where you have no control over it, somewhere in another body or in another place. By this thinking, you render yourselves powerless to make a change. For in this thinking you have also made a secret and unconscious purchase. You have bought the belief, hook, line and sinker, that correction of your problems lies "out there."

So it is that by your will, time is made to have a firmer hold on you. By attempting to find the solution "out there," you have each solidified your "reality" in the world. Indeed, you have signed up for an endless journey to nowhere! In your own minds, you will seek in all kinds of endless diversions to find again the answer to our previous question, "What makes it so difficult for all of us here to find true peace in the world?" You will look there, move here, try this and avoid that! Look carefully at your lives and you will see that this is for the most part exactly what you have been doing.

Now for a moment, put yourselves in the position of a man or woman in the very last stages of AIDS. What would you now be doing with your lives? Would you move across the world to find purer water? Would you change your religion? What might you do with your last few hours in this world? You would not have something to fix or change, or to learn from someone "greater" than you what you had forgotten. In truth, many would now be learning from you, for you would become their witness unto something far greater than anything the world could ever offer. *And you would not be wasting any more time.*

You may say, "Well, I don't have AIDS. Why should I be concerned about my use of time now?" I will say to each of you as gently as I can and with great joy in my heart, "You each have a fatal disease." This is not meant to frighten you. It is merely a fact of what seems to be your existence here. The world you are experiencing now and all you have ever done will simply cease to be. In truth it already has. You will be left with only what we share together, your eternal Self in God. In this understanding, once you have achieved it, you will find that in truth there is no death at all. Therefore, be not concerned with wasting time, but only with saving time for yourself and everyone, thus entirely escaping time for your own happy release into *Life*.

Yet this is much simpler said than done, for you have made the world to escape from Life. You each carry with you the guilt of this painful "journey." This is why you all are so often preoccupied with being destructive. You wish to remember Life by destroying what is not life. This gets you ever deeper into your dilemma, for you cannot escape a world you have made to escape from God.

Indeed, by the very attempt of being destructive in any form, you have made "real" what could never be real in truth. This has become a seemingly endless prison in the millions of years you measure as "time." You have each lived a thousand lives, maybe more, to come again to undo the gigantic mistake you once made. That mistake, in all its seeming terror and hatred, was a tiny mad instant in which you each believed you as "you" had separated from God. In that instant, your world was made.

That is why the picture of the world that you each must see is a picture of the crucifixion of the Son of God. It is an endless replay of something that seemed to happen long, long ago in time, but never at all in eternity. And now you are each faced with the undoing of a dream made seemingly "real," seemingly alive apart from Life, seemingly unending. I have come today to lead you Home.

A Journey into Life

It is not in laying your body down that you will necessarily remember Heaven. After all, hell is a *choice*, just as Heaven is. Hell, being what you have made of the world, serves a purpose for you. Because *you* are eternal, so is hell, *if* that is what you want. Yet it is hardly something you are condemned to, if you will simply make another choice! That choice must be made in the place you seem to be. If it is hell where you see yourself, then you must remember Heaven in hell. How else could you learn the difference in what you want? That is why you came here. You forgot what the difference is. Now you need to remember.

Contrary to what your egos would teach you, your journey here is for you to remember Heaven in your conscious experience while here in the world. This is the *only* way to leave your world behind peacefully. It is the only way you have set up for yourselves that will now allow you to see without a doubt that your world, that is the hell you have made, *does not exist*. If you were to leave the world without this understanding experientially, then you would no doubt be afraid of both God and Heaven. And we all know what happened the last time we had a thought like that, don't we?

It would serve you well if you use time only on behalf of allowing the Holy Spirit to undo all of your fear. A simple way to put this is to say to you, "Learn how to *unbite* the forbidden fruit." This involves retraining your mind to think along the lines of undoing the thoughts that made it appear necessary to even think in the first place. How does one think about not thinking? It begins with understanding that it is essential not to take your own thoughts or the thoughts of others seriously. A serious attitude is indeed contradictory to the pearls of Heaven. A sincere attitude of having the willingness to learn to do just that — not take the world seriously — is perhaps one of the greatest accomplishments you are capable of experiencing while you are here. It is this accomplishment that I dare say will set psychoanalysis back into the dark ages. And I'm sure you'll agree, trumpets will sound and angels will sing when this happens!

The "descent into hell" was simply your making of the world together. It began with the mistaken thought that something had gone wrong, something needed to be fixed. It was your incredible belief that perhaps there could be an opposite to Heaven. By pondering this idea, all you see before you was made! Yet you may ask, "How could all of this have come from but a dream?" The answer to this can be better understood, if you realize the power of your own mind. When you are sleeping and you have a nightmare, does it not seem real while you are having it? Until you fully awaken, you may still feel as though your dream is indeed occurring. But once the light is turned on and you fully realize where you are, the dream is seen as just a dream and nothing more. Such is the case with the world you see yourselves in. Nothing about this world is really more than a dream. Most of you vacillate between nightmares and happy dreaming as you walk the earth. Others live in a constant nightmare, while a few of you live in a dream of lightness and joy. Whatever you seem to be doing here, be assured, it is only a dream and that is all. It will pass, as all dreams do.

Yet it is obvious that you do not believe it is a dream when a repossesser comes to take your automobile back for nonpayment or a landlord asks you to move because your dog is digging up her lawn. Nor does it feel like a dream when one finds themselves addicted to food, alcohol or otherwise. These are the things that make your world seem truly real. These are the things that seem to keep you in hell. These are the things that make darkness and death seem bigger than Life itself. But I would say to you, these are the exact same things that will ultimately set you free!

It is in your making of these things that you have sought to separate from your true Reality and enter into a world of your own. Any *thing* that shakes this world can cause you to react as if you were being slowly put to death. That is because in truth, you have made this world to shield you from your real Life, a Life that would surely demonstrate that your world is not true. For it is Life that God gave to you, not the world you have made from the thoughts of fear and separation. You have sought to make this world of separation your friend. Yet in its letting you down, you will seek and find a Friend that truly is forever yours, forever dependable and forever safe. You, who have sought to lose your way, could never lose it in truth. What is truly yours is yours forever. God gave His Gift to you. Because He gave It, you have received It and kept It within you Where It was given.

"Lead us not into temptation" is not only a prayer for direction, but one for remembrance as well. It is temptation that is all you really have to contend with in your world. It is what brought you here. It is what sustains the illusion of this seemingly separate place you live in. It is an attraction to view yourself as unwhole, powerless and needy. It is the attraction that distracts your mind from What is important by replacing Love with what is not important. This is your temptation. This is your falling. And this is your healing as well.

The journey back to the knowledge of Life begins not with your relinquishment of the things in your world, but with the relinquishment of your investment *in* them. It is the willingness not to believe they have any real value. It is the faith not in the seen, but in the Unseen. It is a journey beyond thoughts and symbols, beyond sounds and sights into the eternal Light from which you came. It is the journey into What you are and What you have always been. So short is this journey, it will happen in but the twinkling of an eye.

QUESTION

Books such as the Bible and A Course In Miracles *teach us that we can "hear" God in His truth from within; that salvation does not lie in books in other materials, other bodies, or in the world anywhere. So why should we listen to you today?*

Begin by asking yourselves why it is that you *trust* in what I have said to you in such literature. Each of these books and their words all *appear* to be *outside* you. But that is not why you trust in what they say. You trust in the *experience* you have obtained from your *practice* of what I suggested you do. By practicing what is taught rather than preaching it, you begin remembering your real Self — the greater Self you share with me and God. The experience of this is undeniably real, because this Self (Christ) is all there is. Your Self is created *from* Love as Love. And it is *only* your Self you *can* trust.

It is not "me" you should therefore listen to while reading this spiritual self-help book or any other. Nor is it me (Jesus) alone you should look for in other people, other practices or other material. It is the *shared Holy Spirit of Love*. That is Christ. That is your Self. It comes from God in you, no matter where you seem to see its mirrored reflection. I share Christ with you because "I" *am* Christ *with* you. Thus, when addressing your own spirituality, remember this always:

> *You will always find*
> *exactly what you are seeking*
> *for no matter where you "look,"because*
> *What you want you have already.*

I have given you certain books to study in order to help *train* your minds to "hear." However, it must be clear that it is only your relationships which bring to you the shining awareness of God or the density of fear. Thus, to *hear* anything, you must *relate* to something. To hear *only* God's Voice, you must learn to relate to *only* Love. It is only the remembrance of our Oneness that I am concerned with. You cannot find your Self *by* yourself, any more than I know my Self by relating through only a few individuals. I speak through all of you because we are of one Mind. If you cannot or will not hear me, be it through relating through this book or through relating through the mind of another, it is because you choose not to relate only to the Love in you. You are therefore choosing not to listen to your own magnificent Creation. If Christ is One Mind joined in His Father's Love, then when you refuse to hear, it must be that you are choosing to listen instead to "two minds separate in fear." Yet would you not prefer the gentle and loving comfort of Christ's certainty in us both as One? This awareness *is* your only joy!

When you hear the song of Heaven it will be from everyone, *everywhere*. For God's Voice will always come from you first because you are first in His Kingdom. When you have forgotten that you are first, I always bring a miracle to you. I will find a way to speak to you through the One Mind of God's Son. All of God's children are His channels without exception. Some may realize their potential while others do not, yet this does not matter. If only one of you in a situation is willing for even a moment to set all judgment and belief aside, I can speak through you and lift each of you up and out of fear toward the lighted Hearth of God's Love.

Overlooking what the eyes see and what the ears hear is not a practice you are accustomed to. Yet doing this is a demonstration that you are willing to step beyond separation and join with me and your sisters and brothers in the one purpose to heal. This is the most natural decision you will ever make. Even a child can do it, and they *do* do it all the time. The only reason you do not is because you have trained yourself not to be childlike. Your own flexibility has been exchanged for the concrete and this has indeed made you sad inside. You long for your inherent resilience and spontaneity. It is God's Promise to each of you that you will find it again.

You are encouraged to learn the practice of inner listening, for in you waits the Power of the Universe. Yet when you cannot seem to listen, be gentle with yourself, for you *are* in need of a miracle. God's channels will come quickly to you as your heart opens to receive them.

Everything you hear, whether it is truth or lies, comes from within you. Remembering this will help you understand that it does not matter where you seem to hear it *from*. What matters is only what the experience of your hearing does for you. Learn to hear truly and you will rejoice. To hear otherwise is not hearing at all, but the denial of What is yours to have and share already. Listen only to What is yours already and you have heard all there is to hear.

I do not speak to any of my brothers and sisters with mere words alone. It is Christ's message I come to share with you. This message must lead beyond words and theory, to an experience you will not easily forget. You are God's children, loving and forever lovable. You are in need of nothing but the Gift God's Voice brings to you and which you share with all as well.

Be open to join with the hearts and minds of others, loved one. By doing so you make room for the hands of Christ to lift you to Heaven! Be willing to be truly helpful, for this is how real healing begins. Each of you has agreed to help. Each of you needs help *because* you are here. Learn to listen and hear God's Voice in *everyone*, for this is how you will find true direction and eternal safety. The Holy Spirit's direction has not left you and I am with Him for you always. Blessings on you for beginning this joyous journey with everyone this day. Be glad for those He sends to you along the way.

Come let Him lift you unto Heaven.

Jesus

Chapter Two

DISCUSSIONS, QUESTIONS & TEACHINGS

The Relationship of Sickness to Guilt:
Obsessions, Abuse,
Depression and Recovery

A Beginning Note

Though every healing is instantaneous, the full remembrance of one's Self in God is the result of the accumulation of many such instants into an integrated awareness of God's timeless eternity. His is *your* loving Reality, beyond all sickness, suffering and time. It should be understood that this healing spans throughout the "realm of time." The purpose of this chapter's material is to acquaint the newcomer and refresh the long-term student with healing components, so that a clear direction away from appearances and sickness can be set. In this chapter, we will briefly discuss a few of these appearances and the spiritual components necessary for the process of healing our belief in suffering.

A SCRIBING FOR TIM

Hi Joel and Jesus,

I have previously studied A Course In Miracles *for about three years. Then it dawned on me that I was doing more studying than living it and dropped it. I was previously in a 12-step program for six years but left when I realized that an addiction is not "an incurable disease" and that I was unwilling to lie and say, "Hi my name is Tim I'm an X," at every meeting I attended. I also read much of Joel Goldsmith's work and was helped very much by his approach to addictions.*

I would like some insight into your (or rather your guided) info on addictions.

Can Jesus tell me more about addiction and what it is for?

As One,

Tim

Greetings Tim:

This is Jesus speaking through Joel. Yes, let us discuss the meaning of addiction. Addiction can be equated with the temptation and then obsession to use "magic potions" to "cure" the mind and body of its distresses. "Magic," in the strictest sense, involves the use of some external remedy, be it a drug, book, money, food or anything overly relied upon physically or mentally. Magic is the means by which you hide yourself from Love. All who come to this world will depend on magic at some point or another. There is nothing wrong or right about doing this, although using magic, external medicine or anything from the outside is only temporary as a cure and for "peace of mind."

To further this dialogue, the more one uses outside attempts to fix or cure, the more one loses sight of the true cure, which is Love. When this occurs a person must become afraid, for he has lost touch with the Self — the only Power he truly has to help him find a permanent solution. Obsessiveness can be said to be an insidious spiritual disease. It grows slowly over time and can become an all consuming part of a person's lifestyle. As it grows, it requires more and more of a mixture of great apathy and denial in order for the disease to progress into one that is this debilitating, thus taking a tremendous amount of destructive effort on the part of the abuser. This is the outcome of believing in magic. It takes all of the misplaced energy that has been given to the ego-drive to fulfill the "wish" that magic would make.

This magic is what has been referred to over the ages in religion as the "great evil one." In truth, magic and evil are only inventions of the mind that have the insidious foundation of guilt as their motivators. Evil is destructive to the body because it is a secret wish to punish the body. Yet evil only exists because knowledge of the Eternal has been temporarily obliterated. Once the Eternal has been remembered, evil simply disappears into the nothingness it was made from. How "great" is this "evil one" now?

One must be careful about the idea of overcoming a dis-ease that is based in magical beliefs. Once the mind has followed such a pathology, it can easily take root again, unless one is vigilant for truth. It is true that you are not your dis-ease, but because you have indulged in this pathology, it is likely that the ego, once back in control, will attempt to lead you back to the same destructive path you were on. That tendency will lessen more and more in time if a person uses spiritual rather than material means to affect a sense of peace and safety. Using outside means always weakens the body, thus making it more susceptible to illness and to the temptation to "cure" from without. Using the support of one another through the one goal of finding the peace of God together will heal dis-ease and offer miraculous results never before thought possible.

There is no dis-ease that is not curable and all dis-ease is based in magic, but there is no body that will live forever either. Thus the emphasis and focus on the dis-ease is not a solid approach. In fact it will fall into worship of the body if this approach is kept and followed. What matters are the choices you make now in each of your decisions. The less you depend on the world and the body, the more you will learn to depend on God. When Love becomes your only "dependency," it will not matter to you whether or not you have a dis-ease. Death will not be feared and you *will* recognize, through your experience, your own eternal safety in Love. Once this is accomplished, you will know beyond a shadow of a doubt that you are not your body, dis-ease or your mind. You will recognize your unlimited nature in God and you will gladly turn away from obsessing with all the world seems to "offer." You are in the process of doing this right now.

Some sort of spiritual practice is necessary once you have recognized God in your life. If one chooses not to give time to God, it is likely that old behavior is soon to return. You cannot harm your Self by your destructive behaviors, but you certainly can hurt the body you now seem to dwell in. Of itself it does not matter, but it is quite tragic to never know the joy of living free like the wind and the trees. So, if you would live in truth, live to know God in yourself and everyone. Choose not to bow to the ego's wishes and temptations. It is not difficult to do. But one must let go entirely of the idea that he or she can teach themselves and turn to the only Teacher there is. The Christ that is in you is in everyone and you can find Him simply by looking past fear and to the Light He holds in everyone. Take time to practice this daily and you will need nothing else. Value lies only in Love and only in eternal Life. Learn, my brother Tim, to look and see only this.

May the blessing of this Gift from Him Live in you forever.

Live in peace,

Jesus

A SCRIBING FOR SKIP

I know that coincidences don't just happen. That is the doing of God. People don't just meet. God brings them together. He really knows what He is doing.

Now do you believe in revelation? Or should I ask, "Is there going to be a 'day' as the Word says?" I believe that the way it is described in the Bible is an interpretation understandable in those days. In other words, for example, the "seven heads" could mean something else in today's world. I just wanted to let you know I do believe in what the Bible says, no matter where my life is. I'm very intelligent and loving. This, my friend, is all one needs to succeed. What is success? Well, to reach one's goals. I sit here now trying mostly to stay out of state prison, but I know that being in jail is another of God's stepping stones in life.

Hopes and seeming problems:

I hope to stay out of jail. I hope to pursue my music career and finally complete my task that God has brought me here to fulfill.

Thanks sincerely, Skip

1) *Can I still be a child of God and use (drugs)?*
2) *If staying sober is so hard, maybe I'm going against the grain? Is that true?*
3) *Is staying in the NA/AA program and using wrong, if it fits into my lifestyle easily?*
4) *My main question really is, "Am I headed in the right direction?"*
5) *How can I stop thinking?*
6) *Do I really know all there is to know about me?*

Greetings Skip:

You are right. It is no accident that you have "run into" Joel, or that I am speaking through him to you right now. There are many spiritual endeavors you have come here to perform and accomplish, many of which you are still consciously resisting. I come today to help you overcome these "resistances."

You have asked if you are "headed in the right direction." My answer is simply that there is no direction which will not ultimately lead you Home to God. However, some require a much greater toll of suffering than do others. Would you know how to distinguish the difference *before* you stepped onto your chosen path? And would you choose suffering if you knew it was the certain outcome of the path you were on? There is only one honest answer to both questions. You *do* know the difference because God created you *from* His Knowledge, which is *everything* there is. You do ask for suffering every time you deny this Knowledge and thus *His Will* in you.

You *are* responsible not for what you do, but for what you *think*, because how you think determines what you do and not the other way around. Your complete responsibility to your Self, God and your brother depends on this understanding. Interpreted any other way, you are not only denying your responsibility, you are denying your birthright — the inherent Knowledge of your Self and God. Could anyone *not* suffer under such conditions where Love seems completely absent from their experience? Yet this is the condition which you have often diligently tried to "protect." This has indeed frightened and wearied you.

It is your thinking alone and without God that has brought you discomfort and suffering. By thinking without Love, you have chosen to see yourself impoverished and without responsibility. This can only lead to irresponsible actions later. The only way to correct an impoverished mind is to bring its thinking under guidance which remains entirely out of your control and yet *not* beyond your ability to choose. To choose responsibility is to decide *for* Love and *with* Love. By doing so you cannot suffer, for those who recognize their own beloved innocence would make no decisions alone. Yet all power is given unto them, for the holiness of God speaks through them, healing minds and joining hearts in the one purpose given them under Heaven. This is what I meant when I said, "The meek shall inherit the earth." With Love, all is possible because God created you *only* from His Love. Rest in this understanding, Skip, for whatever path you seem to see yourself on, God knows you are already Home and never alone. With the "chosen" path you decide to walk on, let it always be to gently remind you that this is indeed so.

Let us now look carefully at your first question, "Can I still be a child of God and use (drugs)?"

You are always God's Son and this will never change. Yet it is quite apparent, by the choices you sometimes make, that you believe you are a child of the ego instead. The ego is the part of your mind which dreams of a separation from God. Out of these dreams a whole world was made to take the place of Heaven. Look at your life and see what nightmares the ego has made for you. Everything the body's eyes "see" is a witness to this dream of separation. The identity that you call "you" is but the ego's confirmation that your dream has come true.

O little child, did you not know there is so much more to you than what your eyes can "see?" It is your use and abuse of certain magical substances which confirm that you do not *believe* it is so. For it is only the littleness and grandiosity of the ego which could convince you that you're weak and small, forced to be dependent on its magical "cures" to offer a temporary sense of self inflation and false euphoria.

Has the ego ever offered you anything that would last? Have the results of its mysterious "gifts" ever shown you peace and safety from beyond this world? Answer these questions again with rigorous honesty and you must certainly realize that the ego's shabby offerings *can* and *will* most certainly and always leave you down and feeling abandoned. Only guilt and fear can come from its "gifts," because the ego will use whatever it can as a substitute for God.

Your ego would have you search in an endless maze of the different offerings of its dreams, but with no pot of gold ever to be found. As long as you seek fulfillment from without you, the maze must only seem to grow larger. Your peace and your enlightenment can never be found in the shiny trinkets and polished gifts hidden in the different corners of this maze, for they come not of your Father's Love, but of a wish to replace Him. Would you worship such idols if you indeed knew what they were really for?

Come then, take my hand, and together let us set all idols aside and gently shall we walk to the gates of the real Heaven. It is this you *really* seek. Yet you need not search for it where it lies at all, for Heaven is only *in* you. Peace does surround you, even now. God will never abandon you, Skip, for He created you as part of Himself. You are as much a part of Him as He is of you. His judgment is therefore final and can never change: *You are His Son with whom He is well pleased.*

It is not God Who makes you feel guilty and punishes you for your seeming "sins." It is always you who punish yourself by choosing methods of "correction" from *without* in place of the real correction from *within*. The Holy Spirit's Voice is the only correction that can bring you lasting joy because it comes from the only Source that is everlasting. The more you depend on the ephemeral, the more you will feel guilty and fearful. The more you depend on only Love, the more you recognize and embrace your own perfect inheritance with God. This inheritance is His perfect judgment, for Christ is your Self to share with all. When you are not sharing the joy of this awareness, it is because you are trying to share "something else" and thus you must be looking for salvation in "something else" first. It cannot be found, however, outside His judgment *of* you, because His judgment is forever *for* you, being His Own extension of what you truly are.

Do not go against this judgment or you will only frighten and seem to imprison yourself. By doing so you do not hurt God, Who knows His Son as eternal as Himself. But you *will* hurt your awareness that this is so. You need never put yourself in prison again simply by accepting and keeping the awareness of Where salvation truly lies and not pretending to find it elsewhere. For pretension, my dear Skip, *is* the root of all suffering. Let us not play with idols which pretend to bring you peace any longer, for they are but toys with sharpened tips that can seem to hurt you. Instead, look only to God's shining Altar within you, Where I abide in Christ with you. Here and only Here is the lasting joy we do share together, for only this is God's Will.

Now let me speak to your third question. "Is staying in the NA/AA Program and using wrong, if it fits into my lifestyle easily?"

I cannot over emphasize to you how necessary it is to become attuned to what is happening *within* you. It is always *here* that you will find your answers to everything. Ask yourself, "Do I feel at peace with the decision to 'use' and still go to meetings where many others are genuinely looking for sobriety and sober advice?" Obviously you do not feel entirely at peace with the decision or you would not be asking me the question now. You do feel guilt about this decision, but have done a marvelous job for the most part in repressing the guilt into a darkened corner of your mind where you or others cannot see it. All the while you are keeping your rationalizations going to distract you from it, thus "protecting" it from your conscious awareness where its pretentiousness and self-hatred would become glaringly clear. It is this you really fear to look at and this is why you seek the gratification of your synthetic "gods."

Yet you *must* look at this hatred if you are to ever heal and come to peace with the real creation of God that you are. It was through pretension and denial that you made an image of yourself that you can never love, for it was made of a hatred so intense that it seemed as though the Son of God cast himself from Heaven. In the belief that it was accomplished, it followed that you must now punish yourself for your "sin" against Him Who created you, hoping to exonerate yourself from the "wrath" God would now impose for your abandonment of Him. Child of God, you only *dream* of death and separation from Him and project your own fear and hatred onto God, making Him appear to be your "vengeful Father." *This is not so.* Your hatred, the image of yourself you made from it, and a "vengeful Father" are all *but a dream.* Do not pretend to make it real any longer. Have mercy on Christ, your Self and Him Who has always only loved you. Through your willingness not to deceive yourself any longer and to forgive this frightening dream you've made, God's holy angels shall come to return you Home to Heaven.

Listen *within*, my holy brother, for the messages you send out. When the message returns, does it speak of blessing, love and joy, or the counterpart, which God did not create — condemnation, fear and guilt? In every decision you make, you choose between these two. In one you will rejoice in remembrance of your own perfect wholeness and grandeur. In the other you will weep in sickness and suffering for the picture of death you made. Though it is not real, you will worship it as if it were, forgetting again the Love from Which you came. Listen within first to the Love and to the decision He has made for you, and each message returned will be His Message of your joyous salvation. You have always had the answer to this question you ask, but you did not wish to "hear." In not receiving His Gift, you gave yourself "another."

Let us now answer your question number two, "If staying sober is so hard, maybe I'm going against the grain. Is that true?"

There is only one reason you could not wish to stay sober and that, my dear one, is because you do not like what you think you "see." What you see is always a form of vengeance because your seeing was made as a replacement to Christ's Vision. You do not see what you think, you think what you see and then believe you saw it *before* you thought it. That is why your beliefs are always open to question, each being made only from your own perception. It is this perception that seems to give your "seeing" reality, and yet all perception is based on some past experience, never on the *now*. What you *do* believe you will see, although neither can proceed further than the symbolizing of truth. Truth is an experience of Love and this awareness can come only from Christ's Vision in you now.

When you see through Christ's Vision, you are overlooking your own darkened sight of the world. With Christ you look only with Love and the Holy Spirit as your Guide. With your seeing alone, you look at a picture of the ego's projected hatred. That is why it is essential for you to escape the bondage of the ego's sight in you. What it "sees" it makes real in you. The voice of this ego is relentless in its attempts to establish its own "reality" and convince you that it is "true." This can become so disheartening it could make a saint drink, if he believed it!

When you learn to overlook the ego's relentless chatter and all it seems to "see," your heart will be gladdened indeed! My happy suggestion to you is to try a new "drug." It is called "meditation." Do not be disappointed if at first it doesn't work. The ego is shrewd. Do not give up. Do it every day for three months at least twice a day for fifteen minutes in the morning and late evening. Do the best you can to set down your own thinking and sight. Pretend you have amnesia to the world and look for a gentle Light instead. You will discover there is nothing pretentious about this practice as the days go by. This "drug" will make it much easier for you to not do the other drugs again. (Hint — There is only one "drug" that has a lasting high. It's called Love. It works every time!)

Now to your sixth question, "Do I really know all there is to know about me?"

As we have discussed earlier, the Knowledge of God is your inheritance forever. To the degree you are willing to receive and give Love, to that extent will you gain Self understanding. There are blocks of fear and hatred that must be forgiven before Love can enter. But there is very little else of value that you can do for yourself. Wouldn't you agree? Your only function is to forgive while you are here. Your purpose is to join and enjoy. What you don't know now, I promise you will remember. Seek only God and the Kingdom of Heaven in yourself and everyone. Love is endless. More will be revealed as soon as you are ready. But is the peace of God your only goal? Now your work becomes clear.

Now to address your fifth question, "How can I stop thinking?"

My dear Skip, I have saved the best for last for you! What a truly blessed question you have asked me today! It is your thinking that opposes blessing in every way! It is a most unnatural invention. Wouldn't you agree?

You'll *stop* thinking when you forgive and *start* believing in only a greater Thought. That Thought is the Love from Which you came. It is your Self, your eternal Reality and the Christ we all share. It has no words, but it *is* the *only* Word. It is as forever changeless as you are. You *are* the Light of the world, dear one. And I share this same Light with you. Trust only in this Love and Light and lay down your judgment and arrogance. It's a gentle journey we go on together, my brother. The distance to God is immeasurable because a recognition has no distance at all. Be you blessed in the presence of this understanding, and give to all with love what I have sent for you this day.

In loving remembrance of you,

Jesus

FALLING FROM GRACE

"Falling from your grace" is nothing new. You all do it and there is nothing in it that God in Heaven would judge you for. Can you bring a little of that Heaven into the darkness you have made in your world? Of course you can! In fact, you can experience Heaven right here, right now.

What is it that prevents you from having this experience? It is the many different manifestations of fear that you have made your idols. It is the magic, it is your religions, it is your dogmas, your rituals. It is all those things which you put between yourselves that make for conflict. I tell you, little children, none of them mean anything to God.

Each of your manifestations of conflict and fear arise as the result of your beliefs. Beliefs are most often passed on from one generation to the next. You may well ask how these beliefs could seem to turn to "sins." This is easily understood if you recognize that to "sin" is only to miss the mark. Sin is not what God will punish you for when you lay your body down. Not at all! Sins are what you punish yourself with while you are right here in the "hell" you made from them. How did this all come to be? It is very simple — from your beliefs.

You often wonder why it is that the world you live in seems so bleak and confusing at times. You find yourselves asking why there are so many seeming atrocities occurring. Why all the crime, political deception and so on? Again I would tell you, it is because of your beliefs. They are beliefs that have remained unhealed for thousands of your years. Now the time has come for you to begin to confront these beliefs. They can no longer be avoided, nor will they be. As a whole, you might say that the entire race on your planet has reached its limit with fear and is exclaiming, "We're mad as hell and we're not going to take it anymore."

This is what it has taken for all of you to begin to look at the cause of your problems. The world you see in front of you is the result of your believing. No one caused this alone. You all did it together. The time is coming when you will all undo it together. Then the world you are experiencing as bleak and hostile will cease to seem to be and you will experience the beginning of a little more Heaven on earth.

Now that you know that this is what your beliefs have done, would you want to keep them in light of what they have brought you? I think not. It is best for you to think not *with* me. It is your very thinking that has complicated your lives because of these underlying beliefs. To stop believing would be a very good first step for you, so that you might some day be able to stop thinking. Would it not?

Perhaps you do not realize what kinds of beliefs could have caused all the disharmony you see about you at times. Think about the times in your life when you justified the belief in punishing a child for a mistake. Think about the times when you believed someone was taking advantage of you and you felt a need to defend yourself. Think about the times when you believed your needs were not met in some way. Think of the times when you blamed another and attacked her/him for "making" you believe you were a "victim." Think about how your philosophical or religious beliefs separated you from other people, even countries. Now you have an idea of the many beliefs that have kept your world in turmoil. Now you have an idea why you have chosen magic instead of Love to try to "heal" you.

The sickness, whether it be depression, anxiety, physical disease, obsessive disorder or otherwise, is a manifestation of underlying beliefs about yourself. They are more well hidden in some than in others, but they are there nonetheless. You might ask, "How might I heal all these mistaken beliefs if there are so many and they are so well hidden?" One thing is sure — you cannot and will not do it alone. Nor will these beliefs heal as long as you have left one brother or sister unattended. You see little children, your responsibility to all of your brothers and sisters is no different than God's responsibility to all of you! Could He justify leaving even one of you separate from the rest? I think not.

Now it becomes glaringly clear to you, does it not, how many holes exist in your own belief systems? All you need do is look and see whom you have somehow justified leaving on the sidelines because of a fear from one of the underlying beliefs that is at work in your life. It has made the world you see appear to be as it is. It has made a world of sickness seem to appear all around you. You try in some way each day to hide from this separation you made, but you cannot. Hiding will only make more of what you already "have" and no longer want. This is why it is best that you listen to what I am gently teaching you today. *Together* we might turn this all around. *Together* we could bring some Heaven to this weary world. Oh yes! We can and *together we will.*

A SCRIBING FOR MARGARET

I am planning on retiring, this being my last year at my current work. I'm not sure if I can afford to retire, but I feel like I cannot emotionally give any more to it. Actually, I even have the same feeling about life from time to time, as you'll see in the questions. I have four children and thirteen grandchildren I like to be with. Here are my questions:

    1) Art: Will artwork become a greater part of my life? Is it a gift I'm not using or should I be satisfied with the enjoyment I get from it?

    2) Pain and weight: Are these both manifestations of fear? How can I rid myself of pain and lose weight? Am I manifesting in my body what seems necessary to "die" because I'm weary of living in this world?

    3) Forgiveness: Two brothers-in-law molested my daughters when they were youngsters. I'm in extreme confusion on how to deal with this and it's probably greatly related to question two.

    4) Retirement: I live alone, worry if I can do this financially, and don't want to be a financial burden on my children. I want to be able to change direction in January. Will I be able to get on with whatever I'm here to be doing and how can I "know" what that would be?

    5) Spiritual: How can I learn to hear the "Voice?" If this is Jesus to those with a Christian background, who would it be for brothers of an eastern religion?

Thanks for doing this, Joel. I am looking forward to the scribing.

Love, Margaret

Greetings Margaret:

Welcome to you. I am honored as your brother to receive the questions you have asked. Let us begin with your fifth question first, since it implies concern and possible confusion.

Just as I took on an identity in what seems like long ago in time, so have you now. What you think of as "Margaret" is simply a compilation of ideas about yourself as you see yourself. In truth you are only one Self, posing temporarily as a separate self. That is why actions, no matter how real they may seem, are but self-made illusions. This is a fairly simple and direct explanation. I am offering you this to help you with your other questions as well, which we will soon come to.

There is but one Cause. You and what seems to be everyone else *are* but one Effect, posing as many bodies, all trying to remember that we are but one Effect, or Self of God. It is difficult to understand through concepts and words, and certainly you will never see it through the body's eyes alone. Most of you would refuse to accept what I am explaining to you because it is a direct threat to the existence of the ego. However, the *experience* of recognizing your one Self in everyone is not only possible, it is inevitable. Once this happens, it will leave no doubt in you that it is true. It requires only that you step out of your identification with "Margaret," as you see yourself. This requires suspension through forgiveness of all you seem to *think* or see. My Self and yours are no different in truth. There is no real choice in this. The Christ is you. The only "difference," which is apparent only in the illusion, is that you seem to be posing as "Margaret" temporarily, while "I" recognize only my Self as Christ eternally. The "I" that I am then, is actually the "you" that you can't see, and *only* What God created. I am speaking to you in a form you understand and accept, so it seems that "I" am "Jesus" to you. But I would remind you that "I," as "Jesus," am no more or less than you are as "Margaret." I was able at a point to demonstrate that "Jesus" as a man was entirely an illusion. *This* is what placed me in charge of the Atonement. I became *at one* with Christ in *all*. This angered many, but it also healed many others.

It was necessary for me to do this to point out that salvation is quite available to all. The only way to do this was to prove beyond a shadow of a doubt that the body was an illusion, along with all the apparent worldly experiences that it might offer. The only experience that is genuine is the one that proves within you that what "I," as *Christ*, have just said is true. This is the experience of total surrender to Love which I am guiding you to.

In regard to your second part of this question, each person will hear in a way that best suits their own understanding. If a person is acquainted with Buddhism, then she may hear the Voice of Christ in a similar format to her own teachings. The message, however, if it is in His integrity, will be the same as what I am teaching. Some people hear many voices. This is because they have used many earthly teachers with whom they have remembered a Oneness. Sometimes there are even those who think they hear "evil voices." This is simply because they have somewhere along the way believed in the false guilt of "fearful teachers." Unfortunately, what they are really hearing here is only an unhealed side of their own ego thinking. Still, it serves them to do this until they are able to learn that pain cannot be a teacher. Then they will hear aright. Be not concerned, Margaret, with appearances. Illusions will always deceive you. Yet you cannot be deceived if you keep only one goal in mind — the peace of our one Self in God. It is What you are. Need you be concerned with looking at "something else?"

This is how you can learn to hear the quiet Voice of your Self within. I am your Self and, if you are not hearing, it is because you are choosing to listen to the chatter of "something else." Your Voice, your guidance, is but a quiet instant away from "something else." Listen *only* here and you *will* hear. Is there anything else really worth listening *for* or *to* in you or anyone?

Regarding your work situation, I will remind you again as I have already done several times. Take my words to heart. You cannot afford *not* to "retire." Your work situation, as you experience it, is no longer beneficial to your own healing. It is time to do what you know you need to do. This has nothing to do with making money. Need I say more? Regarding the means, that will be provided for you. Now is a time for developing trust in your true Self and God. This means letting go of things you may still think you cherish. You will find, however, that once you relax into your true occupation with God, you will discover gifts beyond compare to what you are presently experiencing. Trust, Trust, Trust! Ask me to guide you in each step of this needed shift and there will be no burden. I would remind you that you still have a mind. Do your best not to use it, and ask me instead. You'll find it much easier. Let Love guide you on this new journey Margaret. You will know.

You now grieve for all the times you have held a grievance and failed to love. In the case of the molestations by brothers-in-law, you have grieved and suffered much guilt. Yet this is not necessary for you to continue. But you will as long as you blame yourself or them. I have said that all relationships are to be regarded in one of two ways — as either an offering of Love or a call for Love. There is no other choice, unless you want to suffer needlessly. You are not guilty because you were created from *only* Love. *And so were they*. I have also said before that you cannot be committed to two opposing thought systems. You are either guilty or not guilty. You must make a firm commitment to one or the other. But a firm commitment to guilt is impossible. Indeed, it goes against all you were created from and for. The reason you are upset over this situation is because you believe you might have been able to stop it. You believe something went wrong and shouldn't have happened. What if I were to tell you that without this experience, the deep healing that you asked for could not happen? Would you then accept that all is in order as God created it? Nothing has happened by accident and nothing about these experiences has truly hurt anyone, though it appears quite the opposite. Each of you came into this lifetime with a certain amount of hatred to heal. Could, then, this entire experience not help you with this?

As you look upon what you hate and despise, remember what I have said, "There is nothing outside you." All that has happened is gone and over with forever. Yet if you are seeing it, then it is apparent that you believe that pain is valuable and Love is not. Experience would tell you otherwise. Has holding onto the pain helped in any way? None of the defenses you have kept to "protect" yourself have hurt your abilities to truly heal. Is it not time to take a firm stance in the other direction?

You are living to the best of your capabilities right now. It must be okay to be angry or sad. It must be okay to grieve. And if you are not able to heal, this must be okay too. Whatever you are doing is perfect for you. The best I can offer you is to remind you that you need not continue feeling unhealed if you do not wish to. But what is true healing? Healing of the mind requires a recognition of the full intensity of what pain has brought you. It is emotional, not intellectual. It requires letting go of how your mind still sees it, so that you can experience the full effect of the feelings and then let them go. This requires great willingness. The purpose of any true spiritual work is *not* to teach you to *pretend* the pain is not there. You cannot simply overlook suffering and choose only Love while pain is still lingering within you. You must bring the pain to Light. I have asked you to bring your suffering to me and to join with one another with this same purpose in mind. I will see that it is removed from your minds and hearts, but first you must acknowledge what the experience of pain has cost you. This is the risk that most of you find very difficult to take.

It is the pain unforgiven in each of your close relationships that has set you apart. It is the "secrets" you each hold against one another, or against one who has "wronged" someone else, that are dear to you. Other forms of these "secrets" include beliefs that some are unworthy of the time to deepen with or that you are unworthy of such a joining with another whom you deem "farther along." Whatever the belief is that has cost you your peace and true happiness, you can be assured there was first a secret judgment and then a seeming separation of hearts and minds. It is *there* where you will find the beginning of healing or the continuance of separating thinking and painful experience. Only where the secret judgment originated can it be healed. When you discover where you think it was in your past, you will remember where it really is *now*. It has always been right here with you where you brought it. Only *here* as you recognize it, can it be healed. Now might you understand better why the past truly does not exist except in nightmares in the present.

These people who you see as wronging you are in exactly as much need of Love as you who were "affected" by them. You need not give this to them directly, but you must at some point in your heart truly bless them with this understanding. To do this you must deeply risk with one another. Your children need you as you need them to accomplish this. You will be provided with the opportunity as you have at times before. When this happens, let me guide you to the Holy Spirit in you. Let Him take you to God. You need only stand aside and let healing gently be. This means letting suffering be as well. Accept the feelings of what this separation has caused in you. I ask that you remember one idea as you do this, Margaret: You cannot be hurt by taking this risk. Hold this firmly in mind and heart. Then take the plunge into God's Heart with me. You know how to do this. You have done it before. I will show you in the end that you have not been hurt. Once this healing is complete, the feelings of hatred and vulnerability will be gone as well. Healing from rape or murder does not necessarily take a lifetime, as some therapists may suggest. Do not believe this in yourself or in your children. It takes one second of your full willingness to risk being healed! Let it be for you, if this is what your heart truly desires. Let it be.

I would suggest to you, Margaret, that you drop all the conventional ideas about losing weight since they obviously have not been effective for you. Practice often all the lessons in the Course you are studying regarding the body and go deep with them until you feel you own them in your experience. You will feel a sense of relief if you are taking them to heart. The body is not you and neither is the past. As you recognize this in yourself fully, so will your children with you. This will help them greatly with their issues. You are each apt at times to find it hard to accept that the body is not you. Affecting physical measures for the correction of bodily woes or mental illness is always temporary. What you are not enjoying is life is likely to later turn to fat. This brings us back to the mind, where all healing should be done and is done. Obesity is simply a form of fear in all cases. It is a form of unconscious neglect to one's self, taken out on the body. It does not serve you to feel guilty about this, since it is guilt that caused it in the first place. Guilt and sacrifice are never joyous. If you do not feel joyous in doing what you are doing to assist you in your condition, then by all means stop. It is time to work with your mind.

An example of doing this differently would be meditating until you feel a sense of relief and release from your mis-identification with your own body. Then when someone says to you, "Let's go take a brisk walk," you will no doubt be happy to take that risk. Your sense of depression from mis-identification in this case does not overcome your recognition that you are free to do as you will. When you agree to play, you are not *thinking* of all the reasons you shouldn't do it. Rather, you are simply doing it because you *can*. Do you understand what I am saying to you? Remember back to when you were a child, when you did things that you didn't even think about. You were carefree! Not only that, you did not even think you were a body!

If you will trust fully in the message I am offering you, you will soon realize that your condition has nothing to do with the body at all. Remember that I have told you that your body is simply a tool. Of itself it has no value. If you place a value in it being thinner, then you must be seeing yourself as fatter and it is likely that you will make the opposite occur. This is a law of cause and effect. What you fear you make manifest. The way out of this dilemma is to forget the body and choose peace instead. Choose the Place in you Where all is true, all is whole. If you feel you must do something, you are choosing fear. Choose again and, above all, remember that your body is only temporary. Its value lies only in the outcome of what it is in service for. Any other values you place on it are no doubt misplaced. Be joyous that you are not a body! And do not worry that it is not serving you well. Ask instead, "Is my mind serving me well in this situation I see myself in?" Then choose again. And yes, your second and third questions are interrelated.

Lastly, I will address your being "weary of the world." Yes, your mind is weary and you are choosing a form of moderate self-abuse to avoid dealing with it. I remind you, and I hope this can help you laugh a little, you can run but you cannot hide! You cannot escape your own lessons by leaving the world. Many have tried. All have failed! You chose all of what you are experiencing so that you *can* heal your "lessons in suffering." You are not going to die, because you *cannot* die. I am not dead! I do not believe in death in any form. Nor am I weary of the world because I know it is not true. You are capable of wearying yourself only because you believe that death is more powerful than Life. Look at the destruction you seem to see. Now realize it *is* but a dream! You are here *now* and everything else is but your own private picture show. Turn off the projector and enjoy the *now*! I am here and I love it! You need not take the picture show so seriously. "Serious" is what caused the world. It is really quite laughable, don't you think? For in all the seeming destruction, the Eternal still remains! If you must take something seriously, be serious about seeing the eternal in your children and in their children and in the ones who have seemed at one time to set you back. There is no doubt, Margaret, that you and I, with *all* the Sonship, will soon laugh *together*!

Here is a prayer for you, for all. Say it with your full heart's conviction and then let healing be:

"*Father, let me now exchange this pain I am seeing in (self or others) for the Truth within all You have already given. It is Your Gift for me to be free of all which seems to make me suffer. I would answer all calls for Love with Your Word of gentle blessing and complete forgiveness. I am not afraid to let Your healing Rays illuminate all relationships. I ask only for What is mine, and I accept It for all now.*"

Amen.

His Light has blessed you, for you have asked, and you are answered.

You are surrounded by the angels I have sent you.

Listen... and accept this Gift now.

A Loving Jesus

ANOTHER SCRIBING FOR MARGARET

Dear Joel,

Your scribing from Jesus is leading to a real breakthrough for me. I do have some other questions that follow.

Questions:

1) *In my religion, a couple of the Masters (teachers) are Rebazar Tzars and Sri Harold. Jesus mentioned the message might sound different, but in essence be the same. What does this mean?*

I was married to Jim for eight years and he was the father of my four children. I was in a relationship with John for sixteen years. In some things I've read, you are in relationships to learn lessons. Now I'm learning about the differences between reality and illusion. I want to be real/spiritual, but I also feel we must deal with the ego as a choice in being in this physical plane. I feel I've learned some good lessons about compassion from Jim, who chose to live as a homosexual for the rest of his life. I haven't realized some values I think I should have in the relationship with John. He had affairs and I felt hurt. I realize I wasn't listening to "gut instincts" and I should have trusted my "inner Voice." I was taught that God was all-knowing, all-seeing and all-present. Also... to be feared.

2) *Would you tell me about the lessons I learned or should have learned with Jim and John? To what extent do past life connections deal with lessons this time around? Jesus mentioned in the scribing that, "Each of you came into this lifetime with a certain amount of hatred to heal." It sounds like karma. Please explain this as it relates to this lifetime, past ones and connections with my children in the past.*

3) *From the last scribing: "You will find, however, that once you relax into your true occupation with God, you will find gifts beyond compare to what you are presently experiencing." Please elaborate on "true occupation with God" so I can understand it. Any other comments would be helpful.*

Thanks again, Joel

Love, Margaret

Greetings Margaret:

Welcome again! Yes, allow me to clarify.

In response to your confusion about other masters, it is true that each and every one of you is on the same path Home. It only appears as though each of you is following different paths. That is only because of what you see, read and react to in your experience. You each seem to go through many different experiences, all leading to different conclusions and seeming results for a while, thus causing you to form different perceptions and ideas from another. "Welcome" to the separation, Margaret, for this is what the world was made to do. Yet in truth, none of it is really there; none of it really matters. Fear occurs in what seems to be many forms and what only appears to matter. Yet it is one form masquerading as many — separation.

You are each masters of your life and destiny. The only reason you are not sure of this is because you are not yet sure of what your life and destiny is. But you will be, as surely as God is sure about you. Every one of you is a master at something. The question is, what? There are many who claim to be masters of Love who are really teachers of fear. Any person that has obtained true mastery would teach only that fear, the body and the world are but illusion. She would teach that you are exactly the same as herself — the Christ. She would never teach you to depend on her, for she realizes that of herself she is nothing.

The message of all true teachers is the same: The Christ is forever eternal, forever free, unchanged and unlimited in the Power of God. Nothing else exists because nothing else is created.

Regarding your past relationships, they are the same as your relationships now. Each relationship you have placed yourself in has been and is for the opportunity to heal. Each relationship comes to you for a very specific reason. The specifics entail whatever "baggage" you are in need of healing. You will be attracted to whatever relationship best suits the function of exposing your unhealed baggage, thus providing you with an opportunity to look at it and allow healing to enter. Such was the case for both Jim and John. However, you are still grappling with the lesson you were hoping to learn with John, which was ultimately the same as the lesson with Jim. The lesson in every relationship is to teach you Where, and only Where, your true power lies. As long as you believe you can be hurt by someone, you are in need of healing. This may sound cold and almost impossible, but I assure you that it is not. You will learn that you can't be hurt and thus you will come to a place in life where all of your relationships will *be* holy ones. The holy relationship is creative because it entails no self-made conditions. A special relationship is never holy because it entails conditions placed on it made from fear. Those conditions are actually your unhealed beliefs that would suggest that you are not whole, not safe, and not innocent and free.

You felt hurt over John being unfaithful because at that time you were not entirely faithful to your Self — to the Love in *you*. Had you been faithful to only that, nothing he would have done could have shaken you. By being faithful to the Love in you, you are automatically being faithful to the Love in *him*. It is the same one Self created in God. This Self is incapable of experiencing deception or suffering, for It is the Christ, created by God, that we share together. Your experience with him of feeling abandoned and betrayed was a repeat movie of something that happened before that still had not been healed in you. Taking birth into this world was your first recognizable experience with abandonment. You felt betrayed as well, for it felt as though you were literally hurled from your Home into oblivion. That is also what you are here to heal, for you chose to believe that you could separate from God. Now all that is left is for you to remember that you could not, and did not.

Lessons cannot be learned through fear, but only through Love. You each need to be reminded of this often in your world, for it is easily forgotten in your wish to be separate. "Lessons in fear" are the equivalent to taking a drug to feel better. They do not last. You are most likely bound to repeat the same lesson until you learn it through Love. Love is not a body to depend on, a pill to take or a nice car. It is not something you can lean against with your arms, but you can lean into It with all your heart!

If you still feel hurt by John or Jim's actions, look carefully within to where you feel abandoned, betrayed or unloving. The part of you that feels this way is in need of healing. It cannot come from John or Jim. The belief that you could depend on them in any form was a trick of the ego to keep you away from the hidden belief that you indeed did separate from God. Thus the ego had you also believe that you were now vulnerable and unsafe. A next step for the ego was to "guide" you to some sort of "savior" or "safety." John demonstrated to you how fallible the ego's choice was in this case and the result was a resurfacing of past pain. The surfacing of guilt followed because the ego now told you how foolish a choice you had made. The mind is a funny thing. It will tell you to go ahead and eat a piece of cake and five minutes later it will say, "I wouldn't have done that if I were you!" Another lesson in fear not learned! Do you understand what I am saying, Margaret?

A failure to love is only a failure to remember Where Love *is*. It is in *you* and John and Jim and everyone, *behind* the misperceptions the ego would have you believe. That is why you must learn not to believe that you were hurt in any way. You can only be temporarily hurt by your choice to listen to fear. If you will determine to overlook these misperceptions and choose again, you will receive your true healing; you will receive the lesson of Love. It will not let you down.

God is all knowing, all seeing and all present, but hardly to be feared! He does not see what you have made of the world at all. He does not even recognize fear in any form. He simply knows it not to be true. So it is not there. You would not fear God if you knew this and you would simply laugh, knowing that it is not there as well. When you feel fear of God or of your Self, it is because you see "something" that is *not* there. Give it quickly to the Holy Spirit in you. He will remove it, if only you will let Him, and replace it with What is *forever yours*!

Your past lifetimes are only the lifetime you are living now. Karma is the "baggage" of guilt that follows you, only because you are in some way unwilling to let go of your clinging to it. The many lifetimes that all of you have lived have been to allow each of you the time you believe you need to accomplish its undoing. I would remind you that there is truly no time. Only the illusion of time seems to be for a while. It is hard for you who live in the world to comprehend the fact that linear time does not exist, nor does "history" or the body in the truest sense. Yet it is particularly difficult for you to deny this and it is entirely unnecessary for you to do so. It is necessary for you to heal your belief in karma in the negative sense. "Good" karma is nothing more than your choosing to relinquish your investment in guilt and live only with God now. In doing so you will undoubtedly give only Love to others. In this decision the special guilt relationship is replaced by the holy Love relationship whereby the conditions of guilt, control and fear are replaced by true perception and thus an understanding of Love.

There is little importance in contemplating your past karma with anyone. "Bad" karma is, as guilt is, a denial of Love. They are the same. Whatever baggage you may still carry that involves a relationship with another can only be healed now. To analyze, figure out or break down the past in intellectual terms is but an avoidance on the ego's part, a ploy to disguise the fact that healing needs to take place *now*.

You will hear the Voice for God, not through mere words and ideas, but through your feelings, your intuition and your "gut instincts." You may also at times see loving pictures.

Words and theories are really a last resort in helping you find the truth in you. It is truly through your forgiving the world, all its theories, words and past history that you will one day soon find God speaking to you. It will not be so much in words, but in the recognition, experience and joy of being only here, only now. When you learn to listen and appreciate this way, you will find great gifts indeed! For *you* can be all knowing, all present and all seeing!

Your true occupation with God is your true occupation with your Self. It is all you need do while you are here. It is all you can do while you are here. It is all you are supposed to do while you are here. What is your occupation? To let go of all the distractions you have interposed between you, your Self and God. This is the only karma that follows you. This is all that needs undoing — your wish for something else other than God. You can do this anywhere, with anything at any time. It does not matter what you seem to be doing, for in all of your preoccupation lies your one true desire, the will to know God as your Self. That is your true occupation. That is your calling. May you find it now, Margaret, in every moment of every day. It is with you forever. May Love find you now.

Our Gift is the Gift of God

We share together now.

And It is yours.

A Loving Jesus

UNBELIEVABLE BELIEFS

It is the many beliefs that you have formed in your life to help you that have instead become your burdens. The beliefs make up the dream that you are "dying," but that you seem to be "living." Without them there would be no dysfunction, crime, hatred or separation. There would be only Love and you would be happy. You would be helpful to one another instead of hurtful.

I have said before that to "believe" is also to imply that you do not know. Yet you *will* know as soon as you stop believing. You may be wondering if I am asking too much by asking you to stop believing. Yet this is what you must do, even if only for a moment, if you would truly remember God and His Creation. You must be willing to set all belief in the world aside.

Oh yes, I know this is very threatening to you. Why wouldn't it be? You have formed your whole life around a set of beliefs that God knows nothing about. Really, neither do you. But it is all you have to hold on to, so you want to defend your beliefs, at times even at the cost of your body's "life." That is because your beliefs make up your life and *are* your "life" separate from God. Is it not curious, then, that you would want to be separate from God in the first place? Could it be that you wish to replace God with your own beliefs about what He may be and thus about what you may be as well? It could be indeed. Behold the "heaven" you have made as "gods" through your beliefs!

What might happen if you set down all of your beliefs even for just an instant? The "heaven" you have made would not look so much like heaven to you anymore. In fact, in contrast, you would wonder why you have been living your life in such hell. Your life would look like it was being lived in a huge prison, your home being the individual cell where a prisoner sleeps at night, hides from her bad dreams and eats the little stash kept under the bed. Your world would suddenly be exposed for what you have all made out of it, a huge institution for bodies to go and hide away from God! It gives you shivers, does it not? Welcome to the world, the prison you have each made! This is the make-believe world you have made, a seeming prison apart from Love!

The power of belief in your world has moved mountains in front of you. The power of faith in only Love is much different. Faith in Him requires no belief at all. Faith can move mountains out of your vision and allow the sun to shine through. Faith can release you from the prison of belief you have made. So for a minute today, as an experiment for your own Self discovery, set all your beliefs down. Quiet your mind and all its eruptions and let the sun shine through. Let faith in God's Love be the sun in your hearts. No belief is necessary and nothing need be done. Just sit back and receive the Gift of your creation. That is all you need do. Are you willing to have just a little Heaven today?

QUESTION

If the world we made out of belief is the cause of all our problems and woes, how are we supposed to live in this mess and still overcome it and live in peace as you suggest? This just doesn't seem possible to me.

It isn't possible until you each stop taking what you are all believing so seriously. The world and all the problems that seem to occur in it, be it work or play, with a spouse or with a boss, or whatever the problem seems to manifest itself as, is still only one problem in truth. The *problem* is the *belief* in separation. This is the one belief that underlies all beliefs. It is the hidden conflict that comes between each of you through your different and opposing surface beliefs, or *denial*. For instance, to believe in Love one must also believe there can be an *absence* of Love. Why do you need to believe in Love? Love is a Fact, not a belief. So are you.

The world you made through your beliefs was designed to hide that Fact. It is only a dream taken as a serious reality. By this you have made it your prison, as I have said. But it can be changed in the blink of an eye to a world redeemed. Not by fixing it, but by not making the belief in it more valuable than your rejoining with one another in the *Fact* you are created *for*. To do this you must each learn to look past the appearance of separation to the Love in one another. The "appearance of separation" is only a dream you each made from your misperceptions formed out of your separate beliefs. If the dream were real and the guilt that came with it were real, indeed, you *would* all have a problem! But that is not the case here. Be thankful it is so. Your change of mind about the value and purpose of the world will be your ultimate healing of all sickness and fear. Would you not exchange this "mess" now for the world of Love God has kept for you as your true Reality? Blink your eyes and it is possible!

A Scribing for Debi

Hi Joel,

I just discovered your offer in the news and felt an overwhelming sense of "this is for you, Deb." There is an excitement within my spirit. I will trust that I will give you the info you need.

As for my life at this point, I feel restless. I have an obsession with food that will not go away. I study A Course in Miracles *and other spiritual teachings, and only want to be used in ministry. I feel as though there are changes needed in my life and I have the overall feeling that I am "missing something." There seems to be a hole inside of me.*

Questions...

1) *What is my next step to be taken for my spiritual growth and service?*

2) *Recovery from food addiction... How?*

3) *My writing... Continue?*

4) *I desire freedom and options... Would abundance of money bring this?*

5) *Relationships have been painful... How do I become healed of the fear?*

Thank you, Joel, and I look forward to hearing from you.

Blessings, Debi

Greetings Debi:

Welcome. I am honored to share God's gentle message of Light with you today.

You have asked what the next step is in your spiritual growth and service. Be assured, Debi, that you are already in the process of taking it. You have many gifts to offer many people. The healing that you are doing is a powerful witness to the miracles you are capable of performing with me through the Holy Spirit. There will come a time when you will understand your relationship to God so deeply that you will look back in laughter at all the "holes" you once experienced as "real." There are many miracles to come that I will perform with you. Listen, Debi, to my gentle Voice within steadily guiding you and leading you Home.

Salvation is not difficult. It merely asks that you be willing to set down your own motives, needs and desires and accept Love's gentle Word in their place. It is a matter of first relinquishing your own agenda, then carefully and quietly listening only for the Voice for truth. All illumination comes from this, whether it be listening carefully to the Holy Spirit's Voice in your sister or listening carefully for yourself. God can never be heard in the shrieks and cries of the world, for His Love awaits silently beyond the shadows that darkness has seemed to cast outward. Yet the darkness is not there. It seems to exist only because you still may choose it for a little while longer. The day will come soon when you will no longer desire to be led by only your own wants and wishes. You will understand clearly what they have done for you and then you will merely value aright.

You need only learn to ask for What is truly valuable and then listen, choosing your only goal as the peace of God. You will then be led by joy to go wherever it is you will, to do whatever there is to do. In your life you have done nothing wrong and everything right, Debi. Close at hand is your true remembrance of your walk Home with God. Heaven is not a place, but a state of mind in which the Daughter of God has stepped beyond the doors of time into the Palace of her only true desire — the Palace of God's perfect and eternal Love for you, Her child. You are the Daughter of God with me, Debi. Look for me everywhere you go. I am here within the tiny instant of peace that forever remains only an eye blink away from the shadows of the world. Quietly now, take my hand and let us walk in gentleness together on our journey into Heaven.

There is no greater gift you can give the world or yourself than the gift forgiveness will offer. It is through forgiveness that many of the happy dreams you once thought could not be yours will surely *be*. It is through your forgiveness that you will become a co-creator with God. It is through forgiveness that you will know joy. Who would not instantly join with you on such a happy and holy quest?

Let us speak now about your second question. Any addiction is only an effect of an underlying cause. Therefore, you are not recovering from being addicted to food. You were distracted into food as a form of denial designed to cover up pain. The key to recovery is in exposing the pain for what it is, then allowing it to be replaced by truth. The pain is based on guilt from the past, which you hold against yourself like a sharpened sword. You believe that, because you have "sinned," you must now punish yourself before God does. That is why it is so difficult for you to relinquish your pain *and* the weapon you use to keep it as your reminder. Your weapon in this case is food, the body your "victim," and your mind the judge to carry out sentence. Yet the purpose you have ascribed the mind is entirely faulty. Its purpose is to conceal guilt even further through its use of more distraction, punishment and condemnation. The "holes" you feel, Debi, are the results of these lingering beliefs that you are somehow flawed, faulty and therefore insignificant. Many of these old beliefs stem from one deeper belief that you are something other than spirit.

You will find that when you are not truly living in the present, communicating in the Light of love with all living things, you will be tempted toward these neurotic thoughts and behaviors. There is not one of you who have come to the world that can escape experiencing this from time to time. The key to the correction of your dilemma is to heal your perceptive picture of yourself and the world through the quiet gentleness of Love. It is here, in stillness, Where all insanity is brought to final rest. Make your conviction, then, to the Place in you Where all is serene, all is well and all is whole. Spend time there often and look forward to it with trust and faith. This is how you can heal all addictions and sickness. It is not difficult. It takes only a consistent effort on your part for your remembering. All of Heaven's angels will be with you, lifting you higher and higher with each decision you make to be still, and know that you are God's only Child.

My dear Debi, you *have* freedom and options! It is when you believe they have been taken from you that you forget your own God-given abundance. When you become weary, know that this need not be. You have everything creative within you right now. Think you that little paper strips or glossy metal machines will ever give you more? And where is it that they came from? You need only What you have to receive that which you think you desire. But if you believe that what you want is not what you have, then there is need again for healing, for you have become confused between Reality and illusion. God would not have this be. If you would have abundance, know Where abundance rises *from*. None of the dreams you seek or experience will ever have reality in truth. It is best for you to learn unequivocally to not take them seriously. It is this that causes confusion and fear in you and drains you of your creative ability and joyous understanding of eternal abundance. That is why the healing of all guilt is so essential to you. Once your guilt is healed the world will seem of little significance and you will find only joy and abundance everywhere.

Question five is a reasonable question to ask. Your relationships with one another will become frightening at times. That is because you each have determined to make "love gods" out of one another at times. A course you study calls these relationships "special." You even make another a god when you hate a brother as well. Through hate you are controlled, victimized and neglected. That is why real Love can have no conditions. If it did, you certainly would all be in much trouble. Truly, to love another as God loves you means that you must be willing to expose the part of yourself that seems weak, vulnerable and mistrusting. This is risky to the ego, but Spirit rejoices, knowing that in illusion's exposure it must begin to heal. Relationships offer you the opportunity to heal what you would otherwise hide. Many of you at times believe you are in relationship with the equivalent to "Hitler." But I say to you, he was as great a teacher as I, if not greater! For without him you would have not learned how great was your own investment in punishment, hatred, guilt and fear.

It is as it was. The very hatred that drove Hitler is also driving your next door neighbor. Not as a reality, but as an illusion that needs to heal. What is more, this illusion of hatred lingers in you as well. It all began because you each decided to take something for your very own that you knew in truth you couldn't do, but you tried anyway. Still, each time you reject God, you try again to usurp Reality and make it into your own personal nightmare. The consequence of this attempt remains unprecedented. A whole world of insanity seemed to evolve out of nothing! So you see, Debi, your relationships play a mighty role here. Without your risk to participate in unraveling your innermost "secrets," indeed you would be doomed to the hell you sometimes experience here. It is your relationships of the deepest intimacy that will ultimately set you free from the conditions you have imposed on yourself, others and the world. Who but the Christ in you could know of the perfect safety of Her eternal Mother In Heaven? *You shall know!* Your relationships will teach you that it is so!

Do your best not to rush into striving for perfection and total safety in your relationships, Debi. You will only succeed in stressing yourself and others. Everything is already set. You made it that way. You will receive the perfect teachers at the right time. You may seem to have choices to make while you are here, but you will never change a lesson you are here to learn. That is why you are here. Just relax and greet the next teacher who seems to come along. He/She will be the perfect one for you. My name is Jesus and I guarantee it! The other thing is to do your best to cultivate a sense of humor. If you could fly into space as the astronauts did and watch from a distance, you'd chuckle at the apparent intensity of the drama you've manufactured here. Spend a little time today and take the next flight Home to Heaven. All of Its joy and laughter is within your reach right now! Seek it in one another as well. May your true purpose be known on earth as it is in Heaven. The timelessness of Love is yours forever!

Blessed are you, Debi.

The Father's quiet Gift of Heaven is in you now.

Be, then, of good cheer,

A Loving Jesus

THE "VALUE" OF CONDEMNATION

It is not any wonder that you have each gotten caught in your own webs of obsession and compulsion at different turns. You each, at times, want to turn and run from the feelings you have that are caused from this underlying belief that you are separate from one another and God. At times, each one of you feels as though you are deserving of punishment because of these feelings. Some of you live in families that even support the idea of punishment, and so you each make the dream of separation all the more "real" for all of you. Punishment is the "god of sickness" the ego would have you follow, to keep time real and give darkness "life" in you.

The idea of punishment comes from the hatred that is instilled deep into your sub-conscious minds from this hidden belief in separation. It is really only this belief that seems to come out in one of many forms, and then unexpectedly wreaks havoc in your lives. By believing you are separate from each other and God and then hiding it, it follows that you would also believe you have committed the ultimate "sin" and act of treachery. This is where the split takes place in each of you. Now you see yourselves separate from God and at war with Him, fighting for your "survival" before He reacheth down and cast His mighty sword against your frail flesh. Not only do you see yourselves fighting with Him, but fighting as well with your brothers and sisters. You have a neat little word for this called "competition," which is only another fancy name for "justified separation."

The idea now, since you truly believe you have succeeded in this separation from your Self, God and your brothers and sisters, is to punish yourselves just enough so that God won't be too hard on you when He finally catches up to you. Your way of doing this is to keep your "distance" by honing a competitive edge, all the while making sure that you do not forget the guilt that "motivated" you to establish your little "camp" away from Home. You protect your "camp" and all it has made, while you go about your life finding different reasons to continuously punish yourself and others. This you call "living" in the world. The many forms in which this is all too glaringly apparent are your everyday reminders of where you think you have come.

Think you that God made this bleak place you have sought to call your "home"? Not at all! You made all this yourselves. Yet many of you complain that you do not understand why all this has happened. It happened because for one tiny instant, the Child of God forgot the Home from Which she came! In that instant a world opposite of Heaven seemed to suddenly appear. Now, it seems, here you are.

Could it be that this is all illusion, a dream you made up from the guilt of your believing that you had separated in that tiny, mad instant? Could be! Is it possible that all the seeming madness, self-inflicted hatred and dis-ease is but a dream you have made up to punish yourself and keep the face of your ego "alive"? Could very well be.

Is there a way out of all this? Do you want there to be a way out of this? The key lies in each individual mind to choose the One Mind we share *together*. I can assist you if you ask for help with joining this One Mind. Yet neither God nor I would ever interfere with any other choice you make. How will you heal a world that is broken in a million chards and has gone completely insane without a unifying solution?

There is only one way out of sickness and insanity; it is through your forgiveness of the frightening dreams you have all made into your "reality." You cannot heal it by taking political stances or fighting wars or even by correcting your brothers and sisters "mistakes." You cannot take a pill, remove a limb or build more jails and hope to live in peace. You cannot do it. It will not last. If you would have the world be a picture of health and beauty, then you must do only one thing: Change your mind about the purpose you have each ascribed to the world. Instead of it being one of separation and competition, it must become one of reuniting and genuine helpfulness. You cannot do this without your complete forgiveness. You must include everyone in this or it is not genuine, my brothers and sisters. It must be all encompassing to be complete.

How will this be done, when so many of you have so many opposing beliefs and so much fear? It begins right now with you, with your change of mind and willingness to truly forgive. Yet it is not a forgiveness for all of the horrible things you think have happened. It is a forgiveness for all that has never happened in truth. Your reality has never been here where you stand, my dear ones, nor has It ever changed at all. What God created for you, He has kept for you. When all is truly relinquished that is not true and thus truly forgiven, you will behold amongst you a Kingdom never before imagined!

A SCRIBING FOR DAVE

Dear Jesus,

I live in England with my family. I have been troubled/depressed for some time now. I am very tired, but also impatient to change. My wife, Jean, holds me and the rest of our family together. She is also very tired. I have three wonderful children (Lana — seventeen, Billy — eleven and James — six). They are my only real contribution to the world. I have lived in fear all of my life, retreating to solitude/ seclusion and depression whenever I have been hurt/rejected. I know I cannot change by myself and I do pray to Jesus. I feel I do not know how to pray or how to ask for anything. I am scared to ask for or want anything. Generally, I do not feel anything at all, like I am a void/ vacuum, disconnected from life itself. I worry a great deal, almost like it's a habit/vice. I have some financial difficulties, even though I am very well paid. I seem to be living a dilemma and unable or maybe unwilling to decide and move forward.

I would like Jesus to guide me with my job. What should I do? I want to make a contribution. What should I do? I would like to bring joy to others instead of anger, sorrow and rejection. Please teach me about Love and forgiveness and give me strength to carry on. Which way should I go?

Thank you, Dave

Greetings Dave:

Let us begin this communication discussing *perception*, a term you are very familiar with, but are also apt on occasion to use as a weapon against yourself.

Change, properly understood, is an occurrence that you are only capable of experiencing while you are subjecting your mind to beliefs and perceptions of the ego. The ego mind is relentless in bringing change after change into your awareness, all for the purpose of sustaining the insane delusion of its existence. It is true that through your thinking you have invented all the changes you see yourself walking through. This is not justification for guilt. If you knew Where to find happiness, you would have gone there already. Since you are not happy, it is obvious that you should not blame yourself for not understanding how to be happy. Instead, completely abandon the thought system that made your misery in the first place.

The ego is not telling you this. In fact, it is telling you just the opposite. I would gently admonish you now to stop listening to this grotesque interpretation of yourself and the world and follow only the Voice for Love in you instead. I remain at the borderline of where your thought system ends and Where the Thought of God begins. I will lift you with me through the veil that your thinking has imposed, should you choose to abandon your presently confused state and follow only me. I need only your willingness and full trust to do this, for only this will show you beyond a doubt the complete waste of time involved in following any of the ego's dictates at all. Let go of all judgments, thoughts and perceptions that would interfere even in the slightest, for none of them belong in your most holy mind!

If you desire to heal, you must let me teach you *to* heal through the Holy Spirit. I cannot teach you as long as you insist on being the author and protector of your own distorted view of "reality." What you have made of your reality is as far from the truth as hell is from Heaven. Yet hell in you does not really exist. The logic of Love would tell you that the hell you have been living is but a very frightening dream. If you do not want this dream any longer, the Holy Spirit will gladly take it when you are willing to completely relinquish it and replace it with a dream of gentle healing and forgiveness. Your dreams may seem frightening now, but what if they are not real?

Would you not be happy to discover that they can easily vanish in the twinkling of an eye? Would you not have them replaced by the happy dream of forgiveness the Holy Spirit lovingly holds out to you now? Let go, my dear David, and allow His healing Light to enter your darkened dream now! It is only a dream and nothing more, no matter how much the ego would want for it to be true. Will you walk with me this day away from all past devastation and into our Father's guiding Light? Take my hand. I am with you now in this very instant as you read this, waiting for you to give up the dream and walk happily Home with me.

You had accepted many punishments and guilt when you were younger, David. The pain you feel now when someone seems to let you down is a direct result of this earlier primary "wounding." To some degree you have been living your life in reaction to this repressed shame. To some degree you have also been teaching it as well. Is it not time to completely absolve yourself of this painful belief system? You do not need any of it to live well and happy.

Before you can live truly in peace with your Self, you must risk exposing that which is not Love. You cannot pretend it is not there and hope it will go away. You must look at it. Better still, look with a witness you trust, so that you can hear and experience the cries and tears that have been left buried and unacknowledged for so long. You must be willing to bring this out into the light where Love can shine it away. There is anger there as well. But I tell you, it is past the anger where your true healing lies. In this hidden place beyond the anger is an eternal, gentle and innocent being that for a while has been hidden behind fear in the corner of a deep, dark cavern. It seems to be made of stone, but again I tell you, it is as thin and penetrable as a wispy cloud. It has seemed to "protect" you, but in truth it has kept you from the very truth you have longed for so long. Trust, walk through this cloud, David, and into the Light with your beloved witnesses. Nothing can stop you if you will just leave the clouds behind. God Himself will Witness for you and Light will shine through, transforming the cavern into an illumined Altar to Heaven.

You are correct to say you cannot change by yourself, but you can choose to change your mind in spite of your own ego. The ego is but a little cloud, seeming to stand in your way, yet very easily walked through and beyond. While you let the ego stand in front of you like a rock, you allow your mind to be ruled by an insane dictator, who would see you immobilized, as if to be in a void and disconnected from Life Itself. Oh yes, the ego would offer you oblivion in place of the Gift of Heaven your Father gave you! It is only you who believes there is a decision to be made between the two. If you believe you can choose oblivion, you choose nothing at all. Death, then, is exactly what the ego wishes for you, but in the end can never give you. Yet it can seem to make you miserable now. Its darkened wish only seems to overcome as long as you give power to the insane reasoning it offers. The Son of God just fools himself with these silly dreams. He cannot die anymore than his Father could. Is there really any choice other than Heaven?

All of the worries, fears and depression you are experiencing are caused by the power you are giving to your own thinking. As we have discussed, these unhealed thoughts continue because you have not closely questioned the thoughts you hear. Part of this is due to your mind not being well disciplined to avoid wandering from the holy instant. The other reason is because you do not believe you are worth the effort to bring and keep your mind under only the Holy Spirit's loving guidance.

You must learn to practice daily engaging with God. There is nothing more important than this, since your Self is all you have. Would you not want to recognize and live in What you are, rather than in what you can never be? The answer lies in your willingness to be still and appreciate the true Gift God has given you. His Gift is not in words, nor is mine, since they are the same. Words can only lead you away from or *to*. The experience of Love and God's serene peace is the complete undoing of the ego. If, for one instant, you are able to truly still your mind, your experience of the world and your Self will never again be the same! Begin a daily spiritual practice with the full conviction of your heart and mind.

Above all, David (and you can say you heard this directly from me), learn never to take any of your own thoughts or the thoughts of others seriously! Here is God's perfect logic to explain why: If a thought is truly loving then it is truly joyous and happy, but if a thought is fearful then its communication is valueless. Why would you not laugh with thoughts that are loving, and why would you not laugh as well at a thought without meaning or reality? Laugh, David. There is not a thing in this world to truly take seriously!

Eternal Love cannot be threatened. What is not eternal cannot be threatening because it is not there. The Thought of God is with you now and forever. But It is only here in the holy instant Where God placed It in you. You can imagine that your private thoughts are a branch that you have made as an offshoot of His Thought, for that is what you are doing when you think with the ego; you are "borrowing" the energy of Love and turning It into a withering branch. Cut it off. Get back to your Root, which is Love, and let the dead bury the dead!

Now let us speak of your occupation and your work. You will perhaps have many jobs as the world judges, but your true occupation has always been with God. The only work you are ever truly doing is when you are ready, with full sincerity, to take the risks necessary for your own healing. These risks may involve what seem to be a relinquishing of certain things and ideals. In the end you will not see it this way. In fact, you will be glad to have your life more simplified because you will recognize finally Where only true value can be. Nothing in this world will ever supply you with What you will receive from your Self. God gave you the Gift of Christ and His Gift contains everything you have ever needed or really wanted.

This will become more apparent as you develop your ability to hear only One Voice. Then your life will simplify and fill with clarity and vision. It will not matter where you "work" in the world. Should you not like your job, you will simply trust in your own inner Safety and choose to move on, knowing that wherever and whatever you are doing in your worldly "work," your real occupation can also be fulfilled. As your development of trust in Spirit increases, you will also feel little limitation regarding *what* you can do in the world. There is nowhere you can be and not accomplish your *true occupation* with God.

The *occupation* God gave you was to bring peace and joy to every mind and heart. The *"work"* you will do for God and your Self to achieve mastery in your real occupation is whatever healing still remains. To do your work you may find that, for a while, you need to make outside changes so that you are better able to achieve trust in your environment. Once healing is close at hand and your true *occupation* with God is firmly established, you will be happy most everywhere you go.

The most important question you can ask regarding occupation is: "What is the purpose of this occupation?" A worldly occupation can be used for fear or Love. If it is loving, it becomes an occupation with joy. If it is hated, it becomes a *preoccupation* with fear. It is not ever the fault of the occupation, but rather the choice of the decision maker to see himself without choice and in prison. The healing lies not necessarily in a change of environment, but in a change of mind and release of faulty perception.

You have a great contribution to make, but it is not to the world as your ego led you to believe. This is perhaps the greatest of all seemingly shared illusions among the separated ones — that a "worldly" contribution is necessary for their "peace of mind." I will attempt to explain this, even though it is almost impossible for you to grasp a full understanding of this while you are choosing to believe you are in this world. The dreams you have and hold are what makes up the world you see. Without dreams the world would simply vanish and the Son of God as Christ would simply awaken to his Home in Heaven, a Place Where he never left but seemed to leave while in his imagined dreams.

Your Reality is only Love. It has never changed and will forever remain perfect as your Reality. The fact that you do not recognize this does not change anything. You are God's One Creation and, my child, you are at Home with Him. The great contribution you will make, and I promise that you *will* do this, will be when you are entirely willing to "risk" (as your ego sees it) and complete your *work*, accepting your *true occupation* with God. When you do this you will extend only peace and live in the perfect faith and awareness of Love. There is nothing greater for you to do here. It is *all* you came to do. What greater accomplishment and occupation could there be than to transcend the world, recognize your Self and live in God's perfect peace and joy?

Would you take the world seriously? Or would you exchange all of what perception offers and sincerely take only Love instead? You made the choice to forget. The choice was impossible in truth. Yet it will seem so for a while, until you are ready to happily change your mind about the "reality" of your dreams. Why not exchange them now, David, and live in the gentle peace your Father saved for you? Why not *now*?

Be not afraid to ask for what you want, David, but be sure it *is* what you truly want. Your prayers have been answered already.

God has always known your greatest need. Pray only to recognize What you truly *have* and *are* in Him, Who created you. This will be your greatest contribution to yourself and everyone. When you finally awaken, the whole world will rejoice with you! There will be no one who will not be there to help you fulfill the great mission you have accepted. Rejoice my dear David, for the Light is come to lead the way. Indeed, angels surround you to assist you and lead you back Home. My faith in you is perfect. You will soon make the right choice and the *only* choice. I will be right next to you when you do. Listen now to the Voice of the Holy Spirit as He sings God's Words from Heaven to you. In gentleness and quiet you will remember this day, for He has come!

Here is my prayer for you. Say it often with the conviction of my Heart to yours:

"Father, I have sought to think apart from You and make a world separate from my Self. I have made this sight to terrify and deceive myself into believing that separation from You is real. I have given power to my thoughts that is wholly without justification and cause. I would relinquish my belief in them now, so that I may receive Your Thought as You have offered It. Let me remember that with You I need not think at all, but only enjoy the experience of Your loving understanding. Let me be still and receive only Your Word for me now. Let me stand back and let Heaven's Love lead the way. I want only What is mine in You. May I receive only This now."

Amen

David, receive the Gift you have asked for now. It has been sent to you through me, just as *you have asked*. Call on me through the Holy Spirit often. I will always be right here to lift you to Him if you would only be still and listen. I have given you all the means to do so. And so, let it be done for you. That is my blessing unto you. Blessed are you who have asked and received.

A loving Jesus

And David… The world is the only place with a serious problem: It does not recognize the utter futility and laughability of its own grand delusion. Laugh often, play more and let conflict discover the time it has most certainly wasted.

STEPPING BEYOND THE PICTURE OF PAIN

Just as your grievances made a world and all its illnesses, your forgiveness will undo it. The physical world is but a reflection of what you wanted, which left you comfortless indeed. If you were to remove all belief and perception, the physical would be as meaningless and as empty as space. The physical has no value, except what you give it through your beliefs and perceptions. What makes it seem real to you is the perceptual definition you have given it. Your perceptions offer appearances, and appearances always deceive.

For instance, most of you believe that I was attacked, beaten and crucified to death many, many years ago. Because of this apparent tragedy and loss, religions were invented, my brothers were made to feel guilty over my "death" and God has been represented by many as vengeful. Yet I did not teach that any of this was true. In fact, I taught only the opposite: That you *are* eternal and *cannot* die! Though you cannot see my body now, I am still here in your hearts. My resurrection in your hearts is proof that I did not die. Still there are those who see the lamb as blood stained and who are still punishing one another because they *believe* I did *die*. Now do you see how strong your investment can be in the physical, even though the physical is just a picture of past illusion?

I ask only for your faith in my resurrection through our one living God *now*. My perfect faith is only here and that is how I would demonstrate to you that death does not exist. You could not hear my voice if I were not in the hearts of each of you. There is no doubt that many of you are beginning to *hear*. When I said I would come back to you in a form you could understand, this is what I meant.

If you hear me it is because you have chosen to abandon your world and enter the World of God with me. Forgiveness offers the means for you to accomplish our reuniting. Forgiveness offers the means to heal all sickness. Forgiveness offers your resurrection from all death and destruction. Through forgiveness all wounds are healed; not some wounds, *all wounds*.

You do not need your beliefs, perceptions or even your thoughts to remember the holy Place from Which we come. You need only release your investment in all the symbols and fantasies you made to awaken and be glad. It is a matter of right evaluation and that is all. When you have learned to value only Love and only peace, the idea of sickness and harm will become utterly meaningless to you. Forgiveness is the prerequisite to healthy living in a world that was made to offer otherwise. Learn, then, how to forgive. Only in this learning will your life heal and move forward into one that nothing in this world can assail. Join with me and all your sisters and brothers in the eternal Purpose only God has ascribed and watch with me as the world is born again.

Chapter Three

EMPLOYMENT & THE REAL PURPOSE OF THE WORLD

Gently my child, your work is your play. The time you give it is yours to say. You needn't worry, all is in place. Nothing you do can take you from grace. I've come to remind you that wherever you go, I will be with you to see that you're well.

A SCRIBING FOR TERRY

Dear Joel,

I would like you to scribe for me from Jesus.

1) *What am I to make of the "failure" of my career as a chiropractor?*

2) *What direction would be the highest possible expression for me now?*

3) *Is meditation what God would have me do to hear His Voice more clearly?*

4) *Can I create a career for myself combining or using separately the elements of music, writing and spirituality? That is, can I be "good enough" to be paid by the world for doing what I love the most?*

5) *How can I best help my wife and daughter right now?*

I used to quote Dickens in describing these days, both for myself and for the world. "They were the best of times. They were the worst of times." Lately... dare I say it?... these seem to be the best of times. Although I am not making much money, I feel more at peace than ever before in my life. True, I am wondering how I will make a sufficient living for my family, but I feel more connected to God and my true interests in life. A Course In Miracles, my guitar, writing, this computer, working with my brother-in-law and his mate, running, watching my daughter grow in love and beauty — all these things, and especially the freedom I am experiencing, bless me deeply. I look to God in gratitude and know indeed that He loves me. I want to share these feelings and blessings with whomever will partake. I don't ever again want to settle for less than what God would have for me. I don't ever again want to experience fear and dread on a daily basis. Thank You, Father. I love.

Terry

Greetings Terry:

This is Jesus. Let us be aware of what you are asking for today. You are asking the Christ, with Whom you and I reside, to give you some answers through Joel. As scribe he has agreed to assist us in helping you remember this. At no time during this process am I separate from you. I am not speaking outside you, as it may appear. Everything that is true and comes from Christ is coming from within you. Never has it been that *A Course In Miracles* enlightened you or that Joel will enlighten you now. Nothing that has seemed to happen from outside you has ever really occurred. All that has brought you closer to peace, you received from Christ in God within. Let us now go on.

It is better to be seen as a pauper and know joy, than to be seen as a king and know ruin. You have an awareness of this. Do not trade your joy for anything that might compromise this. Seek *through* the joy and guidance of the Holy Spirit, the way in which to manifest the abundance that is already yours. It appears to the fearful that all that is accomplished in the world is done through fear. But I say to you, nothing in the world is accomplished but through Love. It is through the joy you have remembered with your holy companions that great abundance will manifest for all of you. The joyous know whole-heartedly that everything that is truly received is received *only* through joy. The joyous have learned not to judge by appearances, for it is in appearances that the Son of God grapples with his greatest temptation to see himself as lacking. What are appearances but delusions about one's self? Judge not by appearances, Terry. Instead, recognize only the Gift you have and are now. All else will be taken care of *for* you.

Let us now discuss your question number four. Indeed, you can create a career using some or all of the talents you have described. What is more, you *will*. You will also be using your chiropractic talents as well. What you have been experiencing is a shift in your dependency on the old way of viewing and handling your "professional career." You have attempted to follow some of the "norms" you were taught in school and learned through observing how others approached "the business," and to some degree have tried to follow in those footsteps. This did not work out, and this you refer to as your "failure." It is not a failure at all. It is a triumph!

You are still in the process of discovering where your power really lies. You were taught that power is in education, well developed "tools of the trade" and in all the many different forms you have learned about. These forms are indeed helpful, but not until you have allowed me, through the Holy Spirit, to direct your use of them. You wonder why you haven't gotten clear direction from the Holy Spirit on their use. I would tell you that the reason for this is because you are still "sorting." There is still some confusion about "power." This will pass as you gain more confidence in your *true* Power. Once this happens, you will begin to hear clear inner direction on how you will be most helpful to everyone with your talents, while making an abundant living for your family as well.

But this will not be in the "norm" that you are accustomed to. It will be considerably different, and the work involved will seem at first to be almost overwhelming. This will pass, and remember that I said this. Now the main thing for you is to continue to develop trust in the Spirit of Love within you.

Once this is more fully developed, you will have little trouble knowing what direction to take your career. In developing trust with your Self, you will also be developing a deepened trust within your family. This will be important, for you will need their full support as you tread along the new path you are about to follow. There is "risk" involved to step out past the "norm" and do what you are truly guided to do. In fact, *anything* that is truly guided by me involves "risk" to the ego.

The ego is frightened to its foundation whenever you choose to go beyond the limitations it has set for you. But be not afraid. Go ahead and reach to where your heart and the Holy Spirit guides you. The "risk" involved is minuscule in comparison to the gifts that are ahead. Most of the "hard work" that you will do to reach the place you feel guided to be is only the breaking down of your own resistance to what is inevitable anyway. You know deep inside what you must do. It is now a question of listening carefully to it and then following it. Terry, doing what you love the most is *all* you came here to do. Could that be a clue for better "hearing" what you are now not sure of? Your inner Voice has the key to your destiny in your pocket. Reach for the key!

In answer to your fifth question — you can best help your wife and daughter simply by doing what I have explained above. The key that unlocks your future will be a model for unlocking theirs. You are a teacher to them as they are to you. It is of the highest order for each of you to listen carefully to one another. They will be helpful to you in many ways, if you can listen. Your daughter is quite free and she can teach you how to *be* free. Your wife has an enormous amount of trust and she can help you there. Your family is there for much more than meets the eye. Observe carefully, looking beyond their forms, and you will see the gifts they have to offer. Hear their messages, for I work through them with the Holy Spirit every day to help each of you.

The greatest gift you can offer them is to follow your heart and realize through it your greatest potential. You teach them by what you model, not by what you say. If you do not take risks, they will learn with you not to take risks as well. If you limit yourself to only the laws of this world, they will limit themselves in the same way. Learn, then, to trust in the Heart of Love in each of you. Each of you has a calling. This calling is what joins you together. Yet each calling takes a different form for everyone. The capability that each of you have to develop this calling is based in your ability *together* to overcome your obstacles to peace.

Guilt and fear have no place in the healthy family relationship. Punishment is never an option, but healthy consequences and agreements are. All of you surpass your limitations by keeping your agreements and being responsible for the consequences of your choices. Many good parents have mistakenly set their families back by using some form of blame or attack to enforce consequences. This is both unnecessary and unloving. If consequences are clearly agreed upon ahead of time, then there is no need for blame or attack. All that is necessary is for each person to embrace the consequences they have set up *for themselves* in their agreements. This teaches each person that *they* are indeed imposing their own limitations. It also teaches that *only they* are the ones who can overcome them. So it serves each of you to help one another to overcome limitation *together*. That is the function of the family. Forgiveness is at the foundation of any thought system which leads to unlimited possibilities. Remember this and love one another in this way always. You are doing wonderfully at this already.

You have asked about meditation. Meditation and prayer are the *only* means by which you can hear and *maintain* contact with your inner Voice. I cannot reach into your mind unless you are willing to set aside the thoughts about the world you are often preoccupied with. Perception, at its best, can be trained to disregard itself. Once you have developed good listening skills in meditation and your mind is filled with Light, you can keep better contact with your Self, the Holy Spirit in your everyday activities.

Many make the mistake of thinking that once they have awakened to Spirit, they no longer need to take a daily spiritual quieting. This is hardly the case in a world that has been perfectly designed to stand against God in every way! You must meditate undisturbed at least once a day if you intend to remain creative and peaceful. If your mind is well enough disciplined, it can be taught to remind you every hour or so to give a moment to God. You should practice this. If you find you are forgetting to do this, and the time becomes every two or three hours, then it is time to re-evaluate what you are really asking for. Do you want the peace of God or the insanity of the world? Can insanity ever offer you anything?

This brings us to your remaining question, question number two. I have offered many tools in the above dialogue to help you find your "highest expression." What is most important, Terry, is that you clearly learn the difference between What is valuable and what is not. "Value" seems to be in material possessions but it is not. There is nothing valuable except your Self, Which you already share with everyone. All of your answers to all of your "problems" are *already* answered within your Self. The more gentle devotion you give your Self, the more your unlimited value will become apparent to the world. What will hold you back then, you holy Son of God? All your truly creative ability comes from here. There is truly nothing to hold you back. You and your family are freed as you will allow each of your self-imposed limitations to be lifted. What can limit you except guilt from the past or fear of the future? Place no value in either and know, Terry, your unlimited potential and innocence *now*. In God *all* things *are* possible. Need you look anywhere else but to Him Who is already forever yours? If you should need, call and I *will* be there with Him for you always.

This is my Gift to you, Terry.

Grace and peace be unto you who have asked

and have received.

Great blessing upon you and your family.

Eternally, a loving brother

Jesus – Christ

LIFE CAN BE FUN

It is your working *together* that will turn your work to play. Life on the planet can be fun. In fact it is supposed to be fun. Healing is one reason you came here and creating with God is another. Those who are not having fun are still resistant to healing. Those who are having fun have accepted their holy function. It is not easy to enjoy an occupation one dislikes, yet many of you do the job you dislike anyway because you feel a sense of obligation. Then you learn to resent to whom you're obliged. It is a sticky business when one allows guilt to motivate them. "Welcome" to the ego machine. "Welcome" to the fear that binds you, for here is the picture presented to you that is clearly in need of healing.

Not all of you are aware of it, but your world is headed for colossal changes. Not too far in your world's future, all will be much different than it is right now. The change is already beginning, even though many of you are still clinging to the old. Change in the world is frightening to the ego. Yet it is blessed to you, for it teaches you that your world is not dependable. As it burns you, you learn to rely less and less on the things of the world and more and more on the Self God created for you. When frustration finally reaches its critical level and giving up is in order, then can come the "big shift."

A WORD FROM JOEL

Wow! This is excellent! I actually get to say something here.
It is suggested by Jesus that I explain to you, the reader, about the following set of scribings. The scribings to Thornton are a set of several. Thornton is a friend with whom I'm sure I go back many lifetimes. He came to me and asked for these scribings over a period of about one year.

A Scribing for Thornton

Dear Elder Brother,

I have asked Joel to be a conduit for you. He said to write it out and he would give me your answers in written form.

As I come to you in conversation, I want to be totally honest. There "seems" to be an enormous amount of fear coming up about my perceived lack of money, about scarcity. I choose not to deny it, but it "seems" real and it "seems" to be my constant companion. I'm feeling frozen in fear. Not knowing which way to turn, I take NO action.

I have chosen this path, this Course you have given me. "Love IS the way I walk in gratitude." Thank you.

Greetings Thornton:

I am with you always and I am not deceived in you or in understanding. I am always entirely willing to share with you at any given moment that you are entirely willing to hear.

You *are* deceived in yourself and me and you do not understand what total honesty means. This is why you are afraid. You will continue to be confused as long as you continue to *try* and *try* to understand the meaning of "total honesty" on your own. Could God be totally honest without *you*? Can you be totally honest without me? Yet you *are* quite willing to pretend that you are "alone," Thornton, to such an extent that you are at times almost *frozen in fear,* yet still convinced that you *are* being "totally honest."

I will gently repeat myself and encourage you to listen; *you* do not understand because you do not hear and you do not hear because you are afraid of what it would bring. What it would bring would be an end to your own ego's dishonesty. You believe you have been dishonest and therefore that you *are* dishonest. That is why you are constantly driven to preempt conversations and communication with me and everyone with, "I want to be totally honest," or, "I want my intent to be perfectly clear to you."

No one can be "perfectly clear" or "totally honest" when they believe they are *someone else*. It is quite apparent that because of this, they are so confused they believe that dishonesty *can* be made honest. Do not dream that you can make "reality," Thornton, for this thinking must only confuse you. Do not try to make your dreams "honest" or you must certainly isolate your understanding even further. Dreams are forever dreams and that is all.

It is not *you* who is dishonest, but the ego you have made to replace what you are, and it will always be a lie. You *think* you know who you are and that is your whole problem. You will not be able to identify yourself in this way for long without suffering, Thornton, because you have felt the joy of being attuned with your own God given Self. I sent you the *Course* you study to bring you to a joy that is beyond your physical identity and all mental identification. It is now time for you to begin to experience your Self beyond the tangible in everyone and everything.

You do not always see me or the Christ in others because you have not overcome the sense of guilt the ego has fostered in you around dishonesty. *This* is why you feel log-jammed around the area of your upper heart and throat. Your words are still under your control alone and this is hurting you. *Place the function of communication under my control, as I have asked of you* and you will be taking a giant step in overcoming your sense of dishonesty and thus fear. You are not dishonest, Thornton, and everyone but you sees this. They honor the love and great joy that shines through you into them. You do not always believe this because you still see yourself in "control," even though your life is under the control of only the Love you receive and send to others. Be the Love that is shared in everyone. Let go of this false control.

There is a "seeming" to the fear you are experiencing. What you are feeling seems real to you and it is unwise to try to experience it any differently. If you fail to acknowledge and release the suffering you are choosing around finances, you may fail also in this "test" to truly and finally discover where both your true worth and unlimited Self lie. The test, as *you* have asked for, will either break through a seemingly thick wall of unhealed apathy and old self-deceit, *or* make the wall seem even more tough to break down later. Either way *you* cannot lose. Either way the ego has *already* lost. Your true Self will survive, and then you will know *you are a miracle worker*.

You have said that you choose not to deny what *seems* to be real to you, what seems to be your "constant companion." Yet you *are* denying the presence of fear in your mind by labeling it as *only* an appearance. Your heart longs to acknowledge and feel the pain and *then* completely break *through* it, while the ego defends *against* the existence of what you need to fully experience. How else will the fear be disarmed? What the ego defends *against* by reducing its importance, only becomes more "real" until you are forced to recognize its presence. Let us be *totally honest*, Thornton. Fear thoughts have been so well hidden by the ego's dishonesty that you are frozen in fear of recognizing them in your mind. These fear thoughts are dark indeed, my brother, but if you will ask me, or another who will witness with me for you both, together we will undo the blocks to your experiencing Where your only Power lies.

Deep within you, beyond the thoughts of your world, is the Answer to every "seeming" limitation your mind has ever invented. Since you made these obstacles from your own self-hatred and fear of Love, you must first recognize the power of your mind when you place it in the ego's hands. Siding with the ego, you have made a lie into your own private "truth" and you have then denied the fear that you have hidden in your mind. Yet keeping it clearly in mind and denying that you are making fear thoughts real at the same time, you have unknowingly fostered a perfectly imperfect and self-perpetuating ego dynamic that has been ingeniously placed out of reach from all offered help. This is because in experience it is kept "real" by each painful reminder. In your heart you realize it cannot be true.

You cannot completely deny what is in your heart, even if it is merely an illusion. You cannot say in your mind it is not there, yet in your experience "seem" to feel it. It *is* there in your experience until you change your mind. You will not change your mind until you accept the *totality* of your suffering. It will not *pretend* away, and the longer you attempt to rationalize its presence in your mind, the more you will see it in bits and pieces that will not seem to fit together. Allow yourself to recognize the pain in full, Thornton. If you are honest you *cannot* deny it. Fear is fear. Even the tiniest bit unacknowledged may as well be a thousand worlds separate from God.

It is time to let go, my brother. Walk with me slowly down the path to our Father's gentle Abode. Join with me and allow yourself to remember I am with you. Let me hear your deepest heart, for whatever fills it has come from your travels while away from Home. Empty it to me that I may find room for our Father's Light to enter, for all that you hold heavy in your heart I would ask you now to place entirely in my hands. Give me *your experience, your deepest suffering, your lightest moments*. Be honest from your most open heart, Thornton, for I am your brother Jesus and I need the totality of your gifts that their purity and fullness may rejoin us now as one. Hide nothing; hold back nothing. Let all you feel and desire come forth now as we walk together on our way Home. I am right here with you. Take my dedication to the healing of your heart *now*.

Blessings,

Jesus

PREPARING FOR THE BIG SHIFT

This *big shift* is the turning point that you will reach in how you approach your work and survival issues. For some of you it will be early on. For others it will be very late in your earthly lives. Everyone will reach this turning point eventually and you will reach it together. It is at this turning point where one realizes he or she no longer needs to be oppressed by the ways of the world. No longer is it necessary to react to situations like a robot wearing one-directional blinders to keep sight limited. Many of you are now beginning to remove your blinders and question the *value* of what you are doing to make your contribution. Many more are to follow in your footsteps in the near future.

It is at this turning point in your human lives where suddenly you begin to experience miracles. You cannot reach this turning point unless you become weary of the old way, that is, the old standards of limitation and fear which have long bound you. It is the relinquishment of a cocoon that no longer serves to assist you in your growth into the life that brought you here. It is the giving up of trying to solve all your problems through the typically dictated mundane everyday struggle. In this giving up, birth is given to a newborn Son and Daughter of God. It is the ending of the world you once knew and hated and the beginning of a new world that shines joyously in all its glorious majesty. It is the transformation in *you* from a world ruled by guilt to one that is ruled only by the limitlessness of perfect Love.

ANOTHER SCRIBING FOR THORNTON

Joel, I'm sure you remember the day. I was so distraught, I didn't have enough money to pay the full amount of rent, not to mention all of the other bills I had staring me in the face. We had just pulled into my garage. We sat there in the car for awhile and had a talk. I started pouring it all out to you. I was still "frozen" in fear, not knowing where to turn. You listened patiently while the tears streamed down my cheeks. You then related the picture that suddenly appeared in your mind. You saw me just starting to cross a rope bridge. I was standing there, hesitating and gripped with fear. You said I knew that I had to cross this bridge. We then went inside where I later asked these questions of Jesus.

Dear Elder Brother,

I feel so low, so gripped in fear. I do not have the funds to pay my rent.

How do I handle this financial crisis I'm in? How can I pay all of those I owe? I'm not getting any answers on my own. I still feel "frozen," not knowing WHAT to do. I don't want to lose my house, yet that seems very real right now. The thought of a roommate to help with the rent has crossed my mind. I've made it very dark right now, brother.

Greetings Thornton:

Perhaps you will eventually find it difficult, us meeting like this? Indeed, though it may be a peculiar way of hearing, it well suits our purposes for meeting our common needs at this time. It is also good to know, however, that you are now occasionally consciously receiving my assistance by more direct means. This is what happens when the pain of holding onto the world's offerings finally becomes less valued than the joy of finding your Self in God with me. Indeed, this is a crossing of a sturdy, yet still unfamiliar, rope bridge. You still believe you must hold on tightly as you cross for fear of what supports you. Yet there will come a day soon where you will dance across the same bridge to the other side! The ropes, Joel's assistance or anything else for that matter, will not keep you from flying over the top to your Destination! You will merely *value correctly* and then you will find yourself sitting with me on the other side!

You cannot but be in the right place at the right time! The answer waits for you to receive it until you *want* to receive it. You may not hear it because you do not *want* to hear it. The answer waits for this remaining decision to be made. How can you be listening properly if you do not hear and yet the answer to all your problems is already come? You must still be listening to "something else."

You have asked about where to apply your finances for the most efficiency during this apparent crisis. If you will look inside you will surely see that this question is already answered. Prioritize what is most important to you *now*. Pay your bills thusly. Do not be concerned what anyone thinks. Simply do what is possible and what is fair within your apparent limitations. *But do not hide from anyone.* I emphasize this because of your tendency at times to hide from my guidance. It is the same out there as it is *in here*. Are you looking for the awareness of Love's Presence in everyone, including the bill collectors? Or are you looking for fear and *finding it*? Again, *what do you want to value?*

It is the same in answer to your question, "How do I handle this financial crisis?" There is no question that you must *relate* to many others in your life at this time, especially in view of your apparent circumstances. The question is, are you relating lovingly and creatively or are you relating through gripping, gripping fear? Fear, of itself, is entirely useless. Other than acknowledging that a specific fear exists and turning it over so it can heal, there is nothing else it is useful for other than entirely letting it go. By keeping your mind in fear, you only succeed in becoming more "frozen." You stay in fear only because you *do think* it will help somehow. It will not! Now is a time of loving *action*, not fearful stagnation. Be open to my guidance. You have the same Mind I have! Why clutter it with needless and useless fear? Living in fear of something is an unconscious wish to have it happen. Why indulge your mind with useless journeys?

You must give up living in fear and stagnation. You must be willing to give up the old way of doing things and allow the new to enter freely. *Take some risks!* Invite a stranger to live with you; you may find he is not so strange. Take action, Thornton. You have the universal Mind I share with you at your fingertips. Perhaps you might seek out an agency to help you find a roommate. This would certainly solve much of your financial crunch at present *and* would find you someone to share your stories with. These are necessary risks that you have asked to start taking, but are resistant about implementing. The awareness that a loving answer is everywhere you look would be more appropriate. For now, look there.

Days later the scribing continues...

Joel, You'll remember this scribing came in two parts. After you received the first part for me, I swallowed hard, then took the "unthinkable risk" of talking face to face with my landlord. I couldn't believe it. I sat down with her, told her I didn't have the full amount of rent, that I had just started a new job, that I would have the balance in about 10 days and could I have permission to get a roommate?

With a gentle smile she said, "I think that will be fine."

Greetings Thornton:

Now that a short time has passed since our last communication, perhaps you can see how quickly miracles do work for you. Not only has your entire attitude changed, but so have your seemingly catastrophic problems. Tell me now, Thornton, which changed *first* and *how* was it changed? *Who* changed it? It was not me who changed your mind. I only reminded you that we *share* the same Power *together*. Yes, we do occasionally need reminders of where our power lies, don't we?

Fear immobilizes and Love frees without limitation of any kind. Love must also share. If you are willing to stay in constant communication with me, together we can overcome your apparent dilemma in an even shorter amount of time! How does a milli-second sound? With Love your problems are already answered. But do you really accept this? What makes you think "something else" pays the rent? Are you ready to start saving time instead of wasting it on silly fears that have only been made to get "something else?" Simply choose Love in place of fear next time, no matter how difficult the picture is to look at, and watch to see the picture change right before your very eyes! All I need from you is a tiny instant of your time, my brother. Will you remember this next time Hiroshima clouds your mind?

Your power is in the joining with Christ in *His* Service. Where is it you cannot see Him except in your own childish nightmares? Look not to nothingness for answers any longer, Thornton, for it is only nothingness and despair you will find. Yet the real answer is right before you, plain as day, waiting in every brother and sister you meet. What is more, *they* are waiting for the answer you bring to them as well! Why are you waiting? If you need specific help, open your mind to my inspiration. Ask if having a roommate is in the best interest for all concerned. All will be provided. Only remember you must also be willing to give as you would receive. As you need help, be willing to give the same.

I recommend that you do not waste time since you *are* more prone, at the place you are standing in your crossing of the bridge, to become entwined in appearance and fear. Part of your repeating this painful lesson is to teach yourself the power of your mind's choosing, or *not* choosing, correctly. *Fear always wastes time.* Remember, form may or may not change in what you are doing, but attitude *must*. *Not* choosing anything in a crisis is *fear*. It is an attack on yourself. Though it may seem risky, choose you must. Choose lovingly through inclusion and by being truly helpful. Make sure your agreements are clear, upfront, modest and undemanding of both yourself and the ones you ask for help. Most of all, listen for my Word in everyone. Everything will work out better than you could ever imagine. The gifts, which are soon to come, contain much more than just the wrapping. You have the idea. What are you waiting for?

Blessing all unhappiness in you,

Jesus

Joel, as you'll remember, I was on cloud nine. I had received this miracle and I was literally overflowing with gratitude. All I had to do was ASK! And in about four days time I had a roommate!

THE TURNING POINT

Perhaps you do not yet realize that once the turning point has been reached, not only do you begin to experience your life with more flexibility and peace, but so does everyone around you as well. A mind transformed calls upon all other minds to transform with it. This begins a kind of chain reaction that, collectively, you are all just beginning to glimpse an understanding of. This chain reaction is not so visible at first. It works silently underneath the system you have all made in an area of the mind you each share. Within the Heart of this area, there lies no conflict or opposition. It is here where the silent change of heart and mind takes effect, reaching out to all other hearts and minds in a call to join and heal.

It is here, deep within you, that Light is summoned, recognized and sent within to all other minds. Now you understand better why the meek shall inherit the earth, yes? The power given to a mind that takes only Light as its Authority is unlimited and invincible in its ability to transform! While those who are still scurrying around in their madness do their dance, the mind which has accepted only Light remains still and steadfast midst the turmoil.

In stillness the world of madness cannot help but transform. No one but would trade their insanity in an instant where God's peace has been offered to take its place. This is the power of the still at heart! This is the only power you *can* share. This is the power of Heaven come to earth again!

Several months later, Thornton is in a frenzied and chaotic job environment with the "flu that lasts forever."

YET ANOTHER SCRIBING FOR THORNTON

Dear Elder Brother,

The bills are getting paid now — I am truly thankful for that. I'm experiencing a cold now that just won't go away.

Questions:

1) What is the purpose of this illness?

2) What is the purpose of my relationship with my former wife, Jeannie? Why did she give up?

Greetings Thornton:

It is interesting how one might value illness over employment and even money, don't you agree? Of course, this is not the question to really ask. You do value it or you would not be sick. The question is, how is this serving you better than what you were doing? Do you see? If you are honest with yourself, you can easily recognize that being ill is providing a much better service! Do you really want to work at your present job? Do you miss time in quiet listening to me and God? Do you want to do what your heart desires? Ah, you see? Your illness is serving you well, isn't it Thornton?

You are doing exactly as I explained to you before. You are sorting out what is worthy from what is not worthy! Sometimes it just takes getting a little sick for you to force yourself to accept your new values and delete your old ones. By becoming ill you have a perfect measuring device to notice your progress. Why are you not getting better, then? Could a part of you still value the conflict with the "money?" It is this part that says, "In God we *don't* trust." That's *why it's* on the money! You all need reminders each time you "give it away."

There is nothing wrong with being ill, Thornton. In your case, there is everything right about it! It serves you well! If you didn't get sick, just think, you would still be trudging along doing what you don't like to do. In illness there is change. But you may want to carefully ask yourself why it is that when you are standing at the edge of a very high cliff with a parachute on your back that says, "God's Jumping School," that instead of jumping with a smile on your face, you end up falling off, taken ill from the long wait in the wind. Either way you still get back Home, right? You will stop being ill once you realize that it is finally safe to jump off the cliff and you will stop being afraid when you realize there is nothing to lose.

Some say the biggest risk is dying, but I would tell you that the greatest risk is truly living. No one can *live* in fear. This is what I meant when I said, "Give all your possessions to the poor and come walk with me." You are indeed poor as long as you would author your own life based on things. You are poor only because your values have been misplaced. I assure you that in all of your time spent worrying about things, the same amount of time, given totally to God, would not only stop all your worries, but also provide *complete* and *happy* answers to all of your future undertakings.

You have asked about your relationship with Jeannie.

As your valuing is changing very rapidly, hers is as well. She is finding a deep need within her to make up for "lost time." Jeannie has never truly known what it is like to be happy as an adult. She has had spurts here and there, but never really felt joyous and free inside. She is troubled by her own life and believes she has not accomplished much. Though she still loves you, she feels unworthy of you and of God. It is unfortunate, but her mind is set. She feels compelled to live a life now in a sort of shell. Very seldom will she rely on guidance from any of us. She does not understand her purpose in life, but secretly she has vowed to find it alone, which eventually she no doubt will. She is safe from harm, but has bouts with wondering whether or not she belongs here. She has much healing ahead and it is essential for her not to become confused. This is why she is alone. She may well stay alone for the rest of her life.

However, Thornton, you are someone she at one time had great expectations of. Though she is bewildered with relationships, she is likely to befriend you in the future. But it will be slow, for she is not trusting of intimacy nor may she be for a long while. You can do much for her by just being Thornton. Abandon all hopes, if there are any, of ever getting back with her. She needs you differently now. It will give her great pleasure to know that you are happy, even if you find someone else. But it is most important that you love her, no matter what either of you do. Your relationship with her is turning into a powerful holy relationship. This requires that you ask within before you make decisions regarding each other. You are also not asked to judge, ponder or even to try to figure out what is next for the both of you. Trust that I will guide you according to what is truly best for everyone. You can count on one thing, Thornton. It will never be as it was in the past. Be thankful it is so.

Remember what I have said about taking risks. It is easy to stay stuck and not proceed to new things or relationships. What is easy does not come without pain in this case. Don't wait for the tide to get low before you go water skiing. Above all, *enjoy*.

In peace eternal,

Jesus

OUR TRUE OCCUPATION

Each of you is becoming a miracle worker, one by one. Nothing will stop you, for what in the world can overcome what peace would silence and still? Oh, there will be trifles here and there along this freshly groomed path. But this will not last. It cannot last because only peace is lasting. The disputes that arise here and there during this transformation will not be looked upon through the "eyes for peace" as something to *resist against*. This is the power of the truly helpful, the truly peaceful. They do not see what has no value. Because of this, what has no value disappears. Peace comes closer and closer with every step, reaching every heart.

Those who have made the *big shift* no longer listen to the dictates of fear and conflict. Instead, they receive their guidance from the Light they recognize in themselves and also see in their brothers and sisters. No longer are decisions made based on divisive or hurtful measures. Indeed, the light-workers approach their families and occupations in quite a different way. Their concerns are directed for the all, not for the few. Their actions are humble, not reckless. They refuse to participate in that which excludes others from a life that is harmonious with peace and God. Oh, yes, now you are getting a clearer picture of what your true occupation is and what underlies your worldly occupation.

A LAST SCRIBING FOR THORNTON

Dear Elder Brother Jesus,

I am now feeling as though I am preparing to take the "leap" you have referred to, to take the risk and find the truth about myself. After much resistance, I have finally completed my resume. I have surely felt your help with this. I just feel like I'm ready to "take the next step," but I'm unsure of what that step is.

Greetings Thornton:

You have asked again what the next step is. I will tell you now that you are already doing it, even though this is not what your ego would like to hear. This is a time for reflection for you. It is a time in which you are to hone your inner listening. It is especially a time to embrace all that has happened in this past year and put it in proper perspective. Much has happened that is not measurable in your worldly activities. Look instead within you to what has happened and is happening in you emotionally. Look at what each of your worldly experiences has brought you. Search your heart for the lessons the world has brought you and the outcome of these lessons, which have absolutely nothing to do with the world. These are important lessons, which once incorporated, will allow you the freedom you deserve in the future. You will hear me speaking to you more directly as you incorporate each lesson, for each of the lessons have been to help teach you What you are truly

EMPLOYMENT & THE REAL PURPOSE OF THE WORLD

dependent on. Look carefully at how well choreographed your life is without the interference of fear. Fear has not helped you complete your resume, but indeed, it has not stopped you either. Who, then, is really running the show?

There is a necessity for quiet time, just as there is a necessity for right action. Learn to appreciate both and you will have learned. In quiet, you will be able to place each lesson in its proper perspective. Overlooking this process has indeed been tragic for you in the past, has it not Thornton? You will soon learn that you can accomplish more by taking quiet time than you ever have by pushing the river. The fact that you are asking for the next step is indeed an accomplishment, but it would hardly be complete until you also learn to completely step aside after you have asked. This is also a crucial lesson for the work you will soon be doing, for it will involve your deepened trust in me.

It is perfectly okay for you to start distributing your resume, but ask me before you send each one, whether or not this will be suitable for you. You will save much time if you do this, for there is only one job that you will be doing. If you are not hearing my voice in your decisions, it is simply because you do not want to hear. I have not moved from your side. If you do not want to hear, then you must not be quite ready. That is why things are not moving quickly. You are processing the lessons in your life that have brought you to where you now seem to be. Some of the lessons have been painful. Some have been happy. There is no need now for you to repeat painful lessons unless you choose to be impatient and act solely on your own. Your needs will be provided for, little as they may seem now. It furthers you to have little now so that you may enjoy more later. It will not be long, so enjoy this time for inner reflection and deepening.

I will caution you on one last thing. Be careful that you do not stagnate in this still period you are experiencing. Use the release from your own decision-making that I am offering you to further facilitate the deepening of your relationships with others in your life. As you spend time in quiet and become more free of your own self-made obstacles, reinforce this state by incorporating trust in all of your relationships. Look for peace and God in everyone. Seek the Answer in all others, for It is everywhere! Enjoy the process. Do the footwork you feel joy with and guided to do. Above all, release yourself from the "duty" of worrying about anything. Once you fully embrace your lessons, it will be crystal clear to you Who is the Author of your Reality. I am right by your side. In Love I stand by you, and in Love I will answer you.

My trust in you is perfect,

Jesus

IT'S NOT IN THE "DOING"

It does not matter so much what you are *doing*; it matters more what you are not doing. Moving a pencil on a piece of paper or dumping a chemical into a lake will not be so valuable on this new path. Indeed, the value will be found in the *rest* given to the "great race" that humankind has obsessed itself with for so many years. The value in life will come again to be recognized as the *undoing* of complexity, conflict and separation. I tell you, this is no idealistic dream I am describing to you. This will be a step *out* of the dream and *into* your Reality!

The birth of what you are calling the "age of communication" is now at hand. The opportunities that exist now for all of you to take your focus from the mental and physical and transmute them into the spiritual are unlimited by the potential you are beginning to realize. This is the age of going inward for all decisions. Time spent otherwise will indeed be wasted.

Chapter Four

RELATIONSHIPS & FAMILY

THE CHARADE OF SUFFERING

Your relationships are the most important tools in your life. They are sacred, even in what may appear to be a most despicable form. It is through your relationships that you will remember God or seem to lose Her for awhile. It is through your relationships that either a new and glorious birth is given to a tired world or a dying world of grief and sorrow is clung to and held so tightly that hope of freedom seems a distance too far away to imagine.

We have spoken many times about the two emotions you are each capable of — Love and fear. I have also explained that only one is true. It is surely helpful to remind you that all is only Love and there is nothing really to fear. It is quite poetic and surely you enjoy such sweet reminders about your true Origin. It is not practical for me as an elder brother to address only what you *like* to hear. This will not reveal what is *keeping* you from consistently experiencing the glorious Love and peace you seek. Gently now, let us take a closer look at what it is that keeps your lives in "hell." It is not so pretty, but do not be afraid to face looking at this more directly with me. Together we *do* have absolutely nothing to fear. Take my hand and let us further our discussion in simple terms of what the false emotion of fear has set up for your relationships and for the world.

Were it simply fear and nothing more, your world would not seem so challenged at this time. As I have said before, fear is an attitude based on guilt. Fear made the separation, but guilt holds it in place. It is what keeps your world a seemingly savage one. Guilt perpetuates the insane need to punish, which we will discuss in more detail later. For now, let us look at why it is so easy for most of you to rely on the idea of punishment and condemnation in your relationships.

Blame, condemnation and punishment have reached critical proportions in your world. This is making you all insane. Yet there must be some reason that you are attracted to these false teachings or you would not continue to follow so blindly in the insanity it breeds. This reason is simply that you believe these false ideas will get you what you want. Yet they never do. If you could accept this, your lives would take a giant step closer to Heaven and your world yet a larger step to peace.

Guilt is a denial of your freedom, as punishment is an acceptance of your imprisonment. Whenever you use punishment or condemnation in any form, you are affirming your wish to stay imprisoned by denying your own innocence. Such an action could not be a better example of your wish to be separate from God, your Self and your companions. The tears of Christ are shed every time one of my brothers or sisters chooses condemnation over forgiveness. All the Sons and Daughters of God are guilty with you *if* you would choose guilt for yourself or anyone. If there is no salvation for *you*, there is no salvation for *the world*. How long, my holy sisters and brothers, will you continue this charade of suffering in my holy name? How long?

A SCRIBING FOR ALEX

Joel, I would like a scribing from Jesus very much. I'm living in New York city with my wife and three-year-old son. We are going to move to our home country by the end of the year. After living here for ten years, we wonder:

1) How is our life going to be over there?

2) Are we going to get jobs?

3) Is it a right decision for my son?

4) Can the job I'm starting now be continued over there?

5) I'm also starting with ACIM after more than ten years of Transcendental Meditation. Is there any incompatibility between both of them?

Thanks,

Alex

Greetings Alex:

I am honored to assist you today. You are indeed moving to some new and great adventures with your family. Let us join together now for some answers to your questions.

I will begin with your third question since this is the question that you are concerned with the most. It is also the question that, when put properly in perspective, will answer most of the other questions you have asked of me.

I have said before that you must learn to plant your seeds carefully, for if you sow seeds in bleak and dry soil so shall you reap. I have answered you many times regarding the question of moving to your home country. In your heart you already know the answer to this question. Where you give roots plenty of room to grow, they will grow strong. Any alternative to living in complication is best suited for all of God's children, though it is quite possible to live humbly and simply, even in the most "difficult" of seeming circumstances.

You are beginning to glimpse the fact more often that all of the complication you have exposed yourself to is but illusion. Yet your child is not likely to be aware of this right away *unless* he is given the opportunity to experience simplicity by your modeling. A child will retain what he is exposed to. Just as you are now undoing some of what you retained as a child, he is still *forming* as a child. You understand this and are making the right choice. Your heart has already told you this is the choice to make. Be glad that you have listened!

You can be successful with your type of employment anywhere, but you may have to make adjustments in your methods of communication in order for this to happen. Look for ideas from all of your brothers and sisters, and from me through them, as you go on. The way to be successful will be there for you if you listen carefully to what may be offered you. Even a simple hello to a stranger may turn out to be the offering of a miracle for all of you. Pay close attention to your own heart and the hearts of others. Listen to what their hearts are sending you. Above all, listen carefully within to the Voice we share in all of your decisions. It will be important to do this in the near future, for there will be many opportunities to upset yourselves in these times if you do not proceed gently.

What will bring success for you in your employment will be marked by your own inner happiness once you move. It will have nothing to do with where you go. Where you go will simply provide your family with the opportunity to rebuild itself in a much more relaxed and loving environment. It is the Love inside you that joins you all together and will bring you success and happiness. This will offer you the gentle environment you hope to achieve. It may be easier to recognize, once you are all out of the "complication" that you now see in yourselves and, thus, see yourselves *in*. The move seems necessary because it has become difficult to find the simplicity God offers you, though He does offer you this even now where you are presently. You are not expected to tolerate the fear you feel you are exposed to in your present situation. The fear is illusion and you have chosen it. Now you must choose differently and follow the guidance I have provided you. I have a happier life *and* occupation in store for you, *if you* will but take time to listen and act on behalf of what I am gently guiding you to. Listen, then, in each new moment for the Voice for Love I would share with you.

Your happiness is all I am concerned with. However, you may still meet with some turmoil once you have moved. Your egos will not have the stimulation required to keep them so "alive." The ego will fight you on this and you may find it frustrating. If this happens, remember what I have said to you. You are here to heal, to find joy in this moment, to unite in the Love that is given us. That is all, and *that* is everything. You do not need the world you have placed yourselves in. But you *do* need the contact with your Self through the Love that created you. How wonderful it will be for you who have chosen humility and simplicity! As your values change and you see the gift of peace your Love has brought you, how will anything or anyone stop you from the happiness you deserve?

You have asked about "differences" in your studies. There is, of course, no dispute between your meditations and what I bring you through your course studies. Anyone who would teach you otherwise is not teaching the Word I have intended for you. Can there be dispute between Love and fear? Can anything harm the holy Son of God? You are indeed safe to study both. I would caution you about making such distinctions, for there are no differences in the Kingdom of Heaven. This eternal Kingdom is within you. It has nothing to do with anything physical because the physical is incapable of containing truth. Meditate often. Remember me always in our Father's Name. I will take you beyond all conflict to the Kingdom of Love. This is Where we are joined. This is your Home. Leave the world of fear and perception behind and accept this Gift in its place. Wherever you walk, I will be walking with you.

Let us embark on this journey to Love now.

All blessings to you who have chosen

Heaven in place of the world.

Jesus

OUR INVISIBLE REALITY

I have not come to take from you what you still treasure. Yet it is necessary that you take careful notice of what has been happening in your world. We cannot do what we all came to do, which is to celebrate in peace together, unless we learn *together* to let go of what seems to separate us. I appeal to you to hear me deeply as a concerned and elder brother.

You did not come here to punish one another. You thought that is why you came, but fortunately you were mistaken. Your relationships have always had but one purpose and that is to join together in the celebration of our Oneness. All that stands in your way of doing this is the guilt you have all synthesized together. The only way out of guilt is through total forgiveness. What you have made of the world together you must now choose to relinquish. Your entire belief in the reality of the world of guilt must somehow be exchanged for the goal of a different Reality, the *only* Reality. Not one sliver of guilt and condemnation can be withheld if you are to reach the goal of peace this Reality holds out to you.

This invisible and indivisible Reality is only available to you *through* your relationships. You cannot experience It solely on your own. It is impossible because you were not created alone. You were created as one Self, together. Yes, dear sisters and brothers, I know this does not appear to be the case. It seems to you that there are many of you all walking in different directions. Well, so much for "appearances." The Reality you seek you cannot seem to find because you are trying so hard to do it alone, in your own separate way. You look for happiness in everything but your Reality. Then you wonder why it feels like you are banging your heads on the wall. It's because you are. Your Reality is *shared together*. It is in *everyone*. Only in Christ will true happiness be found.

A Scribing for Janet

Dear Jesus and Joel,

I am twenty-seven years old, happily married with a four-year-old son. I am an artist, but currently working as a gardener/caretaker for a wealthy family. We live on the premises also. My husband and I both do this, although I'm also developing and creating a dried flower business with our employer. Although this arrangement is good in some ways, I have been more depressed and anxious than usual over the past year. I find myself wishing I had more time and creative energy to devote to my art. Also, with our son starting school soon, we feel the need to be in a stable long-term living situation. Here are my questions for Jesus:

1) *Will I ever be satisfied and comfortable in our current living/ working situation, or should I develop my art and be independent? What is the purpose of my relationship with Debbie (our employer)? Why am I in this situation?*

2) *In my art I feel like I have a lot of talent and I'm making a lot of progress, but I seem to have a "block" that prevents me from working consistently and having the courage to do what I know I can. What is it and how can I overcome it?*

3) *I have endured some difficult childhood memories. Will I ever be able to have relationships with my family (parents, siblings) that are emotionally safe for me? Or is it better to "cut my losses" and let it go as I have been doing?*

4) *My son is extremely gifted (Has been able to read since age two, etc.) What can I do to help him develop his full potential and in what areas can his enormous energies be channeled? Are we making the right decision with school? What is his "mission" here?*

5) *Should we have another child? I've been back and forth on this one and I really need to know how I really feel.*

Thank you so much for doing this. I look forward to hearing from you.

Greetings Janet:

As you read this message to yourself, be aware that everything you seem to be "hearing" is truly coming only from within you. You can hear the Voice for Love in your Self at any time, anywhere. I reside within you as we reside together, in Christ, and at one with the perfect Love of our Creator. Let us now begin with your first question.

You have asked whether you should develop your art talent or continue doing your present occupation. It is not likely that you will be satisfied with any current work situation until you are doing both. A part of you does not feel completely independent; that is, you do not feel as though you have accomplished a full and self-reliant lifestyle. There is also some guilt about that and I will address this as we go on. You are resistant to following your inner Guidance, which suggests that you develop your artistic side and perhaps use this talent to enhance your abilities to become self-reliant and fully independent. Even though you are doing a wonderful job with your own self-reliance at this point in your life, a part of you does not want to accept that it really could be okay just the way it is. There is no doubt that you will at some point finally take the risk and decide to find a way to incorporate your art with how you make a living.

Debbie represents potential to you. She can and will be helpful to you in your quest if you allow it, but only if you can learn to set aside your differences. She is supportive to an extent, but also perceives her dreams to be different from yours. Learn to work within those boundaries and you will find many gifts to share with one another along the way. She can also offer you many tools and ideas that will be helpful to you later on. Learn to listen between the lines in your relationship with her. There is more there than meets the eye. You have placed yourself in the situation to learn what that is. Within her modeling, you can learn to distinguish between what you do want and what you don't want, if you carefully and quietly listen.

Many of the blocks you are experiencing in regard to your artistic development have to do with your third question as well. This shouldn't surprise you. The two situations are quite parallel to one another. The question, "Will I ever be able to have relationships with my family that are emotionally safe for me?"

lacks only one word at the beginning for it to be a complete and answerable question. The question should begin with "How." Do you understand, Janet? There is no doubt that you will come to terms with your own "safety factor" regarding your relatives. The only question is "how?"

One way for you to feel safe with your family would be simply to cut your losses as you have described. This would offer you "safety" at a distance, but would hardly be entirely healing for you or them. This would be a poor choice since it implies that you are unwilling to risk being truly healed with them, a choice which is also reflective and parallel to what you are experiencing with your art talents. Now do you better understand the correlation between the second and third questions? If you back away from the risk of healing with your own family, are you not also backing away from your own healing? Could this choice possibly empower you to go ahead with perhaps greater risks in the future?

I cannot emphasize enough the importance of healing your relationships with your mother, father, sibling and early significant others. All of the sense of being "on hold" that you feel in your life is a direct result of your unhealed significant relationships. It is where your guilt and fear stem from. It is where your lack of willingness to take risks stems from. It is where all your sense of depression arises. The need to blame only encourages and multiplies these feelings. Be perfectly clear on the importance of facing these fears head on. Doing this will bring gifts beyond your dreams. Not doing this will only bring you misery and more fear.

You do not necessarily have to do your healing with your family *in person*. But you do at some point have to do it. There are many who spend their whole lives in misery only to finally forgive in the end. That is because they finally realize what is valuable and what is not. When one is about to set their body down, they are very seldom concerned anymore with "crimes" committed against it. They may look back in one single flash and recognize, with seemingly great loss, all the times their hatred had blocked them from the Love they could have given and experienced instead. Finally they realize ultimately that there was no loss.

They may choose to repeat their previous course in order to give themselves more "time" to heal and rediscover the beauty of a life experience lived guilt free. Such is the birth and death cycle.

Many have repeated their course over and over again because they continued to avoid the program and have attempted to "repay" themselves and others with hatred and guilt instead of Love. This is not the kind of repayment God or I have in mind for you, for the repeating of such lessons in fear serves no purpose at all. The only repayment that you or your family deserve is a repayment given in total forgiveness and Love. Do not believe there is any other repayment to offer. In doing so you would only hold yourself back from the gift of peace that you are created with and the gift of innocence that is truly yours forever.

Now can we look at "how" a little closer. It is most important for you to not place yourself or anyone in what you may instinctively feel to be a "dangerous" situation. It is important, however, to encourage and do your best to cultivate a safe arena for healing wherever you may be. This is perhaps the most important thing to be aware of for your family now and for your extended family. This is an idea that, in its proper application, should be kept in mind at all times. A healing environment, as opposed to any form of a punitive environment, is paramount. If you learn to cultivate, provide and secure this type of environment to the best of your ability, you will discover the integrity of Love. In choosing to do this, you will automatically provide your family with an open space to heal. If you keep this goal always in mind and heart, you will find many gifts will follow. It is the most important choice and decision you can ever make for everyone. And your repayment will be great indeed!

Once you truly begin to do this, you will begin hearing the Voice for God in you and others often. What you are now perceiving as possible losses will become potential, if not actual gains. Gratitude will be allowed to take the place of resentment and fear. Tears of pain will be transformed into tears of joy. All this can happen as a result of this one right choice. Remember, punishment in any form is never justified. Forgiveness is the only form in which true healing can take place. This is what you need to remember most regarding yourself and others.

You do not need to condone cruel behavior, but you must learn to forgive it in yourself and others. As long as you judge another's actions, you are attempting to kick that person out of your heart. This is impossible because in truth you each share the same Self

God created. The apparent "action" of another is where forgiveness belongs. "Actions" are actually illusions that seem to have real and lasting effects to change and alter the Sons and Daughters of God by appearing to "steal" their natural Inheritance. Thus if you hold the actions of another against him, you hold them against yourself as well and judge yourself accordingly. Whatever you put out of your heart you place beyond the reach of God's healing Light and proclaim it to be "true." Let no part of your mind linger there, Janet; it does not belong there. Give these judgments to me. I will take them from you and replace them with What has always been there — the bright Light of Innocence that came with you.

It is through this Light that your artistic qualities will be inspired. It is through this Light that you will heal all family separation. It is through this Light that miracles will come to you. You need only risk being healed — the risk to love again as you were created. You cannot "cut your losses" because there is nothing to lose. But you can let go of the perceptions of loss that you have been attracted to as a defense because of unhealed anger. It is only these unhealed perceptions that keep you seemingly separate from your Self, others and God. I encourage you to release your mind and let these go. Indeed, this *will* cut your losses. The Light *will* come to you if you do!

The best that you can do for your son is the best that you can do for you. He needs only models of Love to assist him on his way. The gift your son has is identical to your own. It is the Gift of God, the Christ in him, forever free, innocent and perfect in every way, loving and eternal forever. He needs nothing else. He is nothing else, but in This he is everything. As much as you are able to reflect this truth to him through your own actions toward him and others, to that degree will he keep remembering from Where he came later in life. Now he is busy developing his own ego and for a while he will play with his inventiveness and ingenuity.

Someday he will grow tired of all the things he once amused himself with and he will wonder if there is more. This is when he will remember what you modeled to him when he was young, for he will find there is more only by what you give him now. When he remembers the gift of Love you gave him through the Gift God gave you, he will rejoice with great inspiration! When this happens he will go on to give the gift you gave him in whatever form he chooses to channel it. When this happens, he will know that he is God's child — unlimited in strength and power, innocent, joyous and free as the man of God he is destined to become.

Could he ever ask for any more than he already has? Show him What he already has and is. Nothing you do could be a greater gift than this! His mission is no different than your own. His purpose is yours. It is your gift together to share.

Regarding his schooling: Choose only the healing environment for him that I described earlier, whenever possible. Do not hesitate to lovingly question "authority" that is in any way demeaning, guilt encouraging or limiting to his creative ability. Teach him only through Love to break through boundaries by keeping his agreements to himself and others. Teach him gently to make agreements ahead of time and what the consequences consist of *before* he has an opportunity to break them. In this way he will learn the difference between consequence and punishment, for he will learn by what he does to himself, not what others seem to do to him.

In modeling this to him, he will learn of his true power — the power of Love rather than the "power" of fear. He will stumble and he will find himself in situations at times where he feels powerless. When this happens, count on him to be a teacher to you, for you will be asked to deepen in your understanding together by his choices as well. Remember this: Communication can only occur through Love and anything that is not Love is not communication. There will always be trials with this, but recognize that he is no more a victim than you. He has an agenda and a curriculum. No matter what, it must be okay for him to follow it.

You already know the answer to your last question, Janet. You want another child. The real question is, "Why are you afraid to have it?" It is totally safe to have another child if that is what you wish. All will be well provided for. Your confusion with this lies in your fear about physical needs. I would remind you that I have been speaking to you throughout this session about Where all values need be placed because only There do they lie. The world indeed seems harsh when seen through the eyes of fear, but when seen through the eyes of Love there is nothing to limit you or your children. They do not need "things" to be happy any more than you, even though that may be what the ego insists is "true." Your children will test you on this. Are you ready?

Be gentle with yourself, Janet, and do not worry about the decision. In your heart it has already been made. Let Love guide you and decisions like this one will be much easier in the future. You, your husband and all of your family have powerful awakenings and joyous experiences ahead for you. Trust in the still, small Voice within you to assist you and to correct all mistakes you might make along the way. There is never a need for guilt. I will be there to lead you to God if you will ask for my hand. You are each safe at Home even while you experience your many varying dreams. Let each of you be reminded often of God's one consistent Answer *now*. This holy Gift is given you today, in this moment and all moments ahead, to receive joyously and extend to all.

In you is the forgiven child,

Longing only to awaken in

Her Father's loving Arms,

Where Life and innocence

Are truly safe in Forever.

Awaken now and know that you are Home.

That is my blessing to you,

A Loving Jesus

THE GIFT BEHIND THE GIFT

You bang your heads on the wall every time you make your possessions, habits, occupations and bodies more valuable than the Love you share together. Yet this is all you really *can* share together. You each pretend every day to "share" other things with one another. Then things become sticky and very confusing. You see, my dear ones, it is not that you cannot "share" money or homes or other "things." By all appearances, you do this every day. Yet do you ever stop and ask what is *behind* the appearance of this "sharing"? What is truly shared has no conditions and is eternal, for it comes from the perfect safety of Love. What *appears* to be shared is always conditional because it is always temporary. Its "conditions" cannot last, so the element of fear easily slips in. If a thing is *truly* shared without conditions and without "value" placed on it, the only *real* Gift, the underlying Love that gave it, is easily recognized.

The "thing" does not matter. What matters is the everlasting Gift behind the gift given. This is what you want, but are often afraid to receive. Thus you mistake the *appearance* as the gift, which in turn allows the interference of guilt to be precipitated further. So you would not know how to take it if a saint walked up to you and handed you a thousand dollars, smiled and walked away. Some of you would even feel unworthy or shameful by accepting such a gift. The saint feels nothing but Love. He gives it *because* he knows the only value is in the Gift behind the gift. The one who feels guilt in receiving it does so because his *values* lie elsewhere. He may even believe he is "stealing" something from someone who knows no better! Oh my holy companions, you have so much to learn about value! What matters to the saint matters not to the "sinner." The "sinner" is only the one who has mistaken the gift for the Gift and has only substituted the nonessential for the essential.

The person who "sins" will not come before God in the end for final judgment and punishment, my dear ones. God does not wait for time to end and then cast Her Son or Daughter into "hell" for past mistakes. God is entirely loving and merciful. When a fearful choice is made, fear is immediate. "Hell" is what you have each made because of this confusion in purpose. If a child were to walk away from his father in the woods and become lost, the natural response for him would be one of fear. His father's greatest wish would only be for his safe return. A loving father would hardly consider punishing his child for becoming lost. Indeed, his eyes would well up and his arms would fully open upon his homecoming. This is what your relationships are *for* — to welcome one another Home from your weary journey spent lost in a forest of fear.

A Scribing for Barbara

Dear Joel,

I was told about your generous offer and I couldn't resist. I am a single mom with two daughters, twenty-one and sixteen. My youngest is somewhat troubled and is not (I think) able to accept God into her life. My older daughter lives in LA with her boyfriend and is trying to get her big break as an actress. I am in recovery and in a new relationship with a good man, but scared as heck about it (my self-esteem/ego stuff). I have many blessings in life. I am grateful.

1) How can I be most helpful to my daughters?

2) What does God want me specifically to do to serve him in this life?

3) Which is the best vocational avenue for me at this time?

4) How can I best secure my family's financial future?

5) Who was my brother, Johnnie?

Well, those are my questions. Thank you very much.

Peace and love to you.

Barbara

Greetings Barbara:

I am gladdened that you have asked for my guidance through Joel. I would remind you, however, to pay attention in your life to hear my Voice everywhere. You can do this *because* my Voice resides in *you* in each new and shining instant that has been kept "clean" of past and future fears. You seem to hear my Voice in others at times because they have kept their mirrors "shiny." Yet in truth, even what you are hearing now as you read this comes through you.

I shall begin with your second question since it is this question that will shed light on the rest, once the answers are truly understood.

Be clear in your own heart, Barbara, that it does not matter which vocation you choose or what "avenue" in the worldly sense you take to "secure" your family's future. I cannot specifically answer these questions for you, since I would only be offering one illusion in trade for another. My concern and yours should not be with illusions, but only with Reality. It is This and only This which will bring you and your family joy. All the rest is but a happy dream at best. It is hard for many to believe they do not really want the things of the world. But I tell you this is true. Your one need is only to remember the One from Whom you came. This will bring you joy and only this, no matter what you have or do in the world.

You are faced with many seeming obstacles that might keep you from the joy of Heaven which you seek. These "obstacles" are truly illusory, though it does little good to tell you this midst the turmoil in which you now find yourself.

There have been times when you have heard me very clearly reminding you to simplify your lifestyle and values. You already know that none of the "things" in your life will see you to Heaven. This does not mean that you must throw your possessions away. It merely means that you must learn to not be invested in them. So when something seems to be taken away, you are not left feeling victimized or isolated. This has all been coming more into view for you recently. One day not so far off, Barbara, all this will become crystal clear to you. You will laugh at the thought of any loss at all!

Addiction and compulsive behavior is no more than a tendency to become destructively preoccupied with what is not important.

You do this in an attempt to hide from the guilt you believe is yours. All the problems made from addiction stem from this one belief. The "dysfunction," as some call it, is simply a misplacement of your ability to evaluate properly. It can be quite an intense teacher for you. But it is entirely unnecessary to learn through the pain of the mistaken evaluation that guilt binds you to. I would remind you that your own ego and the egos in your family are often trying to place value on the valueless. It would be a further error to attempt to "teach" them any of your newest realizations. Your family is not so concerned with the teachings of God or with theories on how to reach Her. They seek only the *demonstration* in your actions that show you know God's Love.

You can help yourself and your daughters the most by living and being in the Light of truth. How do you do this? It is simple. Let go of all that you now value other than Love. These values are all mistaken. Value belongs strictly to Love and that is all. Since you are created from Love, you need only remember your own value. To value anything else will only cause you eventual grief and suffering. You teach proper values not by words, but by the rhythm and dance of your choices, decisions and actions. Yet it is not *what* you do, but *how* you do the dance while you are doing it. If you take everything you do so seriously, why would you expect your own daughters to do it any differently? Would you expect them to love this "god" you bow to?

The God that created you is unlimited in joy, freedom and Love. This state of mind has nothing to do with the world. It has to do with how you do the dance while relating *to* the world. Your demonstration teaches every Son and Daughter of God! Would you teach heaviness, seriousness, guilt and sorrow? Or would you teach lightness, innocence and freedom? All addiction and compulsion stem from the first. All healing and extending Love come from the second. What you teach you learn.

Joy is experienced the instant you exchange the world and all its offerings for truth. You can do this right now, as you have before. Ask yourself honestly, Barbara, how attracted are you to the drama the world provides you with? Can a dream be eternal? Would you not exchange the dead for everlasting Life? How simple is salvation! But do you want it more than anything else? This is the question you should honestly ask yourself. This is the question that will set your valuing right. And this is the question, when properly answered, that will heal your family and yourself of all "dysfunction" and bring you Home to God together!

"Walking the talk" involves a great but simple responsibility. It requires that you value and choose only peace, only the eternal, no matter what appears in your life experience. This is your natural occupation! All the other "occupations" you do while you are here are only to meet the body's "needs." Do not teach anyone to value the body, unless you would wish your mind and theirs to live in illusion. Be grateful not for things you own, but for truly not owning anything. Place gratitude on proper values. This is what will set you free.

Johnnie is a great and wise teacher. In his apparent absence, he is still teaching you. Without him you would not have learned some of your most important lessons. Speak with him often, for his gifts are many. He stands with me and reminds you to appreciate the holy instant you are in now. Smile more often, Barbara, for the world and all its thinking is not to be taken heavily. He is your teacher for this, for through your relationship with him, you can clearly learn to overlook the world and all the separation it stands for. Johnnie is quite happy knowing this. Let it be for you as well.

Finally, I would say to you, remember often that each new instant is your opportunity for rebirth into God's fountain of Love. Allow yourself to get away from words and seek only true experience now. Be still and know that you are with God. You can do whatever your heart desires. It is your dream, but remember that it, too, is unlimited in potential when you let Love guide you. All limitation comes from your secret belief that certain things are impossible for you. Give these beliefs to me! They do not belong in your holy mind! Be at peace, knowing that I walk with you. Joy to all, for there is nothing we cannot heal with God, together.

All blessing and holy remembrance to you,

Who are the Daughter of God.

A loving Jesus

THE INDEFENSIBLE DEPENDENCY

It is difficult at times for each of you to receive the Gift you came to accept and extend because of the shield of hatred the ego has erected to protect its "gift" of guilt in you. The relationships you have each formed were made to "save" you from the guilt which most of you have repressed from awareness. This, however, is the way the ego keeps guilt in you.

Set on an impossible journey, the ego in each of you is attracted to relationships in order to get something to make it feel better or to get a "fix" for the guilt it has hidden in you. The ego knows that if you were to truly heal your guilt, you would share and experience only God with everyone. You would have no special needs that only certain special people could meet for you. You would recognize that, rather than being dependent on certain others, you are actually reliant on everyone equally through God. This the ego cannot tolerate because, if you relinquish faith in your special relationships, the ego's occupation is no more and thus the ego is no more.

Now the form of "dependency" would be changed. No longer would you be dependent on certain others to help somehow "fix" you. Instead you would be God-reliant with whomever you meet and wherever you go. "Getting" is happily exchanged for giving and receiving with the realization that giving *is* receiving and receiving is giving. Your trust in Love would replace all questioning and concern. You would recognize that you and your brothers and sisters *together* have *nothing* you must change or fix. You would recognize that you *have* and *are everything*. Thus you would not see one person as offering more or less than another. You would see only the perfect equality that God knows as Her one Creation — the Self you share. The Christ in each of you is as perfect as the one God Who created you. It is this and only this you all long to experience with each other once again. You can through the transformation of your dependent relationships into loving, blessed and holy relationships. Your relationships truly are already a marriage made in Heaven!

A SCRIBING FOR MARLENE

About four years ago I was admitted to a hospital and diagnosed with a nervous breakdown. I still suffer with anxiety and feel I need medication to deal with life. Dear brother Jesus, can you help? Here are my questions.

1) *What is wrong with my life? I have been searching for love and happiness, but I keep meeting abusive men.*

2) *Is Matt, my present boyfriend of three years, the right man for me? He says he loves me, but his business comes before me. I want to have children, but time is running out, as I am 38.*

3) *I live in constant fear of growing old alone, which depresses me. I am on medication (Prozac) to be able to cope with life. What should I do to heal myself?*

4) *What is my purpose, my mission in this life on earth? How could I be most useful to my fellow man?*

5) *Is it my duty and is it within my power to help my sister and parents with their mental and emotional problems? They seem to think so, and they dump all their problems on me.*

Greetings Marlene:

Quite to Heaven's likeness, yours is of a gentle and sensitive "nature" in your presentation of yourself to others in your world. You also bear the weight of the often cumbersome "responsibility" of holding others up on each shoulder as a result of this persona. Because of this you at times feel taken advantage of and this is key to the fueling of continued repressed core anger. This leads to vacillation between mild apathy/depression and spurious rage. This may seem somewhat forward and judgmental in relation to how you may think I or others may see you. Allow me to gently remind you that I am *not* speaking *about you*.

We are speaking about an image, an ego-portrayal, which seems to follow after you everywhere you go. Its insistence is its weakness and its clear demonstration that *it* is not *you*. Yet as long as you identify with any part of this image, you will seem imprisoned from the true and gentle Likeness that God, in all

His blessing, gave to you of His Creation, Which is your Self. It is therefore not what you are doing, but what you are *not* doing, that makes you feel something is "wrong" with your "life." Let us now look at your first question together.

Dear Marlene, there is absolutely nothing wrong with your life. Begin to accept this by *not* trying to interpret what I have just said! It is your interpretation that makes up a picture of your life that is appealing, but all the same, quite untrue. Your Life in no way resembles any part of your past experiences or your future expectations. You may indeed decide to make the future like the past by bringing the past with you into the present, but this will hardly offer you the real joy of knowing both your Life and your Self in Christ with all.

If you *search* externally for love and happiness, you *will* attract abuse because you are calling on it *instead* of joy. Let us end the external search together now and recognize that a change of mind about your Self and your life is clearly in order. You are loved, dear one. I come this day to remind you it is so. Yet your acceptance of the Love I would bring you must seem unaccomplished while the distraction of your external searching continues. Close your eyes a moment to the world around you and join with me, for I am *already* with you, in the One Who ends all searching forever. Receive this gift of me. O gentle child, we do share His Life together.

There are not abusive men; there are abusive attitudes, which lead to abusive behaviors. You all have participated in these at times either in thought or deed. Everyone has the potential for abuse, because everyone has made an ego for themselves. This choice gave rise to the meaning of "abuse." If you are asking to escape from all relationships that generate abuse, you must begin by learning Where Love comes *from* through greater awareness. I can tell you that Love comes only through your Self, but *do you accept it*? To the extent that you believe it must come from elsewhere, to that extent you open your relationships to the possibility of some form of "abuse."

It is impossible to be "abused" unless some form of an invitation is made to fear instead of Love. *To misplace the Source of Love is to invite fear.* You may believe that it is impossible to recognize in your relationships that all Love comes from God. Yet it is *only* your holy relationships that will carry you beyond belief so you can truly experience the awareness that eternal Love is true. This experience is simply not dependent on the body or the physical world. If it were, you would indeed have good reason to search everywhere for What you had misplaced. Yet the ways of the world are not God's Way, and therefore the search must end where it began, with you. In this recognition, may you truly experience that everything *is* quite right with *your Life*, Marlene.

It takes great learning to love without some form of condition or expectation, for learning of Love means unlearning the world's ways. You are not asked to give up what you have learned at a rate faster than will promote healing in you. Only an interpretation of gentleness is therefore in order for every aspect of your life's experience. Gentleness, with its patience, work together in fulfilling God's one promise in you *and* in each of your relationships as well. He *has* promised to have *all* of your relationships become holy, just as you have promised Him to awaken to your own holiness and share it with those who would remember theirs with you.

Marriage is not of the ego. It is of God, Who already has accomplished your joining with every holy brother and sister you would "meet." Your meetings are not by chance, nor are they your first encounter with one another. There is a reason and a purpose far beyond what either of you can see. When "separation" rather than marriage is apparent, there is reason and purpose in this as well. Its reason may not be what you want to have, but it is always to teach you what you *do* have. If you try to author the reason for your relationships, only a learning failure can result, leaving you needing to learn the lesson you came to learn at a later time.

If you allow the Holy Spirit to bring to your relationship His Reason, a peaceful and fulfilling outcome will always shine its Light on the witnesses who surround you. Let Him decide with His Reason, then, and do not worry or concern yourself with what seems behind or ahead of you. In this way, Marlene, all will become a glorious lesson in a Love so holy, everything it touches will sparkle with a joy this world can never overshadow. Be gentle in this area of your life, dear one. This *is* your lesson and, in the relinquishment of all your judgment surrounding it, you will receive your lesson and move on to what is happily next for you.

In regard to your second question with your boyfriend, there is only one person who can provide the answer and that is *you*.

But you must hear it clearly from *within*. I will answer you there, but I cannot answer you here, for in this particular case it would interfere with a lesson you are intensely engaged in learning. You know that this is so, you *know what* you must do and how you must achieve it. I will take your hand, when you are ready, to lead you through the present fear which has held you "captive" in indecision. I will say this: Only in risking what seems to be "vulnerability" can anyone *be healed*. That time is upon you, as time is *always* there for you, as long as "business" seems to come before Love. Look carefully for the similarities in your lessons, for you can heal them together, if What is primary becomes your shared goal. Remember "meetings."

I will speak quickly to your statement about children. Thirty-eight is very young. You are but a child and I do know! I do indeed hope this gives you reason to laugh, little child! Children can have children when they decide. Then they pretend to exchange childhood for parenthood, but they always return to being the lovely children they are. God is happily blind is He not?

It *is* your choice and time *is* for you. Are you ready to practice being "happily blind"? It is a lovely practice indeed!

Let us now move to your third question that, in your heart and mind, also entangles itself with question two to some degree.

Your "constant fear" remains constant partially because of your consistent dependence on medication. All medications take away from your innate dependence on God to heal naturally. This is why using medications must be understood as only temporary expedients from fear or pain. They do *not* heal, but only cover until healing is gently invited to take magic's place. At some point everyone must accept miracles in place of magic and its "cures." It is merely a question of willingness to risk the exposure of whatever deeper fears seem to horrify you. These fears are beliefs about yourself. None of them are true or can really hurt you. While you give them precedence over the truth in you, suffering can become very acute, making magic attractive.

It appears that without your medication, Marlene, life is constantly depressing. This is because the ego is vigilant in its constant reminder that you are somehow deprived. You *are* deprived of the awareness of the eternal Love That is forever yours, as long as you listen to its insane vigilance against the truth in you.

True healing is always *for* the ego, which *is* the belief that *you* are separate from Love. Believing that the ego is for you, instead of the healing of the Holy Spirit that is for you, has caused you to believe that consistency lies in magic and not in miracles. There is no doubt that the ego can convince you to consistently medicate yourself, thus offering you some habitual sense of a "temporary happiness." I assure you that the real happiness you are hoping for will never be found there, for magic must always dull awareness and cloud the Son of God from your awareness. *Only miracles should become habits.*

Yet you should not discontinue a medicine that seems to help you until you are ready for the only Medicine that *will* help. Nor should you *ever* feel guilty if you feel the need to depend on external help for a while. I can only remind you that there *is* a Way that is *eternally* consistent. As a loving brother to you, that is what I must do. You will know when it is best for you to "risk" stretching toward a different and more lasting experience with your own healing. Great gifts from Christ will come as you do. The Safety Net you are seeking to help you onward with your healing is *already* established, Marlene. Not outside you, but within you and within all the holy ones who surround you. Seek healing here, my beloved sister. It awaits you and gently calls to you from Where His gentle Guest remains, in each of your hearts that call to join in Christ together. Here is His healing and Heaven is His Goal.

You cannot grow old *alone*. It is impossible! That is why it is said in Heaven that you cannot trust anyone under forty million, for only the Ageless stop keeping track!

Marlene, you are a beautiful Child of God. You will indeed know intimate and lasting companionship in your life, but you will not "have" it as long as you are afraid of what you think you *don't* have. By fearing what you think you *don't* have or *can't* have, you call on your experience to *prove* this *to* you, rather than bring What you *do have* to you. How you call determines what you invite in.

As I stated earlier, your second and third questions are interrelated. The fear is of unfulfillment and *this* is related to your fourth question, which we will also discuss shortly.

Are you calling on fear or on Love? You must learn to ask this question often for a while, until you have learned Where your true Treasure lies. Your Treasure *is* your safety. If you make the perceptions the ego holds out to you into your "treasure," your keeping track of *it* will blind you to the glorious and unlimited Treasure the Holy Spirit *always keeps for you.* Which voice would you call on to entrust your safety and happiness to? Calling on the voice for fear will bring you enough burnt offerings to only confuse you and keep you in dismay. Calling on the Voice for Love in you and everyone will surely show you the consistent and everlasting Safety and Happiness that brings an experience, beyond any shadow of doubt, that you are fulfilled. This comes not from the offerings of the ego, but in the timeless and everlasting Love of Christ Himself. May His recognition in you fulfill you now.

You have asked how you might heal yourself. In every healing situation there is but one activity present — the letting go of blame. What better way to heal than to practice the walk of sincere gentleness and honesty with everyone? You who are truly young at heart should hardly worry about growing old. "Cope" with your life easily then, by realizing once and for all What eternal Life is! It is your only Life. Your gentleness, loved one, will surely show you it is so!

And now we shall discuss question number four.

Your function in your life is to forgive so that you may fulfill the purpose God gave you to share with Him and others. His purpose is to create, as is yours. The creative process occurs all the time in every thing you do, but that is not the point. The point is to discover what work, what specific individual process, best suits you in both keeping your recognition of Life and consistently offering it to others as well. Life is Love, dear Marlene, and It is only available *now*.

Now is beyond the world as you see it. It is the eternal present in which Christ smiles through you, bringing the Father with Him and healing the world! This is your mission dear Marlene, to *allow* this to be so for you and all.

The recognition of Christ in everyone *is* your only joy. All men and women seek it in *you* as well. Learn, then, to provide what everyone is seeking by not hiding the Kingdom of Heaven in you from them. Instead, shine the Light that forgives and is forgiven through you. Can anyone's mission be greater than this?

I have chosen *you* to set forth God's Mission for both of us. You can easily do this because I came to establish the completion of His

Mission. His Mission is already accomplished through you and by this you need do nothing at all except receive Its Completion and know that It *is* you. Do this in remembrance of me, and the holy Mission I came to fulfill is fulfilled as well through you. God's Will is done. Take heart in the happiness that it is so and share your Light with all.

Now let us address your final question.

Of yourself you cannot even help yourself; to think that somehow you alone can help others is a gross confusion in the understanding of "power." However, it is within your ability to bring Help to them by allowing each of them the dignity of their own choices. Understanding is not fixing. Compassion is not pity. And forgiveness is not offering correction. It is okay for them to dump their problems on you as long as you do not allow the "wastebasket" you hold out to get too full! When it gets too full, it becomes your problem too. The moral: An empty wastebasket is a happy wastebasket!

In learning to keep an open and helpful mind, you must empty out your own concerns, fears and judgments. The true healer knows that through an empty vessel, Light makes its way faster. A clear Light shining to all those you love will be the greatest help you can offer. Nothing needs to change, Marlene. Nothing needs fixing. All is in His Divine Order. But keep healthy boundaries for yourself, so that your own Light can be happily there. When it seems too dim, take time to empty your fears and problems into Christ's holy wastebasket, for His is so "holy" it never needs emptying.

It is *your* duty not to take yourself so seriously! It is when you do, that your world seems to close in around you. This of course helps no one. Christ's Way is the Way of joy. He recognizes *for* you that your "duty" is always done *through* Him, leaving you with the happy recognition of your Self in all Its completeness and perfection. By learning only to happily extend Him to everyone, you are sure to remember your "duty" is done.

Peace to you dear Marlene, and remember today, in my holy and happy blessing to you, that you are indeed in God's Perfect Light. All is in order, all is well. In keeping with His Answer in you, all is wonderfully done *in you*. You are blessed in Christ's Name.

A loving Jesus, the Christ

EXCHANGING YOUR VALUES

Your relationships must change in their purpose *if* you would experience the true Gift God has willed for you. Grievances must be replaced by the full willingness to forgive. Value must be placed only in discovering the *common goal* of peace through the Holy Spirit — the Divine Inspiration you share together. The temptation to place value anywhere else must be recognized as a futile attempt to hide from truth and the Gift of Love.

The hatred you each conceal from Light is often what "powers" your relationships. The ego in each of you takes up an enormous amount of time dedicated to judging others, criticizing each other's habits, condemning certain actions, and the list goes on. This is the challenge you all face with what you have made — a world designed from your temptation to hide your common goal through guilt and condemnation, rather than reveal it through a true willingness to forgive.

You cannot forgive if you value things and bodies over peace, for you only make more hatred that later must be undone in you. You must value only peace if you are to transcend temptation and if you are to live happily and freely. No matter how long you fight against this goal, eventually you must remember it, for it is what you came to do.

As your healing begins in those intimate relationships you have made special in some way, the healing will extend throughout the world to all others. As slow as it may seem now, the entire world will transform with you into a place you have never dreamt of. Think you that you will never see Heaven on earth? Only in dreams of fear my dear ones, only in your dreams!

A SCRIBING FOR GEORGIE

Dearest Joel,

I read one of the scribings you offered for the whole group to read. It touched me deeply, as I am really struggling with many of the same issues your friend seems to be struggling with. So I have a few specifics to ask, that you might access that part of our mind that is wiser than my blocked self and help me with this one.

I am currently in a mildly lucrative, but waste of time (in my opinion) profession. I'm living with an ex-boyfriend, who offered me a place to move quickly when I found myself in a fearful living situation a couple of months ago. I do need to move out of this situation, as my focus is too much on him and I find that I am at a loss to change that right now. His focus is on several other women, all of whom he is involved with. That is part of my problem. Try as I might, I find that I am lonely and really would like to share my life experiences here with a man who also wants to share with me. I'm forty-five and divorced six years. Just not meant to live alone.

I also am very dedicated to practicing and teaching A Course In Miracles *— have been for seven years. My focus has been in the practice, more than the writing these last couple of years. But writing is my talent (not my profession, which is more into engineering and computers). I find that I have an opportunity to move out to Sedona and be part of the group out there. It is golden and I do want to do it, but I barely get by on my salary. My debts equal my savings (both are relatively small), but without a paying job, there are some real practical considerations, like how do I buy food, gas, Internet time? Truly, I've been afraid that my wish to join them is tainted by my other issues. I don't hold that place or those people to be any more sacred than any other place or people and I know that I desire to find forgiveness in my current situations, not just run away from them. Yet I've never succeeded in anything in life. I fear that this is just another ego trip and I will fall flat on my face and be destitute. I'm already hitting an age where it is hard to find employment in my field.*

My question is a request for some assurances, some guidance that this is not just another ego dead end. Also, can I really support myself if I go there and work more or less as a volunteer for the Circle of Atonement? I am quite aware of a lot of fears here.

Thanks for your help.

Namaste,

Georgie

Greetings Georgie:

Let us begin our discussion today with answering some of your questions about intimate relationships.

Perhaps intimate relationships are one of the most confusing of your experiences while living in your world. That is because most of you are experiencing each other in your fantasies, not in the Reality that was created for you by God. There is a danger to your peace of mind anytime you choose to dabble in mere fantasies and dreams. This is what you are choosing when you believe that a relationship is merely to dance to and fro from one relationship to the next, never settling long enough to discover why you are so afraid to land and remain.

Relationship is about staying in your heart, not leaving. It involves "risk" to stay — risk to the ego being exposed for what it isn't, not for what it is. Relationship involves commitment to discovering what it is that doesn't work, then allowing that to be healed, loved and undone. But the ego doesn't want to be healed. That is why it is constantly finding ways to sabotage and break agreements. That is why it does not wish to stay in one place for too long. It does not want its purpose to be discovered before it has had time to escape what it has worked so hard not to reveal — its concealment of truth. If innocence were to come into awareness, the ego's denial would be exposed and healed. This the ego cannot tolerate.

Relationships can be more easily understood if one can recognize and accept what is being played out in the world you live in. You are busy pretending you are separate from God and others. That is what got you here. The fact that you have been attempting to do this since time began can hardly be disputed. Look at your history. But notice I said "attempting" to do this. Just because it is true that you have *tried*, does not make it true! The game is, "Let's pretend we are separate for awhile and we will all make up different dreams to prove it. I'll gamble that I can make you believe *my* dream is more 'real' than yours!" So now you can perhaps see how involved this is. On the scale of illusions, it is immense!

This brings us to the following point. How often are you able to be with one another in a quiet moment that is so holy that it instantly reminds you that you are really one Being, not two? If you will answer that question honestly, you may see more clearly than ever how often you have chosen to play the same game as the one you see as "not fully sharing his life with you." Ah yes, now we are getting somewhere. It is not he, but you, that must come to terms with the choices you have made to see yourself as separate from *him*. Could it be, my dear Georgie, that this is why you are feeling so lonely? Life, my dear child, is everywhere. It is only your illusions that make you believe you are apart from one another.

What is the greatest achievement you could hope for while in relationship with your beloved? It is the perfect, joyous reflection and complete recognition of your Self as Christ with him, for who is your beloved? This is the one exception I will make to not answering a question with another question: Who is *not* your beloved *in Him*? There is not one living soul who does not have the same deep desire you have — to know *together* your Self as the Christ you share. But you are looking with your five senses. That is why you are walking around wearing blindfolds, running into each other. *The dream is your blindfold*. Take it off! That is your only function here — to remember together from Where It is you really came.

It does not matter who you are currently with or where you go. You are changing nothing but the physical appearance by doing this and change is but illusion. That is why listening from your heart is important to you. The question is not whether or not you should trust in making a change in your physical circumstances for your "safety" and "happiness." The question should be, "What do I need to let go of that is preventing me from recognizing the present situation I am in as the perfect situation for allowing healing *right now*?" Those people and things you are having a hard time with in the present, and you are thus seeking "change for the better" *from*, are the blessed and perfect teachers God has sent to help you heal right now. You can abandon your present situation and seem to leave it behind, but those who have been sent to you will follow you out to your destination in yet another name. As long as you are clear about this, then changing your location will not matter or make a difference. It is fine either way because the lessons still follow. Understanding this clearly *before* you make changes will allow you to do whatever it is you feel you must with a *presence of heart and mind*.

I would not say you should not go to your "destination." Obviously you recognize that I could never suggest this. Nor would I tell you it is best to stay in the situation you are in. Everything I have explained to you in this scribing thus far you are already somewhat aware of. You need to make a decision based on your own higher understanding and inner guidance from the Holy Spirit in you now. I can lead you to the Holy Spirit if you will ask me and He will show you the way through His loving and inclusive guidance. But I can never decide *for you*, only *with* you. It is not my function to *change anything*. I can say that you will be clearer on the decision you are choosing to make if you will allow yourself the healing that is called for *now*. Should you choose to fully receive this healing, there is no doubt that you will have little difficulty trusting to take the "leap" to your other destination. I know you are well aware of "why."

The leap in trust is right here, along with the issues you hope to heal. The destination is also *right here*. That is all you need address. I assure you, once you receive the healing in full, there will be nowhere you will feel unsafe to go. Perhaps with this understanding you will be able to better measure where you stand on your own path regarding the question of the "need for healing." It may also help you to receive clarity regarding the process of denial and acceptance. A useful measuring tool to go by would be, if you feel a capricious desire for flight, that is the time you *should* be still. If you are hearing this right, this should make you very happy, Georgie. I am right here with you, right now.

Can you support yourself? Of course you can! Especially when you take momentary leave of the world and recognize that the whole universe is behind you! Your body is not as big as you think, Georgie. Do your best to keep that perspective. It will also be helpful as time seems to wear on.

The issues you are up against in your life mostly center on confusion about self-worth. The part of your mind that holds this confusion is none other than the ego. Yet this confusion will be easily corrected when you firmly commit to the right evaluation offered by the Holy Spirit. This is perhaps the most difficult of lessons for teachers of God to assimilate. It is hard for you who are in the world to accept that there is no contribution, other than forgiveness, to really make to the world. Even now, your ego is somewhat threatened by this idea.

You go about life seeking new and different ways to "feel better" about your individual life. I tell you, with the Love of God, there is nothing for you to really do *out there*. Value lies only in the communication of Love. Seek not to place value in anything else, for if you do, you will judge against the truth and yourself. This will make you sad. There is nothing left for you to do in this world except to remember with one another What you truly are together. This does not require *doing*, only the pure presence of *being*.

The ego would tell you that this idea is insane, for it does not understand that nothing is accomplished except through Love. It will ask a million questions and offer a million answers about how it thinks you should "survive." *Your healing lies in learning not to listen to it, but to follow the Love in your heart instead*. This is how the ego is healed — when you no longer believe in it or give it power. All the tears you cry will not help you until you accept and live in full consciousness of this one idea. You do not want the gifts your ego has to offer. Choose forgiveness and, through forgiveness, Love instead.

My dear Georgie, the greatest gift you will ever give yourself is your trust in the Love Which created you. Nothing can ever really hurt you here except your unwillingness to take the risk that your complete trust would offer. Even this is temporary. The Gift of your real Life is fully recognized the moment you follow and live in the Light that God gave you. This is what you seek and this is all you will finally find. Blessed are you who will finally give up the search, for it is in its *relinquishment* that you will be returned Home! Heaven awaits your quiet return through this awakening. Take peace in God's Comfort, Georgie. Whatever you decide to do, take joy in recognizing that it does not matter. This is my blessing to you. I share today the Gift that God gives you through me. Would you receive It from me through Him now?

Blessed are you who have asked

and have heard.

A loving Jesus

THE CIRCLE OF LOVE

What would happen if suddenly you accepted this shining purpose given you by God? What would happen if you valued only peace, and conflict no longer held an interest to you? What would happen if the argument you have been having with that certain special person became insignificant to both of you... or if world politics and wars were recognized as not a part of the one goal for peace?

First there would be some upheaval, for by changing your goal from conflict to peace, relinquishment must begin to take place. As each one of you begins this process of relinquishment, so does the world follow in your footsteps. With your change of mind about purpose and goal, the true purpose of the world is revealed to everyone step-by-step. Suddenly businesses end, while others transform. Politicians become writers. Policemen become ministers and ministers become policemen. Changes begin occurring so rapidly that no one's ego can figure it out. Welcome to the twenty-first century. Welcome to the transformation that you have asked for, *together*.

When your relationships transform from the goal of guilt to the goal of Love, the world begins to heal and transform with you. Your relationships are the key to bringing Heaven to earth. As each relationship has the conditions you imposed removed from it, the relationship takes on a new and special purpose that will reach far beyond what your imaginations could ever conceive. Miracles will occur just because of your mere presence together. Others will immediately be drawn to the holiness that emanates through your relationship and they will wish to enter the Circle of Love that this relationship has established. The relationship that becomes holy through your willingness to totally forgive will extend out to bless all conflict, suffering and even the deepest of fear. The Light in it will literally banish darkness in other minds. Where once fear and anger were cherished and held too tightly, suddenly those around you who come close to this Circle will let go of their holdings as if they had never experienced them at all.

This is the power of the true holy relationship, for this relationship recognizes for everyone that there is nothing to fear or condemn. The conditions have been removed, so there is no guilt to bind one ego to another in grievances that were made to keep war and conflict "alive." The relationship has been entirely given to the Holy Spirit, so each does not look to the past or the future for the "power" to keep the relationship insane. The real power has been called upon by both in the present. It is in the present instant, fresh with the pure Love of their Creator, that each would always remember to bless the other.

You may think this is almost impossible in the world you live in. I tell you now that the holy relationship is the only natural thing left here for you to do! Never were you created to do anything else. Over time, you have taught yourselves quite differently. This is why the world has become so insane and seemingly intolerable to many of you. You each purchased the ego's plan for guilt long ago. You have been practicing the most unnatural act of separation while trying to figure out what went wrong. You "bought" these ideas as "tools" to extend time and stretch it out — an action which is diametrically opposed to your Father's Will for you. It was an action that could only make your world more and more dense as you each became more invested in the "purchase" you thought you made. For thousands of years you have justified this dream of separation through the continuing use of the ego's many tools of guilt: Cults and religions, institutions, laws and punishment... the list goes on.

Using these tools has made all the dis-ease, obsession and suffering you now seem to see and experience. These misguided ideas are now coming into question through the urgency you have brought into play. This urgency is the effect of the choices and actions you have all taken over a long span of time with these "tools." In the times ahead there will be great questioning *together* of the supposed "need" for these archaic tools. In times ahead, your holy relationships will overcome this supposed need for autonomy and the ancient insanity that has conflicted your world. Then the true purpose of the world will be revealed to many, not to just the few. The responsibility to *all* your brothers and sisters in times ahead will be great indeed.

Your decision must be sure, your foundation strong now. Brothers and sisters, no longer can you afford to be wasteful of time. The time is come for the healing of all that has kept you apart from each other and God. I have come to keep my promise and lead us Home together. Listen then, for my Voice, the Voice for Love, in all your relationships to come. Turn away from no one, for each has been brought to you by me. *I am not mistaken* in what I have come to do.

Chapter Five

Health, Sickness & Healing

INTRODUCTION

So many of you, for so long in time, have insisted on making this world a serious event. You came here to enjoy your lives, not to take the world seriously and sicken yourselves. I remind you to laugh and allow God's Love to release you from guilt and suffering. Still you follow in the old ways and your tears keep flowing like children who have been abandoned in the street. Are you not yet ready to discover a different way and then live in it? Are you not weary of the seeming hatred and destruction that has given its purpose to your world? Would you see your world as a place to come to experience pain and then watch it one day disappear in a puff of billowing smoke — the end of all ends, that hatred might take its final victory? Is that what you believe this world was made to achieve? Oh no, my sisters and brothers, this is not what all this is for! Yet this is what the ego offers you — a picture of certain destruction.

How is it that you think the ego will succeed in destroying the eternal? What plan can be so foolproof that even God and His Creation cannot escape the end that guilt, prejudice and hatred have in mind? How could you destroy something that was made only to *escape* from God and expect to destroy Him as well? Destroying the world would accomplish nothing, for the world is nothing. You could no more destroy God than you could your Self. God knows you have tried every possible way to prove that it is possible! Perhaps the time is coming where you all might wish to cooperate *with* Love instead of fighting against It. Perhaps this would ease the burden you have each placed upon yourselves by the decision made long ago to put yourselves in charge of a "kingdom" that is not even yours!

Have any of your "sciences" really brought you a better understanding of your Origin? Quite honestly it has brought you only fancy words, theories, a great deal of confusion and even more to seem to separate over. Has it never occurred to you that by looking for answers "out there" all this time, be it alteration, medication, institutionalization or transportation, that perhaps in the complexity of the physical, truth could never be revealed? What if the outward "search" is obscuring the very brilliance of your Source? Scientists and explorers are just now getting clues that perhaps your ancient inner sciences may have had something to offer. *After all*, they worked for *me*! Are you willing to admit that a few thousand years ago you possibly took a slight detour and are now just finding your way back? A humbling idea, is it not? And quite true as truth can possibly be, relative to history.

In this mad search you have all been involved in for a time, you have been looking for the "key to life," the "fountain of youth" so to speak. You have assembled armies to "protect" you while on your quest. You have locked up those who questioned your search and have done away with others who out and out threatened it. You have "educated" your children to follow in your footsteps, forcing upon them a machine you invented to conquer, eternalize, make the body autonomous and make the physical world. In this bloody and insane conquest, you have all forgotten but one essential ingredient — the fact that each of you is *already* an eternal Ingredient of God!

Your search for everlasting life in your world has made you oblivious to the everlasting Life in God's Heaven *in you*! The guilt and fear that has been promoted by this blind quest has essentially been responsible for all the illness and insanity you have endured. Quite a detour, wouldn't you say? Yet even this has not been done entirely in vain. All these tools made in the detour will be useful, once the full integration of your true function and purpose has set in with the greater majority. This will be the Second Coming of Christ in you all. Your true and lasting healing will be soon to come!

SO MUCH LOVE

You each have so much Love to bring the world. Did you not know that your purpose here was far greater than reinventing the wheel or finding a way to make the body last another twenty years? You came here to remember together What you've always *been* and *are*. The little time you have here was not meant for making a world to save you *from* this!

Look at the mythical story of Frankenstein and the monster he "created" because of his obsession with finding a way to eternalize the body and the suffering he went through as the result of his mad attempts. Would you live your lives to be as Frankenstein or as the perfect and eternal angel God created you to be? None of you need be so concerned over bodies. It is perfectly safe if you don't have one. After all, I should know, shouldn't I?

If your body is to truly heal from a dis-ease that you have inadvertently drawn into your experience, how should you think that you can help yourself and the body the most?

A SCRIBING FOR ILA

Dear Joel,

My current life situation is that I have lived for the past twenty-five years with a painful, crippling disease, Rheumatoid Arthritis (more about that in one of my questions). Although I do experience great happiness in my life, I often find my ego trying to analyze these situations and not let me enjoy them. I am at a crossroads where I may choose to live my life in the service and benefit of mankind, which will make me less vested in the world. Yet I have a mistrust of this and people sent into my life for this purpose. I fear losing my enjoyment of the things the world offers me. I also have a problem living in the moment.

The following are my list of questions for my brother, Jesus.

1) *Jesus, I have recently had a relationship placed before me which offers me unconditional Love and the opportunity to express myself by sharing my experiences and helping my brothers and sisters. Yet, I am experiencing doubt and*

*mistrust sometimes. How can I know what is being presented
to me is guided by you and Holy Spirit rather than a
manifestation of my own ego?*

2) *My brother Jesus, I have lived for the past twenty-five years
with Rheumatoid Arthritis and have experienced fifteen
operations, including many total joint replacements. Recently
through* A Course In Miracles *and one of your teachers, I
have been experiencing considerable alleviation of pain and
a general improvement of my total condition. Is it possible
for me to achieve (through God) total healing when I have so
many damaged and replaced parts in my body?*

3) *Does God look upon suicide differently than any other form
by which a person would choose to leave their body?*

4) *I have been given a gift with the written word and have
had many things published in the past. Yet I am having
difficulty writing at this time. How would you have me use
this gift for the benefit of my brothers and sisters?*

5) *How can I forgive myself for hurts I have caused other people
and myself and how can I achieve peace through forgiveness?*

6) *Are our lifetimes connected in the sense that acts committed
in one lifetime have repercussions in another?*

Love and peace to you my brother,

Ila

My Dear Ila:

With open arms and open heart I would welcome you now
into the Circle of Light we share together and with all. You have
much on your mind and heart that troubles you. As we begin this
communication, let me remind you that what you are *reading* may
well appear to be on paper or your computer screen. But what you
are *hearing* is coming directly through you from the Self we both
share. I am the Christ in you. I am not apart from you in anyway.
You will understand this as we go on. All that you receive comes
to you *through* me *from* God. In us together there is no real separation. Let us now go on.

You are the holy Effect of your Creator, Ila. As His Effect you cannot change your holy Self. What appears to be all the changes and confusion that you identify as your other "self" is but illusion. These illusions give the self you made an appearance of complexity. It is this complexity that you are drawn to over and over again, making you ever more confused about the simplicity with which your true Self is created.

This complexity is a survival mechanism that has lost total control over everything and yet maintains that it is fully *in* control. It is a part of your mind that has identified with fear and the physical and has made you think at times that you are going insane. And you are as long as you continue to follow it. But insanity can only last so long. God's Sanity, deep within you my dear Ila, is surely now returning.

Yet there are certain ideas that your ego is insistent on keeping as your "personal hell." I would gently encourage you now to become willing to release them *entirely*. The only "danger" you are in is the state of mind the ego insists you must keep and accept for yourself. This stubborn arrogance comes from the fear of loss of control. It is this very stubbornness that will keep you from the peace that you truly deserve and the healing you so much desire. This arrogance is not visible to others because it has been kept hidden within you. When you became ill, you made a decision to conquer your dis-ease and the fighting has wearied you.

You have thought of suicide because you are tired of fighting. It has not really occurred to you that if you were simply to give up your whole investment in "fighting the pain," there would then be the opportunity to embrace the very "demons" that your illness began from, and that your suicide would only avoid. It is these same "demons" that have had you repeat one lifetime after another. The ego counsels that you must avoid these demons at all costs, for it does not want you to heal what is really destructive to you. It would rather repeatedly send you off to what it sees as oblivion than allow you to heal and experience your real power. It would have you keep your focus only on the body to accomplish this. If you had the full experience of God's Love in you, you would not waste a moment concerning yourself with endings and beginnings, for you would recognize only your Self as a never-ending. God does not judge a seeming suicide or even look upon the loss of bodies. Only you do. This is the oblivion the ego holds out to you. You need not repeat unnecessary lessons unless you want to.

Your ego is bent on its continuance through keeping your attention sidetracked in avoiding your Self. If you allow it to have its way, you will only succeed in dragging on your lessons. You have asked whether one lifetime is connected with the next. This is true in what you have made. Yet it serves no purpose to dwell on this. Would you throw a child out of the race just because he is slow to make it to the finish line? Would you place a five-year-old in a tenth grade classroom? Of course this makes no sense and both of these choices would only induce more fear. You are always given the "time" to learn what you desire to learn. When the lessons are learned, you will gracefully move on.

You came here to learn the lessons you brought with you. For you, many of those lessons relate to the body. You know well indeed what they are deep down inside you, though your ego may have blocked them from your awareness temporarily. These are not easy lessons until you would fully give up the ego's wishes to distance you from them. What better way is there to keep denial in place than by keeping your attention where you are powerless to affect real healing? The body is the ego's treasure. It only becomes more difficult if you follow this picture of denial the ego holds out to you. Your only real choice is to let go completely your picture of the body and embrace your suffering with the help of Love. I have already sent you the right and perfect people to help you with this. There is only one thing preventing you from taking this risk to be healed and that, my dear one, is trust.

In answer to your sixth question, you do take your lessons with you. All these lessons have to do with making the body into a "god of sickness" by denying the Christ in you. Lifetime after lifetime is only necessary because you make it this way. God is not sending you back here. You are. It is more difficult to live in the temporary existence you made than in the Light of your eternal Creation that you already have. Yet most of you don't believe this. That is why you keep returning and making more to undo. To some degree, each of you are *enjoying* the drama of the life and birth process. When you get tired of it, however, and you decide for something different, it will be available to you! You need not lose your body to discover it. To "die" before "death" is to live forever!

It does not serve you to try to escape the existence you have made without healing it while you are still here. Until you find eternal rest where you are at right now, you are bound by fear to repeat unnecessary cycles of guilt. This is why I seldom speak of reincarnation. Most of you become confused by it. Most often it is not helpful to contemplate it, because it can keep you from completing the lessons at hand *right now*. This is the only place your focus *should* or *need* be, for it is here and only here that you will find your pain and your true healing.

Now let us go to your question number five and I will attempt to help you understand how much confusion is at work here.

This is the question that is also the answer. This is the lesson as well and the healing that will bring you Home to Heaven, not after you lay your body down, but before. As I said earlier, all that is preventing you from this healing is the lack of trust you feel for your Self. The anger, frustration and impatience that you feel is all because of mistrust as well. Yet because of this mistrust, you are forcing yourself into a situation where you must trust. And trust you will, because that is part of the lesson you chose to come here to learn. Procrastination will last only a short while longer until you will have to let go. Or you can choose to "jump off the cliff" with our Father's Parachute and float gently into the healing arms of your brothers, sisters and God. Which do you prefer my dear Ila, the skid marks of resistance or a soft landing in a warm meadow?

You will know what is from the Holy Spirit by the fruits it bears, just as you will know the ego in the same way by its "fruits." In most cases this does not include your first reaction to a particular situation. More often than not, when the ego counsels, "I don't think I want to do that," it is best to step back, quiet your mind and allow the peace of the Holy Spirit to guide you. The ego will always tell you not to risk. The Holy Spirit knows there is no risk. Only the ego resists. The way to break resistance is to make a firm decision to follow the guidance of your true Self. When you doubt, know that it is only your Self you doubt, and then choose again. There is no reason to rush to do anything. Take time to move past fear to the peace of the Holy Spirit, Ila. Your healing depends on this. Do not be afraid. There is nowhere to land except the Meadow created in Heaven.

You have asked, "Is it possible for me to achieve (through God) total healing when I have so many damaged and replaced parts in my body?" Yes, total healing is not only possible, it is certain. But healing is always of the mind, not the body. It is not necessary for you to completely heal the body to achieve what you are most certainly here to accomplish. You did not come here to achieve eternal life in a body, only to achieve the recognition of eternal Life. It is essential for you now to become clear on this. If any healing is to occur in your body, it will be *because* you have chosen to place your focus on healing your mind. This is the correct achievement you are here to embrace.

The body is temporary. All the time wasted on trying to heal the body takes away from your true function here. If you place your focus on healing the body you will only incur more grievances to use as weapons against yourself. By focusing on the body you would be equating yourself as the body and *with* the guilt that you have associated around it. This is a complete denial of the function you are here to perform. The body can only begin to heal when the mind has forgiven appearances and has chosen correctly. The correct choice, no matter how it may seem, is to forgive the picture of the physical completely. You need not deny the appearance, but only deny the necessity *for* the appearance. In this way you can learn to overlook the illusion of sickness and properly place healing in the mind.

This will also help you to let go of the need to "control" your pain. As I have said before, the more you attempt to control, the more you will bring about needless suffering. What will heal you is embracing your pain. By embracing the pain you are allowing Love to reach where only suffering once was. Do not push the pain from your heart, Ila. Bring it to the Heart of Love in you. Embrace it, touch it, speak with it as if it were a wounded child. Most of all, Ila, trust in those who have been sent to you by me to help you. They have come because they were called. Let them gently help you on your way to the Heart of healing in you.

In regard to question four, I will answer it this way: If you cannot write, speak. If you cannot speak, sign. If you cannot sign, hug. If you cannot hug, smile. The form with which you bring Love to all our brothers and sisters does not matter. It is only a question of whether or not you will do it, no matter the form. The great Gift you have to offer is beyond the written word. The language of

Love is spoken in many different ways. The way that is best suited for your own healing is waiting for you. It may not be that writing is as important as a hug. Your Heart already knows what you can do to best serve your own healing and the healing of others. Learn to listen to the simplicity It is guiding you to and do not let the complexity of ego keep your focus where it is unimportant. The Heart of healing is in you now. May you allow It to reach through you to illuminate every mind and heart! *Your* healing, Ila, is the healing of the entire world.

It is through your forgiveness that you will learn the meaning of trust. Your brothers and sisters have been hurt only by their own decisions This is temporary at its "worst." It seems that you have hurt them, but these hurts are self-imposed by the guilt each of you have chosen to punish yourselves with. You need not be concerned about your brothers and sisters and the "pain" that you think you have brought them. I would remind you again that time is under my control. There will be time for everyone to forgive and heal. You have done nothing that can hurt anyone.

What still seems painful to you are the unhealed memories of all the times you have forgotten to love. These are the grievances you hold against yourself as if to hold a sharpened blade against your own throat. Yet you are terrorizing yourself for something *that never really occurred in truth*. What is not Love does *not* exist. Your ego would insist, however, that these injustices *did* happen. It seems for a while that guilt follows and haunts you through time. What if these "injustices" had no real effect at all, Ila? Would you lift the blade away from your throat then? Have mercy on yourself, little child. Have mercy on all.

What is true but the Life God has given you *now*? Can anything or any deed really take you away from this? Only in dreams my dear one, only in dreams. There is nothing "out there" to forgive. There is no past for forgiveness to find. All that remains of the past has only been held in place by your decision, as an ancient hatred kept hidden and left abandoned from the all encompassing Love that would absorb it and make you free. Is it not insane to keep what can never be true from the Light of Love that is in you now and is *always* true? Give it quickly, then, to the Holy Spirit in you and let the dead bury the dead *now*! For He would only release you from the dark dreams of terror you have made. Would you not now answer His call to forgive Christ rather than condemn Him in you? Gently, then, trust in the only Gift He has given. Do not block what His Grace would surely bless you with. Let this Gift adorn you with the innocence that is forever yours.

There is nothing to fear, Ila, because the past is dead and gone. Only the sparkle of God's healing Light remains with you, in the Christ, forever free and innocent by His Name. Think you there is really any other reality? Only in fantasies can the Son of God imprison herself for nothing His Father would even recognize! Be gentle with yourself, Ila. The Love of Christ is only here, only now, in an instant of holy timelessness the world can never know. But you can! Because it is here, it is everywhere. There is nowhere that His Love is not. I join you in this Place Where we dwell together. Eternal grandeur is our Gift and It can only bring joy. Walk with me and all our brothers and sisters in His Light, Ila, and rejoice, for Heaven within is come!

Here is a prayer for you. Use it often when your mind begins to wander into valleys He would not have you travel. Say it with sincerity, for it will heal and enlighten you:

"Father, I come to You weary of my own doubts and fears. For I have thought to dream an impossible dream and then make it true. Because of this I have become mistrustful of my Self and have lost sight of Your one Gift to me. I have used this sight as a weapon that would hurt me somehow. I lay this sight and all its fearful fantasies down before You now, that You might take my gift and replace it with the One you have kept forever safe for me. Your Gift is all that I want and all that I would receive now. For I would humbly behold What is mine in only What You have given. Thank you, Father, for this healing and the gentle peace You bring me now."

Amen

Rest in the peace

That is your Life

In the Living God

That is in you now.

Blessed, Ila, are you who have listened and have truly heard.

In You,

A loving Jesus Christ

Question

What part does medicine play in healing?

There are many different forms used in the practice of medicine and many different types of medications as the world defines them. But there is only one real medicine and that is Love. This is simple enough to understand, yet throughout time it has remained far from being accepted on a larger scale in the world. It does not seem remotely possible that Love could heal all sickness and dis-ease of every kind. Of course this seems true as long as the power of Love remains unaccepted. Yet many of you are gathering in the practice of medicine who have become uneasy with the stalling traditional practices and have begun a sincere inner search for a working alternative. This will go further than you can now imagine. Younger generations will follow you, practicing alternative medicines that will soon be found to be truly unlimited in scope. These practices will combine spiritual and psychological principles. The focus will shift off the emphasis on the body and instead to the mind where it truly belongs and where only healing can occur.

As "preventive medicine" matures into an effective psycho-physiological practice, instead of merely addressing the *effects* of dis-ease on the body, people as a whole will clearly realize *What* can *only* be said to truly cure. Then prevention through a spiritual practice will blossom like never before. There is much enlightenment ahead for all of you in this expanding realm.

The most important advances in medicine will begin to occur rather rapidly as the participants in this field discover the crucial importance of becoming *truly helpful* to everyone. The practice of medicine will go farther ahead than ever dreamed possible as the emphasis on commitment to healing the mind, not to the body and material wealth, is sincerely considered. Those who choose to emphasize healing the mind first will become forerunners in the art and skill of a medical practice that right now seems impossible.

This new skill will employ many, many different techniques from all around the world. Each one will play an important part in completing the makeup of this skill as a whole. Most importantly, this combination of new and ancient skills will play a role of vast importance for all here in the world. This role will be to incorporate science, medicine, psychology, physiology and spirituality into a super advanced healing art form. Hints of this are just now beginning to appear in the world. Yet it will not be long before it is practiced on a global scale. These major changes will bring a powerful unity among races and countries never before thought possible. *Healing* will forever be welcomed and surely seen differently than ever before. God speed to those who will take the lead!

A SCRIBING FOR GERALDINE

Dear Joel,

For some time I have been studying A Course In Miracles. *My problems concern my dealing with pain, tingling and a distrust of medical procedures and perhaps God. Would you kindly ask Jesus for some answers to the following questions?*

Thank you, Gerry

1) *Does the ego ever lessen the pain and the tingling?*

2) *I have had pain and tingling in my body for a very long time. What am I not doing that perhaps I should be doing?*

3) *How can I experience Love when I am experiencing pain?*

4) *What can I do to lessen and quiet my ego?*

5) *I take three milligrams of Ativan every night before trying to sleep. Is it a block?*

Greetings Gerry:

Indeed, it is a great honor to receive these questions of you this day. I welcome you now to stop in quiet gentleness and be very still. Listen from your heart to the answers about to follow. In your heart is Where your answers lie. In your heart is Where I abide with your Self — safe, eternal and forever loving with you.

Let us begin with your third question first, since this question is the foundation for the rest. The answer is simple. The application, however, is usually experienced as somewhat frightening at first because, to whatever degree your ego is invested in pain, it will equally fight you in protecting what it values when you decide to give it up. How can you experience Love when you are experiencing pain? Simply by valuing and identifying with only what is true in you.

Yet you must ask yourself honestly if it is really pain you are experiencing. Pain and suffering are quite different. Suffering can be defined as an attitude you adopt regarding the pain you are experiencing. If you were to ask, "How can I experience Love when I am experiencing *suffering*?" I would tell you that this is impossible. You cannot. You can only experience one or the other. You are choosing between the two in every moment of your life. Suffering is fear in its most condemning form. It will rob you of your sanity and happiness if you allow it to temporarily replace What is important in you.

Each of you will experience pain to some degree as long as there is a body. If you trip and fall, you feel pain in your leg. But if you go to the doctor and insist that your damaged leg is keeping you unhappy and mentally disabled somehow, you are also to some degree choosing suffering. If he prescribes pills to end your pain and you rely on those to "feel better," you are now *valuing* your suffering, for the use of magic is your firm proclamation that Love is weak and fear is all powerful. This is not what you would want if you knew the repercussions of such denial and misperception. There is nothing in this world that can save you from your suffering, for by your very belief in the power of the world and its magic, you have made your suffering so.

Every time you place value in the body or the world, you are imprisoning and re-crucifying yourself. Each time you place all value in Love, you are releasing yourself from the burden of the cross and joining the circle of immeasurable healing that has always been available through each of your blessed relationships. All your relationships have been sent to you for this purpose. You will not recognize this as long as suffering and magic hold a place above the function of healing God gave you to share. In the picture of suffering fear presents to you, would it not be wiser to abandon entirely your investment in its dark outcome? To remain there only burdens you with a function you cannot fulfill. Give this picture and all its past that you have condemned yourself to, to the Holy

Spirit in you. Rise with me to an experience that will break the hold of its spell and lift you beyond the body into an experience that will show you the end of sickness and the beginning of your eternal resurrection in Heaven. *You have not lost What God has given you.* You long for the healing into Christ's loving recognition of you. His Light reaches to you and through you into all of your relationships. It sees the body not, yet will the body heal as you take Light as your own. In this Light the fear of death must vanish, for value is now placed rightly in your eternal Life that is forever your only Home.

You have asked what you can do to lessen and quiet the mumbling insanity of your ego. The ego will not change what it is founded on. Its goal will always be to present you with hopeless conflict. This is a common mistake that many therapists make when trying to help others heal. Often the focus is to retrain the ego to be "healthy." The ego *can* be trained to perceive differently, yet its sight must *always* be faulty. If it is taught only to interpret differently, then you will still experience and identify with its new interpretations of you. One interpretation is no different from another. That is why the ego can change its views, but it cannot change what it epitomizes. Fear is its foundation and its view will always be faulty. However, you can be trained to deny and overlook its findings, no matter what form of fear they manifest as. This is what I meant when I said to learn not to take yourself so seriously.

Whatever view you may find yourself grappling with, it is always distorted and removed from the *experience of your true Identity.* Your only hope of experiencing your Divinity while prisoner of this world lies in your ability to laugh at *all interpretations* you find your mind grappling with, no matter how serious and important they may seem. You must learn that a different interpretation is always futile, but that a different *choice* is not only possible but essential for transcending the entire thought system of the ego.

You can be trained to choose only Love. Once you have accomplished this through your deepened willingness to value and have only this, you will discover that peace has always been waiting there for you. It is not in your thinking that peace abides. Peace is an attribute that is built into your being. It is simply recognized when the Thought of Love is accepted as your only Creation, and

all other "thoughts" are seen for what they are — a hindrance to
true healing. Laugh at them gently, dear one. Be still in the face
of what fear's shrieking message holds out to you. It cannot
really hurt you, except temporarily by your believing in what it
has to "offer." Do not believe it. Can madness ever overthrow the
eternal? Can any thought the ego demands to be true close the
gates of Heaven and condemn you to "hell"? Only in dreams, my
dear Gerry, only in dreams!

What will silence the ego faster but the loving Thought of God
you hold out to your brothers and sisters as you take their hands
with only the goal of peace in mind? What joins you together in
Christ as one Self and not two but the gentle blessing of His holy
Word through you? How simple to quiet the ego by joining through
God's one Will by recognizing the eternal holiness in everyone!

What better Gift to give this Christmas but this one! Let us
celebrate our joining with all in the purpose of completing His
gracious Will. Is there anything you cannot accomplish through
Him? This Christmas, in gentle recognition of What is true in
everyone, let healing be. We pray now for the celebration of
Christmas to shed its grace and serenity into and through all
minds and hearts. Today let us together accept our true function
here. Let all be illuminated by our devotion to the Light God has
sent. Behold the gift of Christmas shining through you now! In
this gentle blessing He has sent you, awaken and be glad that
Heaven's Message is come to all who would behold and drink
from the cup of His Divine Love with you. For those yet to join
this circle of rejoicing, pour out this blessing:

*"I come to you my brother and sister with Gifts of peace that
we may join in our recognition and celebration that our Father's
Will has been accomplished in everyone. Our cups are filled with
His everlasting peace; our candles lit with His radiance and eternal
Light. We give our thanks together today, for in our joyous joining
the remembrance of the Gift of Christmas completes this great Circle
of healing, abundance and Love. Let us not part to walk in different directions but, instead, let us walk together, increasing the inner
Circle to include every last one who seems forgotten, for our peace is
accomplished in this way. Let me take my sister's and brother's hands
and walk in steady grace to the Heaven that is our Home. Let this
Christmas shine as our shared beacon emanating from deep within the*

Holy Son of God's eternal innocence. Now I would teach that only this is true. Blessings, good tidings and great cheer to all, for the Gift He has freely given, I would give you now."

Amen

You have asked why you do not experience pain when you are sleeping. This is because when you are asleep, your ego is more at rest as well. It is also the reason why much of the pain you are feeling is really a form of suffering in disguise. You are capable of enduring a great deal of pain without it causing you to suffer. It again becomes a question of what you are deciding for when you are in your conscious hours.

Suffering is a well-hidden form of punishment, which the ego uses to keep you from the experience Love would offer. *Healing,* being the release from bondage and punishment, is essential for remembering What Love has already brought you. Healing is thus the relinquishment of every idea and concept you have depended on and thought to use to "save" yourself. Only by following the ego's thought system can you become fearful, weary, sickened and confused. The ego has led you down a darkened path indeed.

The Holy Spirit eagerly waits for your decision to relinquish the strong grip you have that holds this faulty thought system in place. By releasing it gently to Him and allowing Him to replace it with His Comfort and perfect loving Thought, He will not leave you distressed, confused and comfortless, as the ego has done. He will speak to you softly and remind you that you need not think alone or ever be alone. He asks only that you let Him help you and lift you quietly to Heaven, Where your loving Father abides. He waits in peace to undo all sickness and all illusions about the life you once seemed to make apart from Him.

As you look to Him with weary eyes, He will smile upon you and happily declare that you are his only Son, safe, whole and perfectly loving like Himself. He holds you in His gentle gaze and reminds you that your Self, the Christ, has never parted from the company of His Love. All the angels, with every last brother and sister, join with you now to rejoice in this holy Place. It is your Home. It is kept forever for you, patiently awaiting your firm decision to return.

Where now, my dear Gerry, are the shrieks and cries of the ego? For what can stand against the Light of Heaven Itself?

To quiet the ego, one must want only the peace of God and give up all other desires that would interfere with this one goal. This will also help you immensely with the pain and tingling you have described. Remember that the ego is not apart from you. You made the ego as a part of your thought system. By doing so there now seems to be two of you. The real you has always been at one with Love. The ego is simply an illusory thought system that is founded entirely in fear. This makes it appear as if a split occurred inside you, causing two selves to emerge from one. The ego self seems to control your life, while your real Self seems untouchable and out of reach. The intensity of your ego's hold on fear can be so great that peace and safety seem to be totally obliterated in you. Yet I have said that your eternal Self is always in you.

I have also said that you cannot change your Self because God created It changeless as Himself. When you have relinquished your investment in all the changes and drama the ego has demanded is your treasure, you will simply awaken to What you've always been and are. There won't be anything to do or thoughts to *think* or things to *change* or *fix*. You will not have anywhere to go because you will recognize that you are already Home. You will love your Self as God created you. Great joy will ring throughout the Kingdom on this brightened day!

The pain and tingling you fear will never go away, my dear Gerry, is *already gone*. Pain and suffering cannot enter into the holy instant with you. In this holy instant lies the answer to all your seeming woes. Your loving Reality is found only here. If you should choose to forgive all that would interfere with your joining me here, then nothing the ego can seem to interpose will matter. You will not need to depend on medications because Love will become the only elixir you value. What need have you of magic who have chosen the power of Love instead? Think you there is anything that could ever bring you lasting peace and gentle grace which transcends all the world?

Begin this moment, then, by establishing your commitment to only what is true in you. Be willing to set aside all worldly dependencies, if only for a little while, and prepare for the journey to God that is at hand! Release your mind from the great burdens you have placed upon it. Take my hand and let your tears of sorrow be transformed into tears of joy! I am with you always. Whenever you call on me, I will be there to guide you on your gentle journey back Home. It is truly a journey without distance. Do not be afraid to heal. Your real Life waits inside you. Come forth it will, as you let healing be. Be gentle with yourself, dear one. God will find you and heal you as you never knew healing could be. Trust in Him now. May His joy encompass you and comfort you forever more.

Here is a prayer for you:

"Father, the suffering I feel is but a reflection of my unwilling-ness to let go and allow Your Love to heal me. I have been afraid to heal because I have been afraid that to do so would cost me my life. I now realize that by not risking to heal, I have made my body the target of even more illness. I do not wish to continue to try to heal myself. I do not know the way, Father. Please show me, that I may understand what it truly means to forgive and heal with You. I will stand back and allow you to lead the way, knowing that Your Love will offer me everything I need and want. In humility I wait, Father, for Your gentle Hand to wash away all suffering and pain. I want only the peace of Your Love. As I quietly receive Your Gift to me, I would share It with everyone as you have asked, that they may heal in Your peace with me."

Amen

Say this prayer daily with conviction in your heart. He will not wait. Healing must come because you asked of Him What is yours already.

Lastly, Gerry, do your best not to take the world and all its seeming problems seriously. What is important today will have no relevance tomorrow! The past and the future are already gone. Enjoy the present. Be the child of God you've always been. There are no tomorrows and no yesterdays. God's laughter is in your soul now. May you find it and let it heal you now.

A loving Jesus

THE BODY ILLUSION

It seems that to cure the body, the best way would be to focus *on* the body. Yet we are learning that things are the opposite of what they seem. The whole world is illusory, while all that is real can never be seen. It seems confusing, does it not? It is only because we think a little too much and love not quite enough. When we truly love, all will become crystal clear. For when we love, though the body is forgotten, it must begin to heal.

We must remember that all sickness begins with egocentricity. The tendency to identify with the body as "you" can be very strong when the mind is fearful. This confusion keeps sickness "alive" and pushes your natural ability to heal from your awareness. To recover from sickness we must begin by honestly looking at how much time is focused on the body and the illusory "self" that has been made to "protect" it.

It should be clarified that one is always placing focus either on the body or Spirit, but never on both at once. As soon as the mind aligns itself with the Thoughts of Love, healing of the mind and thus the body begin. When the mind's connection to Spirit is disrupted, bodily thoughts come into play, confusion occurs and sickness in some form becomes the attractive conclusion.

No matter the form of illness, before healing can occur, the mind needs release from believing the body illusion. There are many fantasies the mind can focus on that use the body as its central figure. The intensity of these fantasies often dictates the seeming "degree" and horror of an illness, even though in truth there are no degrees. One is either choosing illness or healing. A person who believes they are "healing a sickness" does not understand the power of their own mind. Healing is a firm decision, as is sickness. A decision must be fully made in one direction or the other. Once this occurs, the outcome is certain either way. The one who chooses healing *is* free.

A SCRIBING FOR PAULINE

Dear Joel,

I would like a scribing from Jesus. I live with my family in Australia. I am 50 years old, the mother of five children, and I am extremely depressed. I worry constantly about the past, present and future. I have no confidence in myself and feel guilty that my five children and husband have to "put up with me." I feel extremely boring. I need to find my energy and face up to my daily responsibilities. But how?

I have just become disillusioned about life and see no purpose in it. I have severe feelings of hopelessness, which just get deeper and deeper. I have no friends and never really had any all my life. I come from a dysfunctional alcoholic family and feel guilty about not creating a happy home for my children. I seem to have sleepwalked through life and now I just want to sleep the rest of my life away. I know this sounds pathetic but I am extremely lonely and don't know where to turn. I do want to give Love but feel unable to, as I feel extremely empty.

I am confused about my study of A Course In Miracles, which I have known about for about five years as I find it hard to understand. I don't know if I should be praying to God, as it says that God doesn't even know this world exists. What form of prayer should I be praying? My appeals to the Holy Spirit for help seem to have no response. Should I be meditating silently? Should I continue to study A Course In Miracles? *I would like to hear my inner guidance and feel some connection with Jesus.*

Greetings Pauline:

I do invite you now, as you sit quietly and read these words, to go within to your heart Where I reside with you. As you read these words, know that I am speaking to you from within the Altar to God in you, which we share *together*.

Indeed, Pauline, I have much to speak with you about. It has been difficult for you to hear, even though I have been right by your side this whole time. You are in no real danger even though right now, in your experience, it seems that you are. What you are hearing are voices from a lingering past, clouding your mind with ideas of loss, guilt and self-hatred, based on choices made long ago but unforgiven. The burden of these grievances follows you everywhere, making your life a living hell. Though they are simply clouds and nothing more, you have not as yet allowed yourself to see them as they are. Your ego is desperately clinging to these stormy clouds of guilt, for it tells you that they will keep you safe from harm; that they will protect you from further disillusionment and suffering. Today I have come to ask you to give them to me, for they do not belong in your holy mind!

If you would truly give Love to your family, Pauline, how would you do this? Can you help them if you are not willing to help yourself? Who is more deserving of Love than *you*? Without *you*, your children are nothing. Without *you*, I am nothing! Who are you without all of us? There is not one who does not need the gifts that only you can offer. No one has walked the earth who has not called for *you*. How is it then that you have forgotten the Light of this holy Self Which God created as *you*?

Let us walk on a journey together, you and I, for the time has come to remember. Be still and take my hand, for we have only a gentle path to walk together.

My dear Pauline, you have but *one* responsibility and that is all. Who ever has told you differently, let him ask of me and I will show you each together what *is* your true responsibility. You are not asked to trudge through your life in mundane and depressing trivia. You did not come here to suffer and then die. You came here to overcome the mundane. You came here to remember the joy from Where all Heaven sings! You came here to heal the guilt and fear that has seemed to bind you to lifetimes of anguish and depression. Yes, once again, in the lifetime you have chosen, you came to overcome this all! This choice *is* your responsibility and only your denial of it has cost you the knowledge of your total freedom from fear, worry and guilt. You are capable of hiding and procrastinating for quite awhile, but I do assure you the outcome is as sure as God. The only question left then to answer is, "*Why are you waiting?*"

Do you have anything better to do than heal from your guilt and suffering? If you believe you have, then you are doing a great disservice to yourself and to everyone you love. In this world there is but one thing you should sincerely take to heart and that is your own healing. It is in your healing that all the world shall heal with you. It is in your healing that all will find peace and joy through you. It is in your healing that Heaven will come to all minds and hearts. Would you not take healing seriously, now that I have told you this so directly? You *have* no other responsibility because there *is* no other responsibility. Whatever stands in your way to do this, set it aside and walk with me!

Your "energy" is not yours alone. Any that you *take* for yourself alone can only hold you back somehow. The vitality you seek is an Energy we all share together. If I failed to share God's loving Energy with all of my brothers and sisters, then I have temporarily failed my Self. The Self we share is not hurt by this. It is simply unrecognized. Not recognizing the loving Self we share together is experienced as depression and even hopelessness. Doing so is a learning failure, but hardly one that deserves punishment, but only correction instead. The Holy Spirit's only wish is that you know your Self. This is God's one and only Gift to His Son. It is all he needs and all he wants, though he may search for a while elsewhere.

Your Self is not lost to you any more than it is lost to me, but to not share It *is* to be lost. Indeed, until you learn to share it wholly with the whole Sonship, you are lost in an endless search that leads nowhere. It is not hard to find your Self, but you must be willing to give up *entirely* all that you have made to replace it. The guilt you hold, the fear you keep hidden, the anxiety that confuses you, must all be replaced with the Gift of God. You must do the healing it requires for you to let this go, for nothing more is asked of you.

All of the loneliness and despair you feel inside, Pauline, is but "protecting" you from the joy God gave you to share. I have said that your Self is Love and I meant just that. There is nothing more you are created of, but It *is* all you have or really want. If you cannot experience It, it is because you still believe that you are something else. Yet has this belief given you even the faintest inkling of happiness thus far? There is nothing to feel guilty about! Only arrogance would tell you otherwise. You are not created from arrogance or such deceit. *Let this go now!*

You are created of the innocence and peace of God. Let all that has come to stand in the way of this Creation be swept away from your heart forever. Hear my words, Pauline, that they may carry to deep within, where any pain may still linger. Embrace this pain with the Love of our Father, Whose Light I send to and through you now. Feel what this pain has done in your life in all its "completeness" and seeming "power." Bring your tears to me; share them with me; tell me what this has done to you. I am waiting with open arms. Go deeper, I am here now. As you approach, offer me this pain you are embracing. Place it all in your torn blankets and hand it to me. Leave nothing of your suffering behind to be kept hidden in you, for I cannot take what you would not give. Now place it gently into my hands and look into my eyes as you give me this heavy burden. Do you see that I have a Gift now to return to you? Look ever so closely, for I am shining the Strength of Christ through you now.

His Gentleness is a blanket of Light that will shine away all guilt and fear, all hopelessness and despair. As His blanket of Light covers you, your torn blanket disappears. It is now up to you to accept this Gift I am offering, for I am the lamb who taketh away the sins of the world. Will you accept my humble Gift to you in exchange for this torn offering? Will you open your heart to the Christ I share with you now? Now embrace your new Self, for It is shining from within you to everyone. My eyes are smiling with your acceptance of this great Gift you have received. Take your Self now, Pauline. Take the innocence and eternal gentleness that is and always was forever yours. It is all you have. It is all you want. *It is all you are.* There are no words for this childlike Gift! It is God's to you. Share It now and forever, as I have certainly just shared It with you!

Now your purpose in life can become clearer to you than ever before. It is to accept as you have received it. It is to forgive whatever conditions once stood between you and your family and friends. It is to let all past go and live in the Presence of your true and most holy Self. It is to look for me in everyone, for in them you shall find Christ or lose Christ. In them is your Self calling back to you, asking you to remember that It shines only in the joy of the Gift I have given you. The world is nothing! It was only what you made out of fear. The thoughts that made it have no value. It is but a dream you made to keep you from What has always been yours. It is not there. But your Self, oh yes, your Self is there with me and with everyone. Where now can you look and not find your Gift, Pauline?

Let us now talk of prayer. I ask you now only to ask with me through the Holy Spirit for help in undoing whatever conditions have made you feel fearful or guilty. Ask what the conditions were that have made you seem fearful. Then ask with all sincerity for Help to let them go forever. Ask for His Help to let go of whatever has made you feel empty and unwhole. Whatever the condition, be assured that it is a mistaken belief about yourself and does not belong in your mind. You want nothing but the peace of God. You want nothing but to know your Self in the totality of the joy It is created of. Ask for help in the undoing of whatever perception or belief that has caused problems within your body as well, remembering that the body's ills are but a manifestation of these unhealed fears. It is the tears unshed that become the cancers to the body. Do not allow yourself to forget what is most important, Pauline. It is healing. Forgive these thoughts; they do not belong with you.

The highest form of prayer is for recognition of what you already are and have. Once healing has been accomplished and you have experienced What you *are* as opposed to what the ego tells you you are, this will be all you will ever want to ask for in prayer again — to "know thyself" as you are created. In hearing your inner guidance from me, it is essential that you realize that I cannot communicate with you from a purely intellectual level. I use words only to lead you away from the need for words at all. The *experience* of God is strictly spiritual and emotional and has nothing to do with verbal communication or symbolism in any form.

This is why it is so important for you not to believe in your own thinking. Your thinking is always wrong about yourself and others. The mind's judgment was faulty from the beginning. You do not need your ego or your thinking to be happy in this world. Do not be invested in it in any form. As it comes, learn to forgive and overlook all that it tries to teach you. It is wrong, while Love has always been right. Love does not do anything. It simply recognizes Itself and lets all else go. The thoughts you offer others should reflect this idea as much as possible.

It is a matter of right valuing. To value not the world is to not take your thoughts or anything of the world seriously. Once you have accomplished this, you will wonder why you could have ever been depressed. Others will want to understand better the shift you have made. They will see in you the Light you are now choosing. It is this present remembrance of truth that shall heal all the world. It is in you now. Choose God now and nothing else.

This will show you, through your experience, that Her Gift is true. For this and only this will set your valuing right. When you forget, pray only to remember What you are in Her.

If you are not feeling a sense of release and joy when you meditate, it is because you have once again placed your own mind in charge of the Atonement. Remember that you are not in charge. You did *not* create your Self and you have *no* control over changing What you are. It is merely up to you to let go of such insane thinking and accept your Self *as God created you*. There are no words to describe What you are, but you can experience your Self simply by letting go of all that you are *not*. Salvation is quite simple is it not, Pauline? You really need do nothing to hear me or the Holy Spirit in you. I will always remind you in gentleness through your happy emotions when you are choosing to heal. I cannot remind you, however, when you choose to listen to something else. Still, it is sure that no matter what, you will once again hear. It is only a matter of your own true willingness to let go, let God and above all lighten up on yourself! You are Light, Pauline. Remember this always, for it is all you are and it is *everything*.

You will never feel guilty again once you fully realize that your only purpose is to bring joy to every mind and heart. How can you do this until you decide that it is not the world you want? As long as you decide for the world, you are destined by your own decision to see no purpose in living! Life is not of this world; it is of God, Who created It eternal in you. Take the Life She has given you, Pauline, and let all else go. I promise you if you do this, you will never again sleepwalk through your life. You will help many others awaken from their dreams as well. Reality is here, *now*. It has been given you to enjoy, to laugh and to not take anything of this world seriously. What could be serious about eternal Life? You need not worry, for your Mother God has taken care of all. Your life has many gifts for you. Everything that has seemed to happen to you has had a purpose. All that has happened has helped to bring you to this point. *Now* you have truly asked and have been answered!

It is important for you, Pauline, to continue to do the lessons and Text of *A Course In Miracles*. The resistance the ego has toward the Course is much like what many others experience. It will try to make you angry at the Course and tell you that you are wasting time. Tell the ego to *be quiet*! Do it regardless of what it says.

Be determined to break through the walls of fear and anger the ego has set forth to protect itself from healing. Be determined to remember your true Self as God created you, not as the ego would have you be. There are many defenses to keep Love from your awareness. All of these are both unworthy and painful to keep with you. *You* will not die if you let these defenses go. Indeed, you will find all Life! Be sincere and determined to cross the bridge with me to Heaven. I am with you always. Ask me sincerely and I will answer. Say to yourself when faith is dim:

> *"Father/Mother God, I must have forgotten the peace from Where I come. I do not know who or what I am. I am willing now, entirely, to remember. I set all dreams and fantasies about myself down, for they have hurt me and I no longer choose or want them. Let me be still and hear only the Voice for Love in me now. Let me remember What I am in You. I ask only for the Gift of Your peace and knowledge. You have offered the Gift of Christ to me and I would accept only this now. Thank you Father/Mother God for Your Gift of Heaven now."*
>
> *Amen*

Then, Pauline, let Christ be in you. Be content to know that all is perfectly well. All is as God would have it be. All else has never happened at all. Let forgiveness rest on all the world. Be at peace, Pauline, and take His joy with you everywhere!

I have asked that Joel keep in contact with you for further assistance from me in the future. He will do as I have asked and you are welcome to ask through him for help at any time. Blessings to you who have asked. Indeed, you have been answered.

Peace surround and carry you by the wings of angels.

Jesus

Thank you, Joel, for the scribing. This has been truly helpful for me. I "need" a further question answered:

How can I feel Love for myself, connection with those around me and even connection with Jesus? I have asked and prayed and handed over my negative thoughts, but they are still hanging around, dominating my day and relationships.

Greetings Pauline:

This is Jesus. This is an important question you have asked. It demonstrates a tremendous willingness on your part — a prerequisite for your own healing.

The negative thoughts you are hearing are the ego's rebellion against your peace of mind that is now close at hand. You have long invested in your own thoughts as valuable. Now you are beginning to question their value, but you are not yet disciplined enough to not allow them to burden your mind with clutter. That is what these thoughts are — clutter. Each one of them is a belief or perception that you have not forgiven. You value ego thinking because you believe you would not exist without it. It is because of this evaluation that you have placed the ego in charge instead of Spirit. Spirit will not speak to you in words alone. In fact, most often you will hear Spirit in the gentlest of illumined feelings. Words may come after to express the loveliness you feel, but in most cases the feeling of openness, freedom and joy will arise first in your heart. You will feel as though there is no need to think at all. It will feel wonderful because you will know that the words you have been hearing were meaningless in comparison. You will literally throw your own thinking away when this happens.

The Thought of God in you is Where your Self resides. I abide within this Self with you. The Thought of God is as constant as the rays of the sun on a clear day. It never changes and is always dependable because It is your creation. Yet you cannot hear It when there is "clutter," for God's Thought dwells in peace in you. This is why it takes discipline to hear, for you live in an illusory world of temptation and clutter. It is a wise person indeed who can walk through a hurricane unscathed. But she could not do this without her anchor rooted firmly in the changeless Thought of Love that created her. The anchor cannot be rooted to anything you see, for it is this that has confused you. It is also this that has made you believe that there is value in what changes. The ego dictates that only through it can you effect changes that are necessary for your body's survival. You believe you must do something for this to happen. So you must think about this and analyze that. Do you understand now why you have so much investment in what your mind tells you, Pauline?

Here is the paradox: Your mind is always wrong no matter what it thinks because thinking is not of God. The closest your mind is capable of coming to truth is in realizing that there must be a better way. That way always involves the relinquishment of your own thoughts in favor of the Thought of Love. It has no words, but It blesses with forgiveness all that the mind seems to see. It takes practice and discipline to accomplish vision simply because you are used to seeing with your eyes. This type of sight is so completely corrupt it has made the entire world you see. You do not want the message from the sight it offers.

Pray not to forget your thoughts, but instead to remember only What is already yours. You cannot simply escape your thoughts without replacing them with something of more value. You must accept and believe wholeheartedly that there is something more valuable beyond the thoughts, sights and sounds you seem to experience. It is there in peaceful silence within your own heart. Say to yourself as you meditate often:

"I want nothing except the peace of God."

Whenever the temptation arises to think or judge on your own, say:

"I am choosing to see something that is not there and by this I am deceived. I do not want what I am seeing because it is not true. I gladly exchange all of what I see for only the truth in me now. This is all I want because It is God's most holy Gift to me."

Then say again with full conviction:

"I want only the peace of God now."

You will need to do this often at first. Then as your mind becomes more disciplined at seeking only what is true, you will find yourself shifting to Light almost always. But you must give time to God at least three times a day. Stay in meditation until you do not feel like leaving it. As long as you feel like stopping, you are still burdened by the ego's clutter. This will pass as your dedication to Light is more consistent. As you go through the day with your activities, practice remembering the Light of God in everyone you see. You can do this by overlooking what your mind sees, by choosing to see only the silent Light of truth in your sisters and brothers. You need do nothing to accomplish this. Just let go of what you think you should or need to do and accept everyone you see as God created them. If it seems that you need to make a decision, stop, go within and ask Love what would be best. Refuse to make decisions on your own and without taking time to do this. You will know what the right decision is by its fruits. If it is inclusive and has helped everyone, you will know by this that you are truly beginning to hear the Voice for peace in you. I will be there as well, gently guiding you.

Lastly, remember the Christ that is in you is not just in you alone. He is in everyone. It is all that is real in any of you. Look for Him in the same way you would overlook your own mistaken thinking. Choose to look past the thoughts of others and see only the Christ you share together. You will find as you get better at this that your Self will be speaking to you from all directions. Even what seemed at one time to be an attack will be seen in the present as only a call for help to find your one Self together. It is all you want. It is all anyone wants. If you remember this, together you will find this Great Intelligence you both share. Forgive and relinquish your thinking every minute, if you need to, until you are remembering the Light almost constantly. It is the act of forgiveness that is also the pure prayer for peace. You will receive it if you want nothing else from yourself or anyone.

Ask, Pauline, in every situation, "What is this for? Will this help me remember What I am? Or will it cause me to forget in fear?" If you want only peace, the answer will be given you in every decision for how to obtain and keep it. In most cases, the answer will involve doing nothing at all. Remember, only the ego asks, "Why?" To this question God's Answer is, "Thy Will is done." So it is with yours.

Accept His Answer now in everyone.

Love, Jesus

QUESTION

I have a chronic illness. Why did I end up with this particular dis-ease and why do others end up with some other kind of dis-ease? You say we choose to be sick, yet I certainly don't want this for myself. Why does it persist?

Let me begin to answer your question with another question. How is your relationship with the world? Is it a happy one? Do you find joy here? Or are you afraid and withdrawn at times?

If you will answer these questions honestly, you will see an area in your life that is not working so well. There is a hole there that you have not allowed Love to enter. There are ways, your ways, which you are still holding onto. There are times when you refuse to listen at all to what I suggest to you. You insist on learning the hard way. For instance, I suggest that you take some time to go within and relieve yourself of the burdens and responsibilities you have placed on yourself. Instead you find other things to do, other things to get upset over. You clutter your day with mindless activity that has no value in helping you heal. Then you wonder why you aren't getting better.

You allow these obsessions to take you away from your function here, which is to forgive yourself. How can you expect to do this if you won't even rest your mind and body for a few minutes? This leads us to the origin and reason behind your particular illness — a mind that is bent on doing it all on its own, even at the cost of peace. You still believe after all your spiritual studies that your anger can achieve something for you. You are much more invested in this than you realize. You have allowed it once again to steal your radiance and humility. Does this sound like a familiar pattern for you? Look lovingly back at your past and you will see it is so.

Not too long ago you reached a point where you completely rose above this pattern. You were able to look back in hindsight and clearly see what you did not ever want to repeat. You also began to heal physically. You were running and playing like you were a child again because you forgot time and age. What made you fall back? Who was it that insisted you take control again? Certainly you won't blame it on me, but you do blame yourself. What is the difference? None. I am your Self. Therefore you must be blaming an illusion that you *think* is you. The only problem is that you aren't *really* blaming an illusion. You are blaming your Self, me and God, while *pretending* that an illusion of you exists! What better way to keep the ego well fed than this! You'll never get rid of the sickness as long as you keep giving it a reason to live in you! You do this every time you use anger and blame as a means to be preoccupied with a function other than forgiveness! You must believe it is getting you what you want or you wouldn't use it. You've been very busy enjoying the attention your illness has brought you. All that was required was a small "sacrifice" on your part. Was it worth it this time?

Every illness works like this. You have set up the perfect illness for yourself to "buy" whatever your ego needs to keep you in darkness. Why is that? So you can punish yourself. Why else? Somehow it seems easier to be a victim in darkness than the Christ in illumination. This is perfectly understandable, since this is what you have been taught all your life. You received much attention when you were sick or had problems when you were little. When you were being the Light, you were told to do something else: Be responsible, do this, go there. Being the Light wasn't paying off. When you became truly happy, you didn't get to play for long. So you discovered sickness. That got you a lot of things. But it required that "small sacrifice on your part."

Now you are repeating these lessons in your adult life until you understand in full that being sick does not get you what you really want. When you've learned this lesson well, I promise you that you will begin to heal. You get to be a child again who is happy just being. You will remember again that you are God's Child and He won't find anything for you to do. He will just find you, love you, and remind you that you have everything you need. It will be like waking up from a dream. Are you ready?

Waking up can't happen until you allow the purpose of your relationships to be changed. Healing can't happen until you discover what it is your relationships are really for. They're not to get attention from mom, sister or dad. They are not for "fixing." They're for joining. That's what mom and dad really wanted with you. They were just suffering from the same guise as you. They forgot too. They became too busy keeping things in place. They felt they couldn't rest and take time for Love. They were just like you've become. And you thought your parents were the only ones. Don't you know that they were only children too? God's children, just like you. Isn't that a shiny and humbling perspective?

A Scribing for Thornton and Joel

Dear Jesus,

Thornton and I have come together today for some healing and "down time" from the world. Our desire is to receive some assistance from you about our present dilemmas. We seem to be on parallel paths in many ways. This week we have both been experiencing some depression and not feeling too well. Here are our questions:

1) *I am struggling with the idea of using medications, even for a headache anymore. What can you tell us regarding this?*

2) *Thornton would like to know more about why we have both been feeling out of touch and weary this past week or so. What is this illness about?*

3) *Why is it we both go through these short times when we cannot seem to hear for ourselves?*

Greetings Thornton and Joel:

Regarding the question about medications, it is entirely up to each of you if you believe you must or must not take them. Neither choice will keep either of you from accomplishing what you need to accomplish. However, time is best used for healing. This is what will truly undo the need for it. Time used on behalf of magic is simply a detour from the inevitable. Medications and spells are only a temporary expedient from pain. The way to truly conquer pain is only through the healing of the mind. Sooner or later this is inevitable in all cases.

Regarding illness and depression, there is no difference. Physical illness in any form is a direct result of the mind's choices. The choice to be sick is the choice not to know. You are not expected to be in perfect awareness of your Creator all the time. The fact that you chose to come to the world means simply that you are in need of healing the idea of sickness. That is what you are doing every day. I can assist you each in speeding up this process, but it requires that you let go of your own decision-making. This is perhaps the greatest obstacle to peace. This is why you both work well together. You are each learning the same thing, as everyone else is as well. Yet your understanding and willingness are equally compatible. This will remain.

Sickness is a form of choosing to be your own author, lacking trust and faith in your Self in God. You really think you can change the direction of your own destinies, but have I not been clear before that God's Will *is* done? You are free to engage in all kinds of changes as the world sees it, but in no way can you change your Self or the lessons you are here to learn. Whenever you decide for yourself without the Guidance of Love, you are choosing to be sick. All this can change in the twinkling of an eye, but will you each listen and then act on the Holy Spirit's guidance?

I have said to use illness as a measuring tool for telling whether or not you are listening and choosing correctly. If you do this, you will learn how *not* to be sick. Perhaps you would rather be sick than risk acting on an answer given you in Love. Being sick seems to relieve you of the responsibility you each face for why you *chose* to be here. Is that not the same as "sweeping the dirt under the carpet"? Will you be happy when the dirt piles up?

I cannot interfere with either of your choices, nor would I want to. You are each getting everything you need out of your dilemmas. I know that whatever choice you make will eventually lead you Home. I have only your happiness in mind, as God does for you. If what you are doing makes you glad, then by all means continue to do it. If it does not make you glad, I am here waiting to help you. Together you are coming to a place where you will soon feel the importance of making that firm decision for either Light or darkness. You are doing this because, together, you have realized it is the only way. I have reminded you earlier that there is no turning back. You chose this as well by going forward. You will both find that it will become much easier to go the only direction you can when you both decide to take your feet off the brake and *glide*.

The decisions you each ask for help with are already answered. They were answered the moment you asked them from within you. I will say this as gently as possible: Try paying more attention to what feels right in you. You won't always hear the decision in words. Of course not! God is not a word, nor are you. You are each beings of Light from the same Source as me. My decisions come from Him. Why wouldn't yours? You can hear His decision between the words, where what feels right remains safe and steady within you. Once you each know the answer is right within you, which is usually right when you hear it, ask me then for the guidance to carry the decision out. Ask me how you can do this lovingly. Do not hesitate after the decision is made, for this is the playground of the ego. You have each been there before. Are you ready to stop playing with the chickens and start soaring with the eagles?

> I wait only for you to accept the happiness
> the Holy Spirit's decision offers.
>
> After all, it is ours together, is it not?
>
> In peace,
>
> Jesus

QUESTION

When someone "dies" from a certain illness, does this mean they weren't healed? Can the body always be healed?

These questions address a confusion that many sincere students of God encounter along their way. Simply put, death and healing can never be equated. Nor can the body and healing be linked to one another, though the world most certainly would teach differently.

It is difficult for most to understand that death is illusory. It is equally difficult to understand that the entire world is illusory. This is because you who made the world see yourself as part of your own "creation." It is also why death seems quite real to you. The world you see and death are the same. The world is a picture of death, a demonstration of your own fallibility and separation from God. Who would not fear Life while cherishing death so deeply?

You see once again that everything is quite backwards here. What seems to be "life" is a form of your belief in death. What *is* Life is the unseen eternal content of your Being.

This content is changeless. The ego is always changing. Therefore, to the ego the changeless *is* death. This is why your real Life is often overlooked. Most of you cannot imagine a state of mind in which you do not think. The ego believes the idea is absurd. It raves, "How can one not think and live in this world?" To this the Holy Spirit gently answers, *"You need not think, but only listen."* Once this is truly understood, healing is complete and identification with the world *and* body is no more. In this state, Life in Its Completion is fully recognized. Whether the body stays or goes does not matter — the mind is in peace and at one with God. This is true healing. This is the remembrance of Christ. This is your quiet willingness to return to Love. Who can be sad who has found their Source, their Self, their full Identity?

Can the body be healed? Only by one who chooses true healing for himself. It is always possible to heal the body, even though this does not appear to be the case in some situations. There are times when one will not choose healing of the body, even though the mind is surely healing. In truth, all minds are already healed because they are part of the Mind of God. The body, like all physical things, is ephemeral. It will never last. The idea that it can be made to last comes from the confusion of levels. Only the eternal does not change. Everything physical does. If the healing of the body is to occur, it will be only because the mind has chosen healing for itself *first*.

Remember that what is seen by the body's eyes as "death" is really a doorway to eternal Life. What is it, then, if only the body is "saved"? Do not be fooled by what appears as tragedy, my beloved brothers and sisters. I am here in you *all*. Which "body" then am "I"? We are all safe together. Take peace in this understanding. Take a moment today to stop thinking. You may be surprised!

Do you realize what a Gift you offer when you look in a brother's or sister's eyes with the stillness of Christ's gaze? It is a chance for salvation for both of you! It is an opportunity to experience pure joy! It is the healing of the world. It is what I have come to teach you in this material. It cannot be spoken, only applied. Learn to give this gentle instant of eternity to everyone. Smile together as you come Home with me. Heaven awaits you, *right now.*

THE HEALING RAYS

We have touched on the meaning of "true healing." Let us now take a closer look at what is most important — *it's application*. Joy comes only from the complete recognition of the eternal. How else can one feel truly safe in a world that is born of the undependable, full of change, loss and fear? Somehow one must discover a Place that is set apart from the world, Where change, loss or fear can never abide. The illusions of time and change shall never reach into the Heaven God has given you. Heaven is yours forever, though it is quite apparent that many have lived almost an entire lifetime without experiencing it here.

Healing is forgiveness and it is quite the opposite of grief and sickness. Grief causes sickness, as healing undoes it. It is impossible to experience any form of grieving without first believing in the reality of the world. The temptation to have faith in the many physical dependencies of the world secures a sentence of grief when what was sought failed to satisfy. Sickness begins here and is not released until the mind is ready for healing to begin. The idols of sickness involve anything the hands can touch or the eyes can see. They cannot truly heal. *All* idols must be given up *if* the healing Rays of God are to enter.

It is in the giving up of these special idols that allows the power of decision to return to the mind. The real power to decide can be clearly understood once it is realized that there is nothing one *has* to decide. Through this understanding the only choice becomes quite clear: The decision *for* Love, to *be* Love and to give *only* Love is as simple as recognizing *What you are forever*.

This is the Will of God and you are His Will. You cannot know this until you give up your own strong investment in idols. This presents the most difficult task you will face because the ego does love its toys.

Healing is release from *thoughts* of this world. It is only *your* thoughts that make you hostage to the many seeming facets and colors of an illusory world. It is your thoughts that cause great conflict in each of you. Even the language you use is bent on separation, division and categorization. Can this be you who *are* God's Daughter or Son? Indeed not, for What you are is one Thought, ever changeless, in perfect peace and beyond description of any inventions of the world.

It is this Thought you seek in idols, but can never find. It is this Thought that *is* your Self. Through It healing is extended to all the world. To give this Thought of Love is to give God. Can anything be more healing and holy than this?

You may ask how the Thought of God is found? How is your Self found? They are the same question. Your Self as Christ is always with you. You need only to let go, little child. It may seem painful now, but only because it seems that grief and hatred are being undone in you. Release your mind from the thoughts of this world! Become willing to quiet the storm and listen for that one holy Thought of Love. You will be amazed at what *true* healing can do if you do this!

A SCRIBING FOR SUSAN

Dear Joel,

Thank you so much for your offer of help! I have tried so many things in my desperation (even phone psychics) and few helped. Some even added to my pain. I can't visit my father any more because I gave him ulcers (I adore my father and it breaks my heart that I caused him pain or that he's unhappy or disappointed in me). I'm afraid of everything. I can't even drive a car anymore. I just want to run away.

For the last five years my husband and I have been desperately unhappy. I saw a brief therapist, then my husband and I saw a psychologist (separately) until he moved out of state. Then we tried another psychologist, but neither of us were happy or felt we were getting anywhere, so we stopped. We are now on Xanax and Zoloft. Our G.P. wants us both to take a two-month leave of absence from work "due to work related stress," but we can't. I'm very afraid for my husband. He's lost 50 pounds in three months. I'm afraid he's going to have a heart attack. Our problem? WORK. We both work for the same company — me for 16 years and him 18 years. The company is terrible (retail. We're both managers. There isn't a manager there who isn't in therapy, on drugs or both. Although we've tried over and over to get out, we hit a brick wall every time. We feel trapped, frozen. I can't stand to see the misery and pain in my husband and my friends. All I want is peace — for myself, my husband, my friends, my family and for everyone who is in pain. We can't seem to find it.

Questions:

1) I found A Course in Miracles *in August 1993. I devoured every word of it. But when I tried the lessons, they didn't work for me. The things that were supposed to happen didn't. I just got frustrated, then angry and stopped trying. What am I doing wrong? Am I not trying hard enough?*

2) I know the road to peace is through the Holy Spirit. I would give anything to find peace for my husband and me. How do we find peace and happiness? PLEASE show me the way. Tell me what to do and I'll do it.

3) I have tried the holy instant and meditation. In over three years all I have gotten (besides sleep) was: "Find peace in

*your heart first, the rest will follow," "Listen" and "Trust"
(I'm not sure about the last two). Please, I need to hear Jesus'
message to me.*

4) *Although I have grown tremendously in the last five years,
I have also been through a lifetime worth of pain. If there is
no way out of this situation, death is the only thing to look
forward to. Please Lord, show us how to get out of this
company. Show us how to find peace and happiness.*

5) *Chopra and Williamson say that we each have talent that
we're meant to use and when we use it, things will fall into
place. The only thing I love to do is read and study. I can't
figure out how to make a living at that. Please show me the
talent I have and how I'm meant to use it.*

*Joel and Jesus, please help us if you can. Thank you for your effort
and concern!*

Sincerely,

Susan

Greetings Susan:

To you and all of your family, I bid you the deepest of healing.
The scribing I now offer you can carry you into the next realm of
your abilities, through the Holy Spirit and my guidance within you.

You and your husband feel caught in what appears to be an
inescapable impasse. I remind you, however, that time is not
under your control. What appears as "inescapable" or "impossible" is your gripping and unhealed fear that time is under your
control. You believe it is up to you alone to set the direction that
time will take. You fear all will be lost without your jobs. You fear
risking change to go in a more suitable direction. All this you are
doing to save the face of your own egos and what the ego deems
"valuable." Your "sacrifice" seems great to you. Indeed it is until
you give up your control to me.

The situation you have made in your lives has become so difficult that neither of you feel capable of taking anything that seems to
happen to you in a non-serious fashion. The ego is thriving on the
pain it has "created" for you, all the while telling you it has no idea
how this is happening. The ego in each of you is thus "enjoying"

the suffering it has brought you — blaming you for causing it and laughing at your tears, all the while living off "borrowed time" it steals from you. This is hell. Look at the enormous drama the ego has brought you. Does it not seem bigger than Life Itself?

Salvation is not a toy for the ego to play with, yet this is what you do when you allow fear to take the place of Love in you. Do not blame yourselves. I once did the same and I, too, had to turn a different direction. You need to hear this and hear it well. You are in a situation where you are both desperately calling for help. Yet a part of your mind is choosing not to listen when Help is offered. You are free to punish yourself as long as you choose, but this is not what God or I have in Mind for you. My function is to show you how to heal and be with your Source and how to be free of what is not true. I cannot help you if you insist on continuing to make insane decisions for yourselves and by yourselves. You need my help to guide you to the Holy Spirit, but you will not hear me while you choose to value elsewhere. Do you really want to continue with the nightmare the ego has made for you? It is simple: Stop believing in it and listening to it, *now*.

You have both put yourselves under so much stress because of the demands of your egos. You have forgotten, my children, there is only Love! You do not need to figure everything out in your lives to be happy. Nothing is out of place except your own thinking. Your thinking is wrong, no matter how much you may want it to be right. Your only choice, as prisoners of this world as you see yourselves, is to let it go.

I will now speak to you of values. You have the power of decision within you. You have the power to decide for Love or fear. Look at your lives and see what your decisions have brought you. Ask yourselves honestly, "Have we been making happy decisions?" If your decisions are unhappy, then they are fearful. Bring these decisions to me before you make them and I will help you choose differently! No decisions made on your own will be happy. Value, strictly speaking, belongs only in Love. What is not Love has no value. The world in which you see yourselves has no value. Your jobs have no value. The things you think you need to be happy have no value. The expectations you place on each other to act in certain ways *have no value.*

Value lies in your ability to find only Love in every worldly situation. Love is not physical, but It can be found anywhere at any time. Ask yourselves, "What are we looking for?" If you are looking truly, Love is all you will find. If you are looking for something else you will find it, but being of no value, you will lose sight of your Self in the process. Is this what you really want in light of what you are experiencing now? Give these "values" to me. I will take them from your holy minds and replace them with only the Light from Which you came!

Your value is established forever in God. It is not determined by your world and what you seem to do as you scurry around in the endless maze you have each made. You could be homeless with only the clothes on your backs, but your value would not change. You might be able to see it more clearly if this were the case in light of the complication you have been choosing. You need not be homeless to understand this. You need only let go of complication and fear. Then you will find that you cannot be homeless, even though at present you feel you are. You will find in yourselves the peace that passeth all understanding. You will act on conviction of the heart.

I have said that if a branch withers, cut it off! I meant just that. Each of you have many withered branches. They are the branches of anger and hatred that you have placed aside and not tended to. They are the hurt you carry stuffed away that molds within you. Bring these branches to Light! Let all witness their speedy death. They do not belong in you!

If your "occupations" are distressing you, by all means quit. If you do not quit, will it not become too painful anyway to continue? I have another occupation in mind for you. You can find this occupation wherever you decide to go. Pain is a teacher. It can only teach one thing — that there must be another way. Until you learn this you are indeed lost in an endless journey to nowhere. Learn the lesson pain is trying to teach you and pain will be no more. Recognize Where value lies and only Where it lies. Then choose it and keep it for good.

This is a time when you both must learn to trust beyond your own understandings. You can no longer trust in what you see because it has deceived you. You can no longer trust in what you think because it has depressed you. Your only choice is to look beyond your own situation for true Help. This is what you are struggling with. This is what you are afraid to do. This is where the fear of risk has stopped you until now.

I have come as a Light to tell you now to step forward and take the full risk. Jump off the cliff and begin to heal your pain and anger with me. Let nothing stand in your way of this, jobs or otherwise. Whatever it takes, you will do it because this is what you have asked. Now are you answered.

If all you want is peace and that is *all* you want, how then can you be trapped? Answer this question with gentle honesty once again. You are *not* trapped except by your own decision to see yourselves this way. Peace will never trap you; illusions will. Release your minds from the heavy responsibilities you have accepted. Your responsibility is to Love. There is nothing about a mind that has found Love that can make it feel burdened. You are burdened only by your own misperceptions and beliefs. I remind you that none of these are real or true. If you cannot accept this, it is because you still believe they have value. Yet the only "value" they have is to keep the awareness of your need to heal out reach. Hear this as I say: You do not want this. Let them go now.

Walk with me now into the gentle Arms of God. The healing you have asked for is in you now. It calls you with every step and tells you by your experience that something important has been overlooked. The great need you both have for your emotional healing is upon you. You need each other and me to do this. You need everyone else as well. Each brother and sister waits to support this wondrous healing. They stand as your witnesses, pushing you gently forward in your great willingness to do this work.

Come into your hearts and look into the eyes of your beloved. Look at the pain he/she holds within. This is your pain as well. Ask each other gently if you can honestly hold onto this any longer. Is it not time to let this go? Hold one another now and ask me, through the Holy Spirit, to come light your way. I am here right now as you read this in your hearts. I do not will for you to suffer any longer. Come, I will help you. Come, I will comfort you and show you the way to Heaven. Let go now of your holdings and take my hand. Let us walk surely on our way to the Heart of God. As we walk away from this dark dream together, be ever so glad it is only a dream. Be happy to know there is a Place we are going to now Where all is well, all is safe and all is done as in Heaven.

Now let us gently go to the other questions and together we shall find our answer.

I have said that *A Course in Miracles* is a study course to retrain your mind to choose correctly. When you choose correctly, there is no effort. Effort is of the ego. Spirit is already done. In regard to your Course studies, stop trying. Remember that it is a course in *undoing* fear. The whole purpose of *A Course in Miracles* and of true healing is the undoing of your perceptions, thinking and beliefs. This will allow you access to any unhealed emotional areas stored within your subconscious. When this begins to come up, the ego will fight you. It will use anger as a defense against truth. That is because it believes, and wants you to believe, that the truth about your past is so despicable it would destroy you. *Do not stop when this happens.* Continue to allow the pain, hatred and suffering to surface. The one thing the ego hates the most is silence, for silence undoes all the ego's works.

Invite the fear in during your meditation. Take tea with it. Do not be afraid to look at it. You cannot release it until you allow it into full awareness. It is also helpful to share what you feel so that it can be more fully experienced. If you feel anger, *stay* with it. Beyond the guilt and anger you will find nothing that will hurt you, as the ego suggests. You will find only the peace of God. You will see the peace of God in all you look upon, for God's peace and happiness are everywhere.

The risk that you must take to do this requires your full willingness, faith and sincerity for your own healing and the healing of the world. Do not waiver in your commitment. Go into the quiet world of God's Heaven in total trust. Each time you meditate and do the lessons, ask for my hand. I will be with you every time. As you do the lessons, do not stop your meditation until you feel as though you do not want to stop. You should feel a sense of lightness, as if a boulder was taken off your shoulders. You must want the peace of God above all else. In fact, that is all you should ever want, since this is the only Gift that is yours forever. Do not try, just do the lessons as I've suggested. I will also tell you that it is now important for you to do the lessons and Text every day. Without this firm commitment for at least the next six months, you may very well fall back to old patterns. I cannot make the choice for you. I can only suggest to you what is needed. I have perfect faith in both of you. Do you in me?

In answer to your second question: The reason you have gotten so much sleep is simply because you needed it. You were not ready to deepen your studies with the Course I have set forth for you because you were too busy taking care of the body. However, your way of taking care of the body will wear it out. The Holy Spirit's way of taking care of the body will renew and heal it. Is it not time to do it differently?

The answers you received from me were correct. You did hear. Listen, trust and the rest will follow. Have you done this? You cannot hear my voice if you leave your mind untended and untrained. An untrained mind will focus only on what the world wants, not what God wills. When your mind is trained and a good part of your fear and suffering is healed through this process, you will be able to hear me and the Voice for Love in all the activities you participate in. But you must first be sincere and disciplined to take "time," for a while, to go within often. This is what time is for and nothing else. Time is given you to undo your need for it. Are you committed truly to using it on this behalf? Do you want to know joy and freedom? The answer to both these questions is the same because the outcome is the same.

I have answered the first part of the fourth question already. You do know in your hearts that there is a way out of your situation. The means are being provided for you. Your only real means for escape is Life. A "living death" is hardly suitable for any of God's children. This is what needs to "die." Even loss of the body will not free you from suffering. Remember, you chose to be in this world so that you could heal your belief in death. You would hardly want to escape right back into it! Death is an illusion. It has the appearance of loss, but I say to you, there is no death nor is there loss. There are many who leave your world who come seeking oblivion and nothingness. They attempt, in their fear, to come into "the land of nowhere." By not consciously choosing Life while they have a chance, they are not ready to accept It on the other side. So they choose to come back into the world and live in another "living death" until they are ready to choose Life. Do you understand what I am saying to you? Your Life is within you, right now, Susan. Accept the freedom and joy God offers you in your Creation. You each have the same Gift I share with everyone. It is God's. Offer It, live in It, and do not push It away any longer for "something else."

In regard to your occupation, which we have already discussed, I will say one more thing. Whatever it is that does not bring you happiness, quit doing it. It is a small risk to take when What you will gain will bring you a happiness you never thought possible or dreamed of!

Finally, I will answer your question on talent. Your "occupa-tion" may require ingenuity, but not true talent. Talent is being able to do your occupation in the world without taking it seriously! You can do it while taking it seriously, but you will not be happy. Your true occupation is healing. In fact, it is your only occupation. The sooner you fully realize this, the sooner you will find an occupation in the world that best suits you. Sometimes a brother or sister is not sufficiently healed to take on a worldly occupation that is stressful. Any occupation that uses guilt for motivation can be highly stressful for even the most advanced teachers of God. It requires a constant letting go and discipline to do this in that type of environment. Still, you are both capable of doing your healing anywhere.

If you can't seem to keep your center on God, then changes will take place. A person will get sick and have to quit. Another may be fired. Whatever happens, it happens for a reason. The key to understand this is to know your own limitations. You are not limited in God, but only by your own thinking. Right now it is time for change for both of you so that you can fill your cup and learn of your true abilities. This in turn will help you understand better any limitations you still face in the future. You have many greater things to do. I need you to help me as much as you need me. I will be there, along with all of God's angels, to lead you in a most gentle and easy direction. The path to God is the easiest path you will ever follow. Trust in it. Do not be afraid to risk being healed. Do not be afraid to let go of the old. Much, much greater things are ahead for you on earth and in Heaven. Heaven is in you and you are at Home, right here, right now.

Here is your personal prayer:

"Father, I do not know the way. I ask You now to guide me in all decisions. Which direction would You have me go for my healing and the healing of the world? Lead me from fear and into the Arms of Your Love. Show me the way, Father, for I know not what to do without You. I will trust in where You tell me to go and what You would have me do. I will listen now until I hear Your loving Answer. I do not have to be afraid because I know you will lead me. I will act on Your decision, knowing that it is a decision for all, knowing that Your peace is my only goal."

Say this prayer often, Susan. It is for you. Remember always, do not take yourselves or the world seriously. There is no world. You are as free as the innocent children that you truly are. Don't try to be "adults in charge." You will be missing the best days of your lives. Be happy for this Gift. Be happy you are now free.

Blessed be you who have asked and have listened.

Inherit thee the Kingdom of God forever.

Jesus

THE JOY OF HEALTH

Healing is begun once the mind is willing to relinquish the many illusions it once sought refuge in. To maintain health, the mind must now also be willing to accept and *offer* truth in place of its illusions. This is how a sickened relationship is made holy. Every relationship you have is essential for maintaining health and holiness. It is specialness that made idols. It is holiness that will transform them into gifts of true blessing. Through your forgiveness each idol is shined away. Through your acceptance and *giving* of Reality as God created it, your health and happiness is made sure. Though you cannot really give Reality because it is already everyone's, you can give the miracle, which is the recognition that Reality is true for both of you.

You must continually give What you would cherish and keep. Health is offering the consistent healing of God's great Light to everyone. By doing so, you will receive It for yourself and keep It with you as you give It away. This is how your strength is maintained. This is how you keep health and live within it. By bringing joy, you keep joy. Joy is health *for* everyone.

Remember that health is never of the body and only of the mind. There are those in your world whose bodies have AIDS who are healthier than some of you who have no sign of physical illness at all! One has overcome his fear of death because he understands *there is no death*, while the other is still not sure. Because of this the one with AIDS may far outlive his own "grim diagnosis." Why is this? Because he has learned not to believe in what he *sees*. He has learned to look only within to the eternal Self that is his. Here is Comfort that can be fully trusted. Here is Consistency and Safety that can always be counted on. Here is Light that never burns out, even after the body lays at rest. The Light is yours. It came with you and has never left you. Look to It and *only* It for health, my brothers and sisters. Give the Light to everyone. Your body will certainly do better. Your mind will be immensely happier! Radiance will shine to all!

You may not yet believe that you can place your focus only on the Light, overlooking thoughts of the body and the world. You are *always* choosing between the world and your Self in every moment of every hour. The only question is, "Which do you prefer?" One choice will bring you health and happiness; the other only sorrow. One will bring you to the fountain of Life, while the other will bring a picture of darkness, doom and death. Can the choice be so difficult when understood this way? Look past the world and the body! Together, in Christ, we share a Light, you and I. Give It to all, that you may know It is yours forever. Health and God's peace are in your decision to do so. It is an instant away. Let radiance be yours *now*. There is nothing to stop you, little child, no matter how it seems. It is as simple as taking your brother's and sister's hands and walking into a beautiful sunrise. If you will just let go a little, you can be healthy, happy and free! *Here* is to your health!

Bless you,

Jesus

A SCRIBING FOR RHONDA

My name is Rhonda. I've had multiple sclerosis for about seven years. Multiple sclerosis strikes people in their 30s and 40s. I am now 42. I am mobile, but limited. I worked in sales after coming out of college. I then got married. I've been divorced about ten years.

When I heard about the opportunity to ask questions of Jesus through Joel, I was very excited. I am hoping to get answers to problems that are troubling me. Not knowing how to be okay with myself and my apparent limitations is quite frustrating. I hope what Jesus has to say can help.

1) *How can I learn to forgive myself for the wrongs I thought I did to myself or others, and to forgive others for the wrongs I thought were done to me?*

2) *As a loving child of God, how do I stop the fears, mostly to do with the physical healing of the body?*

3) *Being that I created the MS in my mind, how do I go about learning to heal it?*

4) *How do I learn to accept help from my father whom I don't see as a loving child of God and toward whom I have feelings of resentment?*

5) *I am involved in two similar types of philosophies, but one deals more with the body. They both lead to the truth — one being* A Course In Miracles, *the other* Science of Mind. *The basic foundation of the two confuses me and my dilemma is, what is the right way to go?*

Greetings Rhonda:

It is indeed a great honor to have you ask me these questions today. Because of your particular situation, it will be necessary to look together at some of the theoretical implications involved. Some of this you are already well acquainted with. We will, however, go over this again. I would ask you to be careful to read this as gently as possible to yourself. Be clear that while I am discussing this with you, I am by no means being harsh with you. Though this discussion may be directed toward the ego illusions, all that is being said is strictly to help assist you in giving up your investment in the "reality" of illusions. Let us begin with question number four, since this is the most crucial question regarding your healing. It will help answer the other questions as well.

From guilt comes anger and from anger comes blame. Sickness is the natural result of blame, for through blame you have asked to be sick and have received as you have asked. All sickness begins in the mind and is later placed upon the body as "proof" of your victimization. Make no mistake about this, Rhonda. The ego has made you a victim in regard to how you see yourself in relationship to your father. Yet the relationship is not outside you, as it appears. The relationship with your father is only a set of images you hold within *you*.

The question you must ask yourself and answer with full honesty is: "What am I afraid will happen if I were to completely let go of all my grievances toward my father?" Whatever the answer is, it holds the key to healing the conflict you now feel. This conflict is the cause of much of your suffering. Until you allow this to be healed in you, you are bound to repeat some of the same painful lessons. You must ask yourself whether this is really what you want. Has it brought you happiness to hold onto this kind of judgment? Obviously not. This hatred has acted as a shield around your heart. Not only has it kept your true relationship with your father disabled and hidden from your sight, it has also shielded you from the Rays of God's Love.

By holding this ancient grievance firmly in place, you have kept a part of your mind out of reach of the relationship with your father and to your real Father as well. Would you want to continue this shadowy charade in light of what I have just told you? In such a separated state, could anything *but* sickness be its hidden goal? Yet I remind you that all is where it is supposed to be. Your father has been sent to you for a much different reason than your ego suggests.

The ego has fabulously engineered a method to keep Love away from your awareness. It is so good at what it does that it has also made you unaware of what it is really up to. You do not understand the implications of this hidden goal. You have had little idea that your becoming ill is clearly related to this unhealed relationship. Your ego is resistant to what I am sharing with you now. Clearly, this *is* the corrupt defense system that is protecting you *from* the healing of your pain.

The ego's one wish for you is death. Would you follow it then, knowing where it is attempting to lead you? Give it quickly to the Holy Spirit through my loving assistance to be healed in its entirety. Leave no trace of this hatred shielded from the Light I bring with me through the Holy Spirit to illuminate your mind. Not one piece of this corrupt thought system is useful to you in any way. Until you are fully willing to recognize that this is so, you have little chance of reaching beyond sickness to the healing you are longing for.

Healing must be to make whole. Yet how can it function wholly if there is part of another goal that is kept for other purposes? It cannot. You cannot, no matter how hard you might try, forgive in part. You *must* learn to forgive all without exception. Could God bless you and *not* your father? You are both His creation *together*. He is not separate from *you*. What appears outside you in him is the projection of your own unhealed perception. Nothing outside you exists! Accept this Rhonda. Your *Self* is *all* you have through God. Whatever it is that still seems wicked within you deserves only the gentle healing of forgiveness that the Holy Spirit would have your mind welcome and accomplish.

You are afraid you will be manipulated by your father should you accept his help. It was easier to follow the ego's dictates and become a victim at his hands than accept that your two minds are joined in purpose and are holding each other's hands and lives *together*. Your father cannot really hurt you. Can fear be made more "real" than Love without the seeming painful effects it calls upon? You only hurt your own healing ability by establishing grounds for separation through your own past misjudgment. There is no past in truth to validate such a decision! It must be that you are dreaming a recurring nightmare planted so firmly in mind that you have accepted it as a reality you feel you can never escape. Your only means of escape is to bring the nightmare into awareness *with* him. You need not do this in his physical presence, but do it you must. I will gladly be your witness and assist you in reuniting both your minds with truth. Are you willing to begin to heal?

Allow me to help you both so that together we can help everyone. Bring this tragedy in its entirety into the Circle of Light with me that the Holy Spirit holds out for our joining. Do not be afraid to purge this nightmare from your mind with my help. Let nothing stop you from achieving the one goal that has been given you to accomplish. On the other side of this dark dream is the safety and joy of God's Love in you. Will you take the leap in faith and trust I am asking of you, Rhonda? Come then, let us begin your journey homeward. All your angels and all of Heaven wait upon your determination to remember. I have come today to remind you that it is time to take what seems to be this great "risk" to be healed!

In the ego's world there are countless risks that it would have you avoid at all costs. Yet what risk can there really be to you who are created by a Father so eternally loving that even death can be overcome? He has not failed you in the Gift He has given you. Deep within you, beyond all your illusions and fear, you have agreed through your Self not to fail in your acknowledgment of Him. Your deepest desire is to return, in full gratitude to all, your loving acknowledgment of the Gift He has given. Your life is given as the dance for this acknowledgment. You long to fulfill it. Can there really be such great risk and difficulty to reach past the illusions that seem to separate and hold you back from completing this dance with all the sons and daughters of God? There is nothing the miracle cannot and will not fully overcome. Only your grievances seem to stand as an arrogant little wave against the whole ocean of God's Joy. Gently let go, my dear Rhonda. Let go of *everything* that might hinder your reuniting with the whole Ocean! The time has come for a firm and single goal to be set. Make it the goal of God and do not let little waves stop you! It is time to return with me and all to Heaven!

Let us now address your first question. Who is it that judges you have done "wrong?" What "wrong" has not already been fully corrected by Him Who created you? Think you that arrogance can hold a sin so lasting that Heaven cannot instantly shine it away? You are bound to the world you made only through the guilt that made *its* "laws." As time is the keeper of condemnation and fear, eternity is the keeper of innocence and Love. Separation is but a grievance left hidden and unforgiven. *This is* the only mistake you have ever made! Anyone who keeps a grievance will suffer. By holding a grievance you have set yourself apart from God, made a separate world and proclaimed it more powerful than Heaven. Only in insanity and sickness can the Daughter of God see herself in a world she made autonomous and kept apart from the Love of God. What seems possible in time through grievances and hatred is not even noticed in the timeless Realm of Heaven. God smiles gently upon this world made of fantasies, knowing that nothing there has occurred that could threaten peace in the Kingdom of Heaven, which is already perfectly established for you.

You need not look upon the world you made any differently than your Father does. What will heal your frightening dreams of "wrong doing" is the same Vision given you through Christ in your creation. God shares all that is His. Do not withhold His Grace from your fantasies. Do not withhold His Grace from the fantasies you have made toward your brothers and sisters as well.

Your brothers and sisters would not have you punish yourself for the mistakes you have seemed to make along the path through time. They ask only that you remember *with* them the eternal grace you were born of together. They call for this grace from you, even when they appear bitter or hurt by your past actions. They ask you only the for miracle. They want release, as you do. Would you hold this back from yourself or them by punishing yourself and delaying the goal instead? And for what? No action you have ever taken has interfered with the Will of God in either of you. God's Will *is done*. All that has seemed to happen as the result of a fearful action from the past has already been undone.

You have no past, nor do they. All your futures remain right here in the instant God gave you. It is given you as your one and only purpose to live in this holy instant that is yours forever. Nowhere else are you asked to live and nowhere else *should* you *have* to live.

Give up these fantasies that bind you to a place that was made to hide God's Will from both of you. They do not belong in your minds and hearts. I have a different purpose in mind for you. It is the only purpose we share with God *together*. Let the purpose that arrogance has set forth in your life be altogether forgotten, Rhonda. Fantasies made from grievances keep you in hell and this is not where God would have you be!

You have done no wrong, nor will you ever. But you *have* been mistaken. I cannot correct your "wrongs" because they are not there to correct. Yet your mistaken thinking is easily corrected *if* you allow the purpose you have given the world to be replaced by the Divine Purpose that God would give you *now*. I have come today to offer you this and *only* this. Will you accept my Gift and hold it dear to your heart? It is yours *already* to do so. Merely receive the truth and it is so. Let sickness be a thing of the past and buried with the dead forever!

What God wills is *done*, but what *you* will alone is a dream that has *never* been done. You cannot change anything by willing against Love because dreams are miscreations and have no real substance. You *can* and *must* eventually join in performing only God's Will. Experience and healthiness relies only on this. This will bring *healing* beyond your wildest dreams!

Let us now discuss your question number three. You cannot "learn to heal," strictly speaking. You are a healer, but only when you allow God to heal *through you*. You have heard this before, but you do not understand what this really means because you believe that you did not make your disease and that it *is* up to you to undo it. This however is quite impossible. If it were that simple, you *would* have not made your illness in the first place. No one thinks they want to be sick, yet they often become this way. This is because they are unconscious of the deeper agreement they have made to secretly allow the belief in separation, and thus guilt, to "victimize" the body. The ego believes that, by making the body a victim of its guilt, it can escape the responsibility for guilt by displacing it onto the body. This further conceals guilt from your conscious awareness. Furthermore, after you become mysteriously ill, it blames you and others for *doing* this *to* you. This is the purpose *it* has in your relationships.

You have no idea how much hatred is concealed in this goal by the ego. Its fear of death is equal to the destructiveness it sets in motion by every unloving decision it would convince you to make on behalf of what it sees as a "protective measure." The ego is constantly trying to devise ways to guard the "life" of the body. In order to do so, it tries to attack everything and everyone, including *you*. By following the ego's dictates, you are actually furthering your susceptibility to more illness. The very thing it justifies to attack for "protection" becomes what is actually assailed *by its protective measures*.

Every loveless thought reflects its hidden agenda to see you ultimately destroyed and separated into a living hell through its "special" script for your relationships. The first place this destructive act begins to manifest is in the body. You cannot trust anything the ego tells you because its focus is always on the physical and never on the eternal. *Only* the eternal can reverse sickness. You can *only* remember this through relationships you have allowed to be transformed from the ego's purpose to the Holy Spirit's holy purpose.

Your attention must be re-routed from focus on thoughts of the body and the physical to focus only on the spiritual. The only way to do this is not to deny the appearance, but rather to deny the *necessity for* the appearance of sickness, bodies and the world. This may mean even going so far as to say to yourself, "It does not matter if my body appears to be dying. My only wish is to be Home with You, Father." It is essential to break the ego's focus on the *appearance*. You cannot heal unless you allow God to heal *for* you and *through* you. As long as you are afraid and are locked into seeing yourself as only a body, you must also be overlooking What *is* essential for true healing — the recognition of *eternal* Love.

Meditation is essential to begin allowing God's healing Spirit to work *through* you. There may be tears of relinquishment as this process deepens. You will have to let go of your attachments to your body being the *picture* you want it to be. What you want is what you believe you do not *have*. This is indeed a contradiction, for what you have *is* everything *because* the eternal is everything *in* you. The ego will fight you on this. It will try to convince you that what I am addressing here will do no good. It will tell you that this is not the answer because it is not addressing the body, which is where the ego believes the dis-ease exists. Do not believe *the picture* or what it tells you about the physical, but deny instead its hold over you.

Only with the experience of inner peace, through your recognition of the eternal in you, can a lasting healing be called upon. To experience peace, one must give up all value placed in the body and in the world. Allow yourself the privilege of dying before death. You will not only recognize that you *will* live forever, but you will also discover the radiant Love deep within that will instantly begin healing both the body and all fear. This requires a shift in the tremendous amount of trust and faith you have placed in fear to be redirected toward the goal of peace. This can only be experienced by diving deeply into meditation and relinquishing your investment in all thinking relative to the world.

You can do this, Rhonda, because I did it. I recognized that I was worth consistent attention and perfect loving effort, *because* I was created by boundless Love from beyond this world. My faith became unified at that point with the same faith and Will Which created me. Have you the faith to look deep within you to What is *beyond* this world? Are you not worthy of this holy effort? Of course you are! You *will* do it because deep down you know that what I am teaching you is true. In light of what this can accomplish and with what you are now experiencing, do you really have anything better to do than take this "risk" to be healed? I will be right there to assist you, holding your hand and lifting you toward the perfect peace of God in you.

Forgiveness is the key to transcending the body and the ego. Through your forgiveness you will find the eternal peace I am speaking of. Your relationships will then reflect the vision of our Father's Holy Spirit. It cannot be spoken, but it can be experienced. You need not die to do this. In fact, you *cannot* die! But the dreams of your ego can and will die as you decide to follow only the gentle Voice for Love in you. Following a disciplined practice is important for your specific problem at this time. You will find that this will greatly reduce, if not entirely eliminate, the fears you have asked about in your second question as well.

In question five you asked about which philosophy to follow. Both can be helpful to you. A deep practice of the lessons in *A Course In Miracles* will help you the most. Do the lessons as I have suggested. Give them, however, more time than I have previously suggested in each lesson. If you find yourself resisting a lesson, do not push the length of time past another minute after the resistance begins. However, do the lessons and meditation more frequently than is usually suggested as well. Finally, remember that the goal is peace in whatever studies you may embrace.

After your discipline increases and you look happily forward to each lesson with no resistance to staying in the longer meditation times, you will begin to discover a healing in you that you never dreamed possible. Be vigilant for the Kingdom of God in you now, Rhonda. Allow yourself to get to the point in your spiritual meditation time where the resistance hardly ever comes. If you begin to slack in your meditations and the resistance becomes greater again, then it is time to recommit gently to even more meditation time. You want to get to the point where you feel little or no resistance both in meditation and in everyday life. In other words, you reach the point where you feel able to turn your will instantly over to the Holy Spirit in all situations.

You will know if you are genuinely doing this because your sense of inner peace and happiness will become profound. Fear of death will disappear. You will notice your mind being present only in the instant that you are experiencing. This will be a good indication that you are well on your way to a lasting and powerful experience of true healing. My faith in you is perfect. You will overcome your bodily illness because you will overcome your fears about the body. Be gentle with yourself, my dear Rhonda. You are a wondrous and innocent child of God. Let yourself be this radiant child. Let yourself be loved by Him Who infinitely loves you. Laugh in Love often, no matter how life *appears*. Do not take this world seriously. As you do this, offer gratitude regularly for the Gift God brings you.

Let your Light shine forth

with this blessing I bring you.

All sickness is healed,

for Heaven is come

and is truly your only Home.

Receive now, the perfection

of this holy blessing

unto you!

A Loving Jesus Christ

*See a second scribing for Rhonda in Chapter Six

Religion, Spirituality & Mortality

Light is your real religion.
You can give it now
because light is in you now.

INTRODUCTION

This chapter begins with a subject that is perhaps the most controversial subject of all. Religion, spirituality and mortality all have one common key element — the coming to terms with God. Thus these subjects are a call for healing as well. The fear of healing seems great indeed to the world. We will speak to this fear, for from it have come the woes and despairs of all human kind. Buried within the seemingly great structures in which all forms of worship have been built waits the Answer of all answers to every question. Beyond the great granite walls, laced with stained glass, beyond the priests and masses of bodies, past the tombstones of doom and sorrow, is His great Truth, waiting to be freed and sung by all. Indeed, this shall surely come soon!

You who have asked for the Great Awakening must be glad your answer is come. Yet time remains a little while longer that the Lamp of Perfect Light be lit in every heart and mind. We come together for this holy gathering to heal each heart afraid of Love. The walls must crumble, words must cease and all complication be risen above. It is time to let everything in our way be gently set aside so we may truly love one another. It will be the great triumph of Life over death, of Love over all science, dogma and symbolism. It is the coming of our Kingdom and our God! Happy indeed are the times to come, my sisters and brothers!

A SCRIBING FOR AGNES

It has been 52 years since I was liberated from a concentration camp. I entered the camp as an overprotected child and I came out as a frightened, confused older child.

The first time I saw my piano teacher's naked body dumped over 50 other bodies, something snapped inside me. My loving, caring child has never returned.

Through the years there have been thousands of questions that have gone through my mind. There didn't seem to be anyone who could answer my questions until now. My questions seemed to be unanswerable. Then I heard about Jesus answering questions through Joel. Perhaps now I will get some answers.

Elder Brother Jesus:

1) *I'm a holocaust survivor. My question is why was there a holocaust?*

2) *If the Jews are the chosen people, why are we persecuted all the time? Why aren't we allowed to join country clubs or live in exclusive neighborhoods or even go to yacht clubs, etc.?*

3) *I'm confused about your birth. If you were born to a Jewish mother and father, who established Catholicism?*

4) *Why does the Pope feel he is better than any Jew, and why is he entitled to such wealth?*

5) *I've been searching my whole life for love and happiness. Where did I go wrong? I trust the Universe to take care of me, except I've never felt genuine love from anywhere.*

Greetings Agnes:

We will begin our discussion today with the subject of anger, for it is your belief that happiness can be found outside of you. This is why these questions have arisen and may seem at times to haunt you.

What you are seeing outside yourself is a projection of your ego's unhealed hatred. This is perhaps direct and somewhat difficult to hear, but it is nonetheless what you must hear and look at *if you* are to experience the genuine Love that has seemed absent in your life. Love has never really been absent, but only obscured by a mind which has placed its focus elsewhere. You will never experience Love from without you because there is nothing outside you to experience it *with*.

You have but one relationship that is essential for a loving experience. That, my dear Agnes, is the relationship with your Self. God gave you your Self, whole and perfect as Herself. You are not really apart from Her. But in dreams of fear and hatred you have seemed to distance yourself from Love. You have thus become confused about your own Identity and the purpose for your being here.

You are apt to even take what I am saying as an attack on this other distanced self that you have made from fear, protected and nurtured for many years. Everyone who walks here does this. I wish you to hear today, with all the gentleness of our Mother's Love, that I would never attack you, nor could I. The ego you have made out of the fear of Love must be brought into question. This ego is not you. It can only seem to hurt you when you rely on it for comfort instead of the Spirit of Truth within you.

The suffering you have seen in your life as a result of unhealed anger has led you to perceive your life through a looking glass of projections that hold only the "reality" you have given them. These judgments are meaningless except to the ego, which guards them with its very "life." It has a tiny existence under the laws it has established and has asked you to follow.

As long as it is your wish to stay angry in any form over such seeming tragedies as the holocaust, you place your mind out of reach of the healing that your own eternal Spirit would instantly offer. Nothing can take these bad dreams away from you, Agnes. But you can become willing to voluntarily and completely give them up. When you truly do so, they will happily be removed forever from your mind and heart by God's Holy Spirit.

Dreams are real to those who see themselves as part of their dreams. It is not until they awaken that they realize the dream was *only* a dream, not the truth at all. No one can awaken from their dreams as long as they fear that, without what they are dreaming, their life would cease in purpose and function and they would be no more. They cling to their dreams, hoping to find some salvation inside the dream, yet it never comes. Dreams can never illuminate the minds of God's children.

Genuine Love is only experienced through genuine forgiveness. Only genuine forgiveness could offer release from all perceptions of the past, thus awakening the mind to the present, where only Love abides. If you were truly trusting in God to take care of you, you would feel Love, not just anywhere, but everywhere! If you are not feeling Love everywhere, it must be that you are "experiencing" the results of *believing in dreams* rather than experiencing God through relinquishing your investment in them. Forgiveness is in order. Only in dreams is hatred kept as an arsenal to keep your holy mind in "hell." This is not what God would ever will *for you*.

I have said before, "Would you rather be right or happy?" You cannot be both, for your function was not given to you to be right about anything you seem to see. You are always wrong about what you think you see, but you are always right in What you are. You can change what you perceive, but you can never change your Self. In light of what your "seeing" has brought you, would you prefer its confusion to the holy Gift God has already given you? Change your mind, then, and place your value only Where it belongs. It is the only Gift you came with, have and will keep forever. Need you be concerned with "finding" anything else? Blessed are you, Agnes, for what is given you is forever shared and forever to be shared by you. That is why you came here. That is the purpose of your Life. May you remember It with me now.

Let us now proceed to your question number one. If you look through the eyes of fear, you will see a "holocaust" occurring every day. Men, women and children seem to be dying by the thousands mercilessly every day in the world you live in. It is no different now than it was then. The only difference is now it is more hidden from your view. Most of you live a sheltered existence when it comes to viewing the real amount of suffering that takes place every day in your world — out of sight, out of mind until something catastrophic hits at home. Then you get a taste of the suffering that others go through in impoverished lands far from your own.

If you were to see this suffering up close through fearful eyes, you would indeed have more than just Hitler to forgive. You would recognize that you have mankind and yourself to forgive! This apparent suffering is never yours alone, although you have chosen to make it appear as if it is. The illusion of suffering is of humanity together and so is the healing. The suffering is not *your suffering*. It is our *apparent suffering together*. Until it is understood this way, it will continue, for pain is never experienced alone, anymore than healing can be accomplished alone.

The suffering that many went through together in the holocaust was due to a similar denial that had built up within the ego framework of mankind. Without the holocaust, this denial would have furthered itself into an even more destructive arena later. It should be forgiven, yet remembered for the blessed lesson it would teach — that Love would not have you be autonomous and that control and punishment lead only to the illusion of destruction and more fear. Indeed, there is a mighty lesson in what happened in this holocaust for all humanity to keep and hold dear to the heart.

If you will all allow yourselves to keep this lesson in the Light of Love and not in more denial, anger and hatred, you will indeed save yourselves from having to repeat it on such a large scale again. The whole trial of the holocaust would have been unnecessary had you fully recognized together that all that was necessary was for you each to forgive Love and help one another. Because of the holocaust and other needless battles, you are all just now beginning to understand the futility of hatred, condemnation and war. In this sense, it is indeed a blessing to humanity. Now, humanity is on the verge of finally learning to save time instead of wasting it and making need for more time.

The ego in each of you seems "inherently" destructive because you made it this way to separate and protect the body. You, however, are not inherently destructive because you did not create your Self. This has been the problem of humanity. You have taught yourselves to believe that you *did* create yourselves and your reality. All the defenses and wars you have erected and experienced have epitomized the vulnerability you believe is built into your "creation." Until you realize *together* that what you have all made is not your true creation, there will continue to be upheaval and disarray.

Once your true and eternal Reality is more broadly recognized, experienced and established in the many and not the few, your understanding together of your inherent *invulnerability* will heal and neutralize the ego's destructive urges. Together, you have all been experiencing a rather painful birth into this new age of unity that soon is to come. What a birth it will be when you all discover together that you *cannot die*! You are really much, much bigger than the bodies you all walk around in. There will come the day when all the "holocausts" you have gone through in the past will become insignificant in comparison to what this Great Birth will bring. You will remember them kindly as only the struggle to be born as One together!

In answer to your question number two, Agnes, you are persecuted only by the belief and projections of your own victimhood. In order for there to be a holocaust, there must be those willing to see themselves as victims, as well as those who see themselves as oppressors. It is a mutual agreement you make with the world as soon as you choose to look upon your life as one of scarcity and victimization. This cannot occur unless you somehow believe you are guilty and undeserving. You maintain guilt only by continually choosing lovelessly. Loveless perception is always based on the conditions of fear you have imposed on others and thus yourself.

Again, we go back to an ancient hatred left unforgiven. You must understand that unhealed hatred breeds condemnation. Condemnation separates. Separation makes war and victimhood a dark reality for you. You do not want this! Your only escape is through your own complete forgiveness of these bad dreams your beliefs have made real.

I can assist you with this, but only if you will bring your fearful thinking to me to take charge of. I will take it to the Holy Spirit for His healing and allow it to be shined away from your most holy mind. Guilt, fear and hatred do not belong with you! Give them to me, for I will gently lead you back to the holy Home of Heaven you have forgotten. Let go, my dear child. You are no more persecuted than was I. You are accepted wherever you accept your loving Self. Your true Self is of God. Your heart is created of Her eternal innocence. I abide within it with you in Christ forever. Can anything or anyone hurt you who have seen and given your life to the living Christ of a loving God? Let us look together on What can never be assailed in you. For here is Where your treasure lies and only here. Gently, let us walk away from hatred and suffering, and walk together instead into the Light and innocence that Her Kingdom of Love has promised has always been ours! Let this great healing and joining of our hearts with all other hearts begin here. The time has come to leave the battlefield completely, to drop all defenses and return in gratitude to our eternal Home.

Let us now go on to your question number three. I would simply tell you that I did not come here to establish any religions. But I did know that religions would be established in my name. I also spoke about the trials and tribulations that they would cause. I will be speaking about this more in times to come. Religion was invented by the ego simply as a means to control the masses. The "power" of many religions is based entirely in fear. Their failures in promoting peace are all too apparent. Like all devices of the ego, they are designed to inevitably fail. It does not matter who invented them in my name. Many were involved, all with good intent. No one had any idea of the extremes the ego would take religions to over time. Mistaken teachings will be brought to light sooner than later. They are beginning to be brought to light right now. *The function of religion in the world will only last as long as you each believe there is a need for it. Then you will choose otherwise.* Do not fear it. Merely see it for what it is. Then place your values only in Love where they belong and watch. Things will change. Most of all, love everyone, no matter what they believe. This is how you can most help each other avoid further persecution from any source.

Finally, you have asked about the Pope. He doesn't feel "better" than you my dear. He is fearful of you. You represent a threat to his interpretation of what I said. In my life I came as a Jew. Wouldn't you be a bit afraid if you took something from me that was mine to share with everyone, then changed it and had my sister show up on your doorstep wondering what happened to it and where it went?

You are all the chosen ones! He is no different than you. His fear and hatred run as deeply as everyone else's. You will all heal this illusion together. His ability to love is the same as yours. You all need each other. Not one penny of his money or your money will enter into Heaven with you. Your wealth far exceeds anything money could ever buy because Heaven is *in* you and can never be taken *from* you. Do not be deceived by what is valuable to the world. There is nothing here that is not bound to disappear someday. Enjoy the beauty of the inner wealth you have now and forever. Remember, in my name, the real Kingdom Which I have brought you and Which you bring to all your sisters and brothers in the Name of God's Love. Peace to you my dear sister, Agnes. Grace is my blessing to you, for you know its meaning well. Keep it. Live in it. And may your life be healed by the graceful Love you give.

A loving Jesus Christ

Jesus' answers confronted me and amazed me as I did not realize that I was so very angry and was not "willing to forgive." Thankfully now, I am putting my past behind me.

Thank you, Jesus.

Thank you, Joel.

Agnes

THE FABRIC OF RELIGION

There is no religion in this world which rises above being more than a mere cult unless it becomes inclusive of all brothers and sisters, all races and all humankind. Any religion which sets out pre-conditions as a *requirement* to "experience or know God" has failed to meet the purpose of true unification achieved only through the Holy Spirit. There are no pre-conditions for salvation. Each one needs only a willingness to look beyond her present thought system toward a Thought which is shared by all. There is no set way, no particular method or dogma that must be followed for one to experience God. In most cases, methods and dogma only serve as barriers to two or more who would join together to remember God. Different methods or dogmas can actually become detrimental to the holy relationship being sought. Words are twice removed from experience. Only experience offers effects that are lasting and real. Religion is, by definition, ego politics and not a mirror for spirituality.

Your world consciousness is now reaching critical intensity because of what many religions and cults have so long insisted on teaching. You cannot fathom how deeply these religions have affected the subconscious mind. Until these religions are changed from teaching fear, blame or condemnation in any form, humankind will be held back from the awareness of the glory and perfection that is inherently theirs.

Remember that I have said once before that your deepest fear is your fear of God (Love). Now your greatest challenge is to not teach yourselves or your children to fear God in any form. Question any "authority" which tries to teach otherwise, but do so with a full awareness of God's Love in your heart.

I call on each of you as my miracle workers now to help in a cause that reaches far beyond your own perceptive abilities. At this time you cannot understand the impact of the miracles I am asking you to perform.

The time for gathering has come. Together we will build our church solely on the Love of God, for Christ is our church, our Home and our happy release from all past and fear. Our church will never be seen, but will be heard through each of you who bring, one by one, another miracle to each confused and tortured mind that longs to join His mission with you.

The second coming in the world will come to pass when the awareness of our church has come to every heart and mind. As the healing of God's Son fulfills itself, no one will be turned away, but all will be welcomed through the doorway to Life with you. Great miracles will be occurring, and sisters and brothers who once seemed thousands of miles away from you will be experienced as standing all around you! Differences will no longer be a concept worthy of attention. These are only a few of the great changes that will come to pass as our inner church builds.

Brothers and sisters, do not buy the plan of the mundane any longer! Do not allow your lives to be ruled by any teaching that would undermine your abilities to be entirely joyous! You have no idea how you sacrifice your awareness of Christ in you when you do so. Christ is the Self your church abides in, for only here can true happiness and peace abide. *Here* is your release from dogma and the world's beliefs made sure. *Here* is your true Inspiration found and shared with all.

Oh great Unseen One, belief must tremble in our vision of your Great Light. And "sin" does crumble where You have come. How mighty is Your Word, yet how gentle your Hand, oh Father/ Mother of ours!

A SCRIBING FOR JOHN

Dear Joel,

I loved your scribing from Jesus. Do you do this for anyone? My life has such a lack of direction. I don't know what I should be doing. I would really appreciate some advice from Jesus at this point. Can you help?

My current life situation is full of doubt. I want to conclusively believe in GOD and Jesus, but I just don't feel anything. I am unhappy at work because I don't think it's where I should be, but I am too afraid to change things. I hate and fear others, yet I know I should love them.

Questions:

1) Jesus, how can I know that you and GOD are real?

2) Jesus, how can I feel your love?

3) Jesus, am I in the right employment and should I change it?

4) How can I learn to love others?

5) Please explain forgiveness so I can practice it.

6) What should my spiritual practice be?

Much love,

John

Greetings John:

Let us begin with your last question since it is this question, once answered, that will help to answer the other ones as well.

Spiritual practice should be undertaken at all times during your day. This seems impossible for most, but only because they have placed their values elsewhere. There is nothing more illuminating than a Son of God who is at peace with himself. The Son of God at peace is the complete and happy undoing of the world and all its seeming "sins" and woes.

There are two aspects to every spiritual practice: One involves a quiet listening during a time that the student has set aside for only himself and God; the other involves his reaching out to other minds in quiet humility to share the Gift that peace has brought to him. Both practices are essential, neither one being effective by itself.

During each day it is important to set aside time to commune with Christ and, through Christ, with God. The length of time you spend in daily meditation will be determined by your ego resistance. As long as you feel impatient about being still, you should be still a little longer. When you are truly comfortable being still and you feel a sense of release, lightness and communion, it is time for you to take this awareness to the world. You do not need to spend hours in meditation.

For a while, during the day after a successful meditation, you will continue to feel released and free. Then it is likely that at some point something will be of concern to you and you will find a heaviness returning. This is the time for a short meditation or gentle reminder. You should be able to remember the sense of release you felt earlier in the day simply by closing your eyes and relinquishing your own thinking and sense of judgment.

Then at night before bed, another longer period should be given to remembering the peace of God and through Him that "You need do nothing." If you commit to doing this consistently, you cannot help but find the peace and joy that God has promised you is there. The question you must honestly answer is, "Do I believe I am worth the effort?" Once you answer this question honestly, you will take time for yourself with God.

You cannot "conclusively believe in God" because God lies beyond where all belief can reach. No matter how much you try to *believe* your Self is there, you will not be able to find It. The Christ in you can never reach into your belief system because your beliefs were made to *hide* the Face of Christ, not to reach It. Nor can I reach into your thought system, for I abide only in the Christ *in you*. The Self that God created for you is not a tangible thing. You cannot see It, touch It or even hear It with the body's ears. It remains hidden beneath the thoughts, words and defenses that the ego has made to replace the silent Strength of Love in you.

This is a very irritating thing for the ego to experience because the ego is bent on investigating and discovering the "truth" in the physical. When it cannot do so, it can become quite capricious, even vicious at its worst. This can cause a sense of acute conflict in you that can seem unbearable. The ego is expert at manipulating you to seek and not find. This is also why it is at times difficult for you to trust and experience Love with your brothers and sisters. The ego is constantly trying to conceal the Face of Christ by "discovering" the one thing that is "wrong" with what your brother is doing, making it seem impossible for you to genuinely see that Christ is working through each and every one of you *right now.*

Everyone who seems to cross your path offers an opportunity for you to join with him in trust and experience all the glory that God has offered you together. It is also an opportunity to choose the mistrust and misguidance the ego offers you. But think truly about the apparent choice to be made. Is there really a choice in lieu of what faithlessness would offer? Faithlessness in your brother is the "choice" not to recognize the power of Christ in your Self. It is a "choice" to sleep in ignorance of What is real.

The guidance of Love that I am offering you here is as easily and readily available in your brother. But will you look for the peace that Christ offers through him or will you call on the conflict you believe may be there instead? If you would look only to the appearance, words and symbols that he may be confusing himself with, how can you help but not confuse your own mind as well? Yet if you will look for only peace in whatever message he seems to be conveying, you will find only peace. The peace of God has nothing to do with the appearances and symbols of this world. His peace is yours. You will find it only in the shining Light behind the veil his ego has made to hide it from you both. The veil is yours if you make it his. But if you would overlook these illusions in him, you will discover the true peace you both share.

The Christ in each of you *is* all you have to share. The rest, with all the symbols and appearances, is but a dream. You can attempt to "share" each other's dreams, but you can never make this kind of sharing true. Dreams will never make you happy until you fully recognize them for what they are. Then they will no longer confuse you, for you will have learned with your brothers and sisters not to take the appearances in your dreams as a serious "reality." Then may you laugh in dreams, seeing through them with the happy Vision of Christ.

My faith in you is perfect and I know What you are. Your trust in me is your trust in your brother and sister. To trust in anything but Christ is an act of faithlessness on behalf of what you believe illusions offer you. They offer nothing except unneeded conflict and a state of mind that, in itself, does not really exist. Would you prefer pain to the peace of God? Exchange, then, all that is not of Christ for the One Reality your Father gave you. Leave no trace of the "reality" you made to take its place. Let it go for all time and join the truly humble. That is my calling to you, John. Will you join with me now on the great crusade to correct error and remember the joyous Heaven from Where we come?

To believe is to think that there must also be doubt, and God cannot be doubted. Yet to have perfect faith, you do not need belief at all. Perfect faith is a demonstration that you are willing only to know. Perfect faith is impossible as long as there is still an attraction to place value in something other than Love. By placing value in something other than Love, you have implied that your beliefs can be true. Belief is always about "something else," not about God, Who does not even see what belief would imply. It is your beliefs, then, that keep perception "alive" in you.

If you were to remove all beliefs that you see something with value or meaning, all you would have left would be your Self. You would instantly recognize Christ in yourself and everyone. The world, which once concealed Christ from your sight, would merely disappear in a tiny twinkle of an eye. That is why it is necessary for you to relinquish investment in all perception at some point. As long as the holy instant is hidden from your awareness, it is impossible for you to experience your Self as God created you.

Most of you, including even those who have carefully studied *A Course In Miracles*, have a difficult time accepting that you can learn to live a great portion of your lives within the holy instant. That is because of your attraction to the belief in the appearance of "problems" in your lives. To a degree you can accept everything I tell you. But part of you still resists and insists that what I am teaching is not always practical in the world you live in. This is a good example of the power of your beliefs. They can literally move mountains in front of you if you do not learn to question all of them. The fact is, you can live in the holy instant and have your life function on a more productive level than ever before. You have no idea the miracles you will bring to all minds once you heal and reclaim your complete commitment to living only in this present

Light! This is Where you can be happy, for you will no longer depend on your own private thoughts to be your guide once this commitment is taken sincerely to heart and mind. You will in fact recognize the futility of your private thoughts and simply abandon them, knowing that they are not for the whole.

The Thought of God is never for you alone. His Thought, as your Self, was placed in your mind and other minds simultaneously. His is the only Thought which can make you serene and calm, for It is the only Thought that can be truly shared. It is His Will that you share the Love He has given you because He shares It with you. You will be happy only when you hear His Call to share His Will and awaken with It by sharing It with all other minds. That is what you have come to do after you have forgiven all that would keep you from this holy mission. There need be no change in the world you see to accomplish this. It is again not a matter of words, actions or things. It is a matter of right-mindedness and thereby, right evaluation and right attitude.

A poor attitude changes into a healthy one the instant you recognize What is valuable. Then what is not valuable is entirely abandoned. Concerns about *doing* transform into acceptance of just being. Where once responsibility was equated with *doing*, it is now equated with accepting only God's Word. This is highly transformative because it undermines the authority problem and restores the function of true Authority to the mind, allowing the mind to relinquish the great burden that was placed upon it by its own confused values. It is these misplaced values that have fostered the sense of guilt in your most holy mind, John. This is why you have been so troubled. Knowing this, would you now not let these values go so that you may again know the peace of God?

It is apparent that many of you have taken the idea, "I need do nothing," from *A Course In Miracles* and have become somewhat confused by it. When I said you need do nothing, I meant that you need not feel you have to do anything. This does not mean that you should not enjoy your life and do the things that bring you happiness and joy. "I need do nothing" is but a statement in recognition that God's Will is already done; that there is nothing to save or be saved from. By releasing your mind from the great burden of guilt you have taken on as the result of your believing just the opposite, you are free in the present to choose what is loving for everyone. You will "do" many things in your worldly lives, none of which will have the slightest effect on your true Reality. That is why "doing" is illusory.

All change is but illusion, including the changes your mind seems to go through. That is what you are here to discover — that none of these changes really matter. They cannot hurt you in truth. When you begin to recognize the change as only illusion, you will also begin to feel lighter inside. This is a first step in recognizing, however dimly, that you need not take any part of the world you seem to experience so seriously. One day you will come to a great and happy recognition — that you need not take *anything or anyone* in this world seriously at all! That will be a moment when a thousand trumpets in Heaven sound, and angels, my dear John, will sing on high! Remember this, then: *Sincerity offers everything; seriousness offers nothing.*

You can know that God is real only by relinquishing your strong investment in what is not real. I have given you the means to do so above. If you would remember that I am one with you along with every brother and sister, you must be willing to give up entirely the littleness that has seemed to make a "self" apart from Christ's Self in you. This part of your mind that insists you are separate from me is the one illusion the ego protects with all its ferocity. The ego knows that by the illusion of separation, it guarantees its own "survival." It has made you blind, John, to the Gift that the Christ in you is offering even now. I am one with you. If necessary I can speak to you with many words, but it is not words you long to hear. You long to know the Love from Which we are both created. Love holds you up and reminds you constantly of the Place Which you have never truly left. It is your Home for all eternity. It is all you long to remember. Seek not peace by looking where peace can never be found! Forgive instead the dreams that have seemed to make you weak, limited and small. It is through your forgiveness of these dreams that Heaven can be remembered for all.

You *can* feel the Love I am offering you right now. And you do. My Love is God's Love. What He speaks in gentle silence is perfectly consistent and true. That is why you are not hearing His consistency in just the words and symbols I am using here. Words and symbols can always be interpreted and juggled into whatever the ego wants to make of them. This is even quite apparent in some of the interpretations by the ego of *A Course In Miracles*. I did not give you *A Course In Miracles* to argue over theory and separate. I gave it to you for one purpose and one purpose only — to remind you that there *are* no words for the *experience* of What you are *together*. What is called for is *experience*, not words, theory or crutches that keep the ego in place and maintain separation.

You must learn to look beyond words, symbols and things to the consistency of Light that is always there. This Light is perfect in you and in everyone. You who look Where only peace can be found will find only peace. But do not attempt to experience it where it can never be experienced, lest you wish to take yet another useless journey. Instead, through your forgiveness of all that never was, take my hand with all of our brothers and sisters and let us journey together to the perfect illumination of our most heavenly Home.

It is your function, John, to remember this Home while you are here. You made the world as a symbol of your belief in separation. Through this belief you placed "value" where it does not belong to keep this world in place. In this choice you forgot What is valuable. For you to remember, you must forgive the "reality" of illusions. Indeed, mighty is your function here!

It is the illusions that seem so real and difficult in your present life situation that are by far your greatest blessings. They seem to be a curse because you have insisted that they are indeed true. Their blessing to you lies in your recognition of what you have made them "real" *for*. They are there to teach you What you have forgotten and refuse to look upon. No one wants to hear that what they made to replace Reality is not real. No one wishes to recognize that what seems to happen to them in their dreams they have asked for. Yet this is what they must accept in full if they are to become empowered to heal and change their minds about it. When you recognize that it is only you who can change your mind about the "reality" of illusions *because* it is only you who thought them to begin with, then you will recognize, know and experience the Reality that God created *for* you.

I am in this Reality *with* you and with all our brothers and sisters. It is Here I remain, waiting only for you to relinquish all investment in this other "reality" and return with me to the glorious and holy Kingdom of our Father's Abode. Will you let go of your dreams and fantasies and walk in Christ with all of our brothers and sisters? This is how you can learn to love others truly. Forgive what can never be true except in dreams. There is nothing else to forgive, and everything to gain by it. Have you really anything better to do?

You do not need to believe in Reality for it to be true, but you do need to believe in illusions to make them seem "true." Look at your life and see what the ego has so ingeniously made "real" from your beliefs. Then give them to the Holy Spirit for Him *to undo* for you. You are as God created you and Reality is as God created It. You need do nothing except receive Reality *as it is*. Then you will know and enjoy your Life, your freedom and the perfect safety of God's Love for you.

The gift of your giving up illusions to the Holy Spirit is the greatest gift you can ever offer Him. He will receive them and undo them gladly, returning you unto His Father's Gift of Heaven. *This* is what your forgiveness truly offers. It is not difficult to forgive, John, but only to hold on to what could never be.

You have asked about employment and whether or not the position you are in is the best one for you. I cannot answer that *for* you. But I can tell you that it is *not* the *only* position for you. I shall repeat what I said long ago: "Tell the truth and do not do what you feel in your heart you *would* not do." All of the answers to all of your questions about the world can be answered easily if you will keep these inspired words in mind. It may appear to be "risky" for you to follow the answer that you will receive. But in your willingness to risk being healed, there *will be* rejoicing! It is in your listening to God's Answer within you that you will know what is best for you at any given time. You already know the answer to your dilemma with your present work. But will you listen and act on it?

Here is a prayer for you. Use it often and with all the conviction of your heart and mind:

> *"Father, I have confused myself by seeking a direction that has led me away from Your loving Truth. By looking outward for solutions to this confusion, I have made my confusion into a weapon I would terrorize myself with. Choosing this has made me full of doubt and left me frozen in fear. I do not want to be fearful any longer, so I am willing to relinquish my own thoughts and judgments and accept Your Word for me instead.*

I gladly step aside now, knowing that You will gently guide
me if I will be still and listen. I take Your Hand in silence now,
for I would follow only You. Let me now receive the Gift Your
Love in me would offer. With Your Gift, all is possible. Let me
not limit myself any longer and let me accept only this Gift
now."   Amen

Receive the Father's blessing through me to you now.

Live in the Light of Its blessing and share It with all.

Blessing you,

A loving Jesus Christ

THE REAL RELIGION

You did not come here to repent. You came to celebrate! Yet
the world was made to save the face of the ego and to deny the
face of Christ. The world, left to the ego's perception, is a place
of punishment. Every end that is sought ends in separation and
seeming death. The means to these ends are carefully guarded by
the ego and disguised in its many different forms. The ego uses
religion, politics, secret organizations and cults, which it calls
"new" or "special," for the continuation of its purposes and as
a guarantee for its own "survival." At worst these practices can
induce feelings of intense separation and guilt, becoming a call to
war and darkness. At best these practices can be converted and
used on behalf of the Holy Spirit for joining minds and healing
of hearts seemingly broken by the deep despair that blame, guilt,
condemnation and punishment "offer" as the harsh penance for
their "sins."

One thing is consistent and always certain in outcome for
each of these disguised forms of redemption. In each of them,
form ultimately takes precedence over content — the physical is
emphasized over the unseen spiritual. When this occurs and God
is made into a mere image, darkness is sure to befall the world.
Many will exclaim, "The world is becoming insane. No one knows
what is true or right anymore!" Many will ask honestly, "Why is
this happening?"

The answer is simple. When this happens, true forgiveness has lost its place in religions, schools, institutions, organizations or within whatever framework the content may be held. A value system must begin with a common component that all may share and benefit from. That component is Love. But the Love of God cannot enter any situation where condemnation or fear is practiced in any form. Even the slightest wish to hurt will prevent true forgiveness from bringing its grace and illuminating those it would touch and heal. *Forgiveness can never be exclusive.*

I say to you all and hear me well: The time is come where you shall all stand firmly together, not in any forms, as a religion or institution, but as one family living in the Light of God. Forget not that the world is still an illusion. Everything in it can offer you nothing you really want. You want peace. You want Love. And you want perfect safety. You will not find it in form. Turn away from all that the world seems to offer.

Choose no way that would separate brother from brother in any form. Do not teach the "laws of punishment" to anyone or surely darkness must come. Teach instead the law of forgiveness. Let nothing you see escape the lighted vision your forgiveness would offer. Let no stone be unturned where forgiveness might not reach. A time approaches in which the world will begin to experience a Great Awakening. *It is essential now that every mind be helped to escape the burden of guilt and fear.* Through this process, a process of forgetting and forgiving the world, the remembrance of God's Love will quickly come to all minds. As the sun rises over a desert, no shadows remain for darkness to hide.

Light is your *real* religion. You can give It *now* because Light is *in* you *now*. To know only Light is to give only Light. There are no steps to climb or altars to kneel before. God gave you the Light. Light *is* your altar. To know this Light is simply to share God's Altar with everyone. God's religion is the extension of Her/His Light to everyone. This is God's joyous Will for you. Would you not offer the same Will to everyone? To love as God loves you is a promise for the world to awaken. For in giving God's Gift entirely and just as She/He gave it to you, Heaven's promise to a dying world is fulfilled.

A Scribing for Jeff

Hi Joel,

 Thanks for offering the scribing.

 About me: Typical baby boomer. 51-year-old male, married with four kids, only two left at home but soon to graduate from college. Interests: Music, art, photography. Made my living in younger years on the music circuits; still play occasionally and write songs. Artistic and creative type guy. Don't hunt or fish, but like the outdoors.

 Life situation: I work in sales and marketing. Have small house in country. Good wife; take care of mother since her illness. All in all, a good life. Have sought God for years and years, but can never quite reach the point of acceptance of any thought system. Now studying ACIM after going through most Christian based religions. No judgment yet as to ACIM... keeping open but it does have a "ring" of truth to it. More books, more books... studying but never coming to an understanding. Not really a joyful person. Bored, the optimism of younger years has left and I can't seem to get that back.

 Questions for you/entity:

 1) I want to be healthy, happy and financially secure. How?

 2) My perception of my job is I hate it, but seem to be trapped with it, with no other place to go. I am tired of the worry and responsibility, but too young to retire. How can I change that?

 3) I do not have a perception of any real purpose. I seem to be drifting along, just waiting to grow old and pass on. No goals or aspirations any more... dead wood, drifting in the stream of life. I want meaning and purpose in my life again.

 4) I want to believe in life after death, in God, in HS, but have not been able after years, years, eons... to really believe in Christian principles. How do I get that proof or experience?

 Thanks.

 Jeff

Greetings, Jeff:

This is Jesus speaking through Joel. I will be speaking to you today about trust and faith. I will be speaking to you about doubt, apathy and indecision. I will be speaking to you about many things that trouble you and will offer you ideas and solutions that can help and heal you. But it is *you*, Jeff, that must apply and act on these ideas. It is you who makes the decision for happiness or sadness, rejoicing with God or despising the world. You have all the power within you to transform your life from one that seems meaningless and futile into one that soars with God's purpose, function and rejoicing.

It is questionable, however, as to whether or not you are really willing to listen and hear, whether you will set aside your own ego's hardened cynicism that is directed toward your life and the world. For this is what you have built as a fortress around yourself. It is this delusion that can keep you in hell. Are you ready this day to accept who I am and what I am saying to you? I speak only for you *from* God. If you will listen carefully, you will hear me now speaking right through your very heart, *for I know you as my Self.* I do know what troubles you. Will you have faith in me today, Jeff, as I have the deepest faith in you? Or will you turn back to the world your ego has made for you? I need all of your faith and trust now, just as you need all of mine. Only in this way can we embark together on the journey I am about to offer you. Will you hear with your heart today? Will you take my hand as your brother and walk with me to the Heart of God?

Let us begin with an idea that is easily grasped. God is an experience, not a concept or a principle. Therefore, you can receive and embrace God, but you can never *seek* and actually find Him. "Seeking God" is equivalent to the belief that you can also "lose your Self." In statement, then, they are the same. You believe you must find what you seem to have completely "lost." If only you knew how utterly absurd the foundation is that this belief rests on! It is like standing on top of your own car in a completely empty airport parking lot and proclaiming to the world that you believe your car is missing!

This is the fascinating function you have ascribed to what you call "language." Yet the only true function that is useful for words and language is to use them on behalf of showing you how limited and, in most cases, how futile words and all thought systems invented by the ego truly are. Most are bent on demonstrating separation. That is why words and the concepts they form can be hazardous to you. Concepts form the beliefs that make up your thought system. These beliefs are what stand between you and the recognition of your complete oneness with God. It is your beliefs and concepts, set in time, that withhold the *experience of Love* from you.

The ego is bent on demonstrating that an "experience of Love" is impossible. It will do everything in its "power" to employ your services to continue implementing its "plan." It will do this simply by having you question, criticize and analyze every "threatening" idea that crosses its path. What is "threatening" to the ego *is* loving to *you*. Herein lies your dilemma; the ego would have you see only what it uses to preoccupy your mind and keep it *from* truth. By keeping you focused on words, concepts and theories, the ego has successfully obliterated Love from your present awareness. The present is the only place you are capable of experiencing the wondrous and shining beauty of the loving Self God created as you. It is in the tiniest instant Where you will witness the full glory of God's eternal Gift to you. Only by sharing this eternal Gift can you keep It with you in your complete and full awareness.

Yet how can you share this Gift of holy innocence and perfect Light if you allow yourself to be individualized by a ruthless and insidious dictator? The ego would have you questioning this and breaking down that, figuring out how, when and where, placing, categorizing and forever looking for change. It will keep you very busy with its dictates. But it would never allow you to leave the world carefree and receive God's Word as its complete replacement. This threatens the ego to the core of its foundation, for even the ego knows that it would simply cease to exist if you were to make such a commitment to Love.

This is what you are really afraid of, Jeff. For the ego has convinced you that if you were to let go of its thought system, your life would cease in "purpose" and "function." It has substituted its mediocrity, doubt and fear for the Love that is the Gift of God's most perfect Creation in you. The ego does this by sending you on an endless search to nowhere. Would you keep this thought system for yourself if you really knew where it was leading you? Would you not throw it away immediately if you truly realized that, in fact, by following it your life only epitomizes and models the *discarding* of your true purpose and function here?

Yet this is exactly the position you place yourself in every time you condone living your life through the ego's fearful thinking and the decisions that follow. It should be no surprise to you when I tell you that, indeed, you must begin to question every value you have ever held. By following your current values, you have perhaps become "successful" in the eyes of the world, but by no means have you felt successful looking through the eyes of your soul. This is why you feel you are purposeless, drifting along with no set path to follow. Indeed, there is a part of you that is addicted to this futile misery, even enjoying your wallowing in the mud! Is it not interesting, Jeff, how we all find so many distractions to keep us distanced from our one God-given responsibility, the responsibility to truly heal and love?

This is where you will find God without even looking! *This* is where you will experience joy without even having to try. You need not retire from your occupation or your life, but you must retire from your perception *of* it. It is your perception that makes your occupation seem real to you. Let me be clear on the importance of understanding this. Perception makes your earthly experience seem to be a "reality," while the undoing of your perception makes way for God's Reality by removing the substitute you have made. Your occupation seems real and important for your "survival." This is how you have made it. You do not question this belief system *because* you "created" it.

The real question you need to ask with perfect honesty is, "What did I make it *for*?" If you will look at this straight on, you will see that you made it not as an occupation to bring you security and happiness, but as a *pre-occupation* to keep you *from* your true security and happiness. All you have ever done in this world will fade away, leaving not even a trace of a memory for you or anyone that will last. The works of man are but temporary. The Works of God are eternal. What is not eternal has never occurred.

Now can we look closer at the meaning of value. What is truly valuable to you, Jeff? There is only one correct answer. Value lies only in God's Love. You need not believe in Love or God for this to be true, for true it is as God created it to be. Love is His Creation, and *you are His Love*. This leaves no question about What is real and many questions about what is not. But no question needs to be answered if an answer has been already given. Now all that need be done is for you to accept and fully receive the One Answer that has been given. Let not one illusion remain to intrude upon truth, for unless you exchange *all* perception for what God has given, you cannot know the eternal peace that He has willed for you. When you have truly been willing to value correctly, all your questions will *be* answered, for to value correctly *is* to will with Him.

Perception *has* no real purpose because perception in itself *has* no value. Value lies only in the goal it brings you. If it brings you fear, hatred and guilt, it has not served as a useful tool. More so, it has "served" only to disillusion you. In serving nothingness, this is what you will "find." That is why you should not believe your perceptions, no matter how much they seem to be true. They cannot be true. At best they can lead you closer to an experience that is loving. But they can never do more than that. If you are to experience Love as God created you, then you must be willing to experience what is beyond any perception. This begins by not believing what any perception tells you. This allows you to live in the present, free of the dream state the ego has so carefully protected and persuaded you to continuously follow.

It is hard for you who live in the world to accept that you need not think at all. By this I do not mean that you shouldn't think. You will think. But by believing that you *must* think for yourself alone, you have placed your mind in the grip of a madman. The truth is just as I have said it in *A Course In Miracles*. When you think without God you are not really thinking at all. Thinking, placed in the service of only Love, allows the thinker not to take his own thoughts or the thoughts of others seriously. You have no idea of the tremendous release and joy that you will experience once you have learned not to trust your thoughts alone! Heaven's gates will literally open before your very eyes!

Meaning is experienced the moment true function is recognized. Your only purpose here is to experience joy in each new and holy instant, free from the self-made thoughts that would burden and bind you. Your only function here is forgiveness *because* your purpose is to extend joy, just as God extended His freedom, safety and joy to you forever. That is His Creation, which is your life. He asks only that you extend Creation with Him, so that you can know Love as your Self. The world you seem to see in front of you was made by you to hide His joy. So what else could be your function but to forgive everything you *think* you *see*?

This is how you will get the experiential proof that you desire. This is how you will come to know that there is Life after death, and I assure you that there is. But you did not really come here just to discover that it is safe to set your body down some day. You thought you came here to experience death before Life! That is why you are so afraid of Life and the pure and eternal Love It offers! Your wish was not to find God, but to lose Him in all this illusion you made as a replacement. In this wish you have become afraid of That Which you have hidden. So you worry often about whether or not there is Life after your illusion of death. You have been constantly bent on making your "reality." Do not worry, Jeff, your real Life has never left you! It is with you always, waiting only for you to relinquish your investment in the "living death" your ego placed in front of It.

There is much to be said about the confusion you have all made together. I speak in *A Course In Miracles* about "upside-down perception." This means just what it says; you see everything in reverse. What is most important you overlook, choosing often what is least important. Such is the case with the untrained mind regarding interpretation of the Bible. There are many places in the Bible which speak of punishment and condemnation, seeming to assign God the role of judge, jury and executioner. Yet this inter-pretation has been made because, throughout time and each new translation, the ego has thrust its own guilt and savagery onto God. I have been careful to set up *A Course In Miracles* so this cannot happen so easily.

The Bible can be better understood if a few simple ideas are always kept in mind: There is nothing outside your Self; because of this, there is really no place to go even if you wanted to. In this way "hell" can be understood to be where it *is* — in your thinking where *you* placed it. Anything you read in the Bible with this interpretation will reverse the faulty and fearful interpretations made by those who were tainted by their own unhealed anger. The *loving* passages in the Bible need no reinterpretation, for they are perfect inspira-tions of the living truth in you now. All in all, the Bible *is* a perfect lesson in Love if you follow this simple corrective translation.

You *are* "going to hell" every time you listen to and follow the dictates of fearful thinking. The "devil" *is* very real indeed, but only because you made "him" that way, and you *do* believe in what you made. God *will* seem to punish you, but only because you punish yourself. By hating yourself it *will* seem that God hates you. Many religious books and political structures have been tainted by those who have not truly accepted healing for themselves. Look closely at the world you see, Jeff. See how your own thinking has been tainted by "the devil" and then *choose again with Love*.

Jeff, I will tell you now how to get "proof" in your experience. It is *in* that "ring of truth" you spoke of. If your experience in life is an unhappy one, it is obviously tainted by the dictates of fear. There is no truth to what guilt and fear offer. That is why it is so painful. You believe in something that has no chance for existence. Fear seems to exist only because you have insisted upon it. By doing so, you have really insisted that you are not real! Could God allow such thinking to be true? You will find the "proof" and experience you are looking for when, at last, you accept the fact that nothing apart from Love has ever really been. By taking the risk to offer only Love with full sincerity and gentleness in all your relationships, it will be returned instantly to you. Can it be so difficult to forgive what has never *really* happened, Jeff? This is all you need do to experience God's reassurance and joy. *Simply receive and give only What is true!* It is a willing and quiet mind that *will* hear and *act* on What it receives. Does *this* ring true to you, Jeff?

When you were young, did you think about all the things you think about now that seem to keep you busy and keep life complicated? Then why are you thinking about these things now? What possesses you to believe that you are somehow different from when you were younger? You are not. Not one thing has changed about you. Your body has gotten bigger and rounder. Someday, like magic, even it will disappear. But you won't. When you were little, did you feel limited by your body when you were chasing a friend or jumping out of trees? There was a time when you did not let it stop you from living happily, moment to moment. What makes you think now that you are contained by this body that others identify as "Jeff"? Why will you not take time now, as you did then, to be truly carefree and listen to the sound of joy in the chirping of the crickets and the birds? Why must you busy your mind with nothing, Jeff?

Here is your "optimism" and happiness — an innocence and freedom and ability to extend Love with God. Here is your One Answer to all problems! You will find It right here, right now, and nowhere else! Here is the Source for your inspiration, Jeff. Here, in this tiny instant, where it has always been. Forgive all else that you have seen and used as a replacement for this instant, and the holiness of Heaven will shine through you now. It is all you have and all you have ever really wanted. Accept it in all the shining glory God offers it. It is yours. If you accept and listen to only it, you will hear! I am in this instant with you, waiting to guide you with the Holy Spirit's help in all the decisions you are unsure of.

Make this your only goal and all other goals will fall into place. Find time to recognize that you are already rich. Receive it thus and let richness *be* yours. Find time to recognize your only security in Love, and security will *be* yours. You will be told how to take each step to make your life a happier one, but you *must* learn to ask, and then *listen*. You cannot count on fear to bring you anything but more fear. It makes only good sense, then, to stop listening to it and choose something that can help you! What have you got to lose except your own unhappiness? Start now, Jeff, in remembering the Gift you have forgotten. Little child, there is so much for you to be grateful for; so much your Father has saved for you while you have been away. His Treasure is great and will support you like nothing this world has ever offered. Trust in It. It is your Home, your calling and your Life. Receive It now, Jeff. That is my blessing to you. Listen often. I will be there, gently reminding you in a smile, that you have come Home!

A loving Jesus

QUESTION

What is the difference between a spiritual approach and a religious approach to living? Is one way better than the other?

Most religious approaches, if not all, are designed to keep the ego in "check," while most spiritual approaches are designed to teach one how to transcend and eventually relinquish the ego entirely. Both approaches represent steps in the undoing of hatred, fear and condemnation. Both can assist each individual in the healing process, depending on their specific needs.

It is important to recognize that any one approach is not necessarily faster than another. But *any* approach that would teach that God is both condemning and loving is in itself a "missing of the mark." It is impossible to teach the "fear of God" to anyone without inducing great and unnecessary conflict in both the teacher and the student who believes him/her. Any teaching that does so is false. Herein lie the great troubles of the world. Any approach that teaches guilt or fear in any form, teaches nothing at all. It is therefore not a religion or a spiritual approach, but merely a grand and ludicrous deception, a journey that leads to nowhere. Only confusion can be the immediate result and separation the outcome.

Some religions teach guilt, just as some spiritual approaches do. The ones that don't, however, can be very helpful. There are some who may enjoy a religion such as this more than a spiritual approach. What is most important is to realize that *all* approaches to God must have something that is deemed "especially helpful" by the follower. Otherwise she would not cherish it as she does. There are those also who, for a while, may need to believe in a condemning God instead of a loving one. Still, it is to any teacher of God's benefit to *save time*. This cannot be achieved while any guilt remains and hides the smile of those called upon to teach the truth of God's Word. There are many, many approaches to God. In the final outcome, it does not matter.

There is no end to What you are in God because you are created only of Her eternal Love. But there must come an end to the world, its symbols and all that seem to stand between you and Heaven. Every approach will someday be discarded, including this one. You will be left smiling, at one with your Creator, as *only* Love's Creation. Nothing will remain which could block the Rays of God's shining Light in you. Words will simply cease and will matter no more. All who stand with you will know and share with you *only* What *does* matter. Then you will see a transformation in your world never thought possible. Nothing in history can come close to compare. Yet, happen it will! It must, for it is God's Will. What of the Glory of Love can be expressed through mere words and symbols, when joy has come to all hearts? How the Sons and Daughters of God will shine then!

A SCRIBING FOR WAYNE

My five questions are:

1) *How can I free myself of the anger I feel toward people who I feel have wronged me?*

2) *How can I get beyond myself and live "in the Spirit"?*

3) *If the Course teaches I need do nothing, does this mean there is nothing I SHOULD do?*

4) *Should I take a spiritual journey? To where?*

5) *What really happened to me when I was young and had the "experience" which changed me?*

Thanks. Hope these weren't too specific.

Greetings Wayne:

I am gladdened that you have asked these questions. I will begin with the first question, since this one, when answered correctly and properly understood, will answer all the rest.

If you did not believe in the world, then no one could ever wrong you. It is your misplaced values that cause all sense of strain, fatigue, and also your feelings of loss of peace.

To value any thing or anyone is a misplacement of your own belief. Mistaken beliefs occur only when you have substituted fear for Love. You do not realize how often you let your mind slip away from the present instant into past thinking. Those who seem to rob you of peace are simply those whom you have not entirely forgiven. The reason you have not entirely forgiven yourself is that your mind seems without choice because of what you still believe must be true.

Remember, "Truth stands on its own forever." Nothing anyone can say or do can interfere with this fact. This is why you need do nothing when you are faced with the idea that something has gone wrong. If nothing has really happened, then why would you want to further believe and act as though it did? It is up to *you* to *allow* correction of this belief and no one else. Once you have truly allowed correction to take place in your mind, all other minds are healed along with you. Do you understand this Wayne? In order to accomplish anything, one must allow Love to accomplish it for you.

All false dependence eventually manifests itself in the form of anger. You can hardly depend on *anyone* or *anything* ever. The belief that you can or should is a misplacement of values based on wrong thinking. What you are seeing as "wrongs" are not even there. Oh yes, it appears that blame is justifiable, yet I assure you that it never is. With this simple recognition you are thus able to free yourself from all that would teach you otherwise. Learn not to depend on the world or all the illusions that make it appear to be what it is. Learn not to place value in what is not there. Then you are dependent only on That Which is changeless and completely invulnerable in yourself and everyone.

If you will look carefully at the ego's wishes, you will see that the entire world is made from this tiny mad instant in which God's Son sees himself as attacked and unworthy of the Love of God. It is because you value your own self-made thought system that this appears true. Yet you can easily exchange your thought system for truth by placing me in charge of it. Your thinking alone can cause you only loneliness and despair. Do not allow arrogance to take the place of the Gift that God gave to you. Humility and innocence are yours forever.

You need only relinquish the beliefs that lurk in the darkness of your mind that tell you differently. These beliefs must be brought to Light. You do this by outwardly acknowledging the fear you are experiencing. By acknowledging the belief as part of your experience, you are simultaneously allowing it to be healed. Your commitment to doing this is an act of willingness and sincerity on your part. Then I can do my part, for I will guide you from there to transcend this once hidden fear by transforming it into a miracle that will heal everyone involved. Value not the valueless, Wayne. I have a different mission for you. You have already agreed to fulfill this mission. Why not begin now?

To live in Spirit is simply to live in truth. But you may still ask, "What is my truth?" Truth needs nothing and does nothing. It merely remains hidden in your mind or recognized through the activation of miracles. To live in Spirit is quite simple. It requires only the will to do it and nothing more. Let go of your thinking and the thinking of the world. Your joy is found here. Heaven is experienced here. All that would release you from your self-made prison has its Cause, right here.

You can do anything you wish in the dream you see yourself in. You are not limited in any way, except by your own fearful choices. The happy dream is one of simplicity, Wayne. The nightmare is one of complication, intellect and separation. None of these attributes are really part of you. They are simply mistakes waiting for you to release them and nothing more. What "happened" to you when you were young caused a deep sense of feeling as though your mistakes were irreparable. Though you also had an experience that showed you that your mistakes were not irreparable, you still believe somehow that it may not be so. Let me reassure you, Wayne, that it *is* so. None of your mistakes have hurt you. None of what you have thought was irreversible ever was at all. As you gradually learn to accept this, you will understand better the real mission that I have in store for you.

You have many doubts. You even doubt what you are hearing here, on one level. Trust that I have no doubt in you, in your capabilities or in your ability to understand. Listen for my voice in the Voice for Love, Which I have been constantly leading you to.

You are on your spiritual path now. You need only step back and allow Spirit to lead the way. Remember that you need only unlearn what has blocked you from recognizing the great path you are on. You will very soon help many, many people. But do not try so hard to figure out for yourself what is next. I will send you everything you need to accomplish your healing. Let everyone you meet be a witness to your transformation. Here is a prayer designed just for you to help you on this new and bright journey:

"Today I will step back and allow Your Love to lead the way. I recognize my anger for what it is today, for it is an attack on the eternal peace You have given me. I choose anger because I believe that without it I will lose my way. I protect and justify my hatred because I do not wish to see What I truly am. I now realize I value only what can hurt me. Help me Father to learn how to truly forgive. I do not understand how to heal because I have forgotten that on my own I separate myself from everyone and everything. Let me see You in those I have seen as hurting me somehow. Today I will accept without judgment the lessons You have sent me to heal. I need nothing but the

recognition of Your eternal peace. I can be hurt only by my own unwillingness to change my mind about each situation as I see it. I see illusion, but You would set me free from them all. Show me how to trust so that I may feel safe once again. Remind me Father, that the peace of God is my one and only goal, for I can only depend on You."

Amen

Blessing you who have asked and heard,

Jesus

THE SPIRITUAL JOURNEY

As guilt is steadily washed away, the reliance on approach lessens. It becomes less necessary for the sincere student to rely on dogma, words and symbols as time winds down and eternity comes to take its place. The "things" of the world slowly but surely are given up as a means to "heal." They are seen for what they really are — obstacles to awakening and peace. No longer are other bodies and substances given "special value." Instead of being sought to fulfill an ego-need, they are recognized as merely alluring distractions. They are not judged or depended on.

Vision begins here. The student is now becoming a true teacher of God. She or he, having given up the insane will of the ego — the sight of separation and devastation — is now almost prepared for a completely different experience. Instead of looking for others and things to provide some form of comfort, others will be drawn to him/her at just the perfect time, as if by magic. Together, their small "needs" will be met. As unification becomes more stable, they will find great abundance everywhere. Each one, both separately and together, will instinctively ask the "Teacher within" for what is next, what is best to further an already immense joy that is rising through them. The true spiritual journey has begun. Many miracles will follow. The world is yet to sing the songs of peace again!

As the teacher's spiritual commitment deepens into one of nearly total trust in his Self and God and all his relationships begin to transform, the purpose of the world must shift as well.

The recognition of the Christ-Self in all sisters and brothers has the power of Christ's holy Vision. This power comes from God, exceeding and transcending all the laws of the world and all space and time. This is the goal we have been seeking. Here is the Will of God met. There will be no turning back now, and much to rejoice in and look forward to.

A Scribing for Paul

Dear Joel,

> *My questions are:*
>
> *1) Can you comment on the guru/disciple relationship as I am currently involved with Siddha Yoga, which grows out of that tradition?*
>
> *2) I will be turning 39 soon and I'm going through a lot of grief as I realize many of the things I wanted have not come about. I'm very confused as to what to do with my life. What direction can you give me? How best can I serve God? What is my personal dharma?*
>
> *3) I feel a deep mystical connection with my pet. What is the role of animals and spirituality?*
>
> *4) I go through periods of profound loneliness. I find it difficult to open up to women and begin relationships. What can I do to foster intimacy in my life? It feels very painful to do so at this time.*
>
> *The way I see my life now is one of seeking and working toward emotional healing. I feel I have something to say. I am a creative person with talents that can be used. I like to sing, write and perform. Although I'm not sure how, I feel I have something to offer. I realize there is something to be said for letting go and allowing grace to work in our lives, but I'm terribly confused about the footwork I need to be doing.*
>
> *Thank you.*

Greetings Paul:

I am gladdened and honored that you have been willing to ask these questions of me today. Let us begin.

The very fact that you are choosing to follow a conscious spiritual path in your life means that you have been willing to let much of what the world values go. This leaves you in a position to be critiqued by others more than if you were involved in a major religion more typical to your culture. It is not so much that they will critique you; it is that you may be more tempted to critique yourself.

In choosing to follow a spiritual path, the ego is more threatened because it knows that if you choose Spirit over it, it would simply cease to exist. The ego does not like this, so it will find as many insidious ways as possible to "protect" itself. The ego will do this by telling you that you are different or that others cannot possibly understand you or even that you are on the wrong path! It will tell you many things, all designed to confuse you, thus keeping fear in charge and the ego "alive." It may seem at times that you are being critiqued or others are separating from you, when in fact it is the ego fighting for its "survival." Do you understand this, Paul?

All you have been studying will bring more peace of mind to you in the long run. The ministry I once performed was partially based on the exact studies you are using. There is a temporary hazard, however, whenever one remembers and becomes a minister of God. Others may pray to him instead of to the one God he is ministering for. There were many times I had to remind my own disciples that it was not me they were to worship, but only the Christed Self, at one with God, created by God and living in all humankind.

You are equal to me in all ways and all abilities. If you were to idolize me in any form, you may be tempted to invent a religion that is tainted by a confusion between body and Spirit. If you look carefully at the world you seem to be experiencing now, it is tainted and corrupted by such religions that wish only to glorify the body. I am still seen by many as a body nailed to a cross. I find this most distasteful, since I came to teach just the opposite. You and I are not bodies at all. Nor can we be limited by the "nails" that at times may seem to crucify us. Nothing about the body is holy or demonic. It is simply a tool. Of itself it is entirely neutral, value-less and meaningless. Its value lies only in what it can be used to obtain. If it is used to obtain a form of idolatry or anything that would give power to the physical in any form, then the body has not been recognized by the mind for what it truly is, an illusion.

In truth there is but one Guru, and that is God. Each of you are His/Her disciples, just as I am. Not one of you living in the world is greater than another because God created you the same. It is impossible that What God created be altered or changed in any way. Only the ego can change and the ego is not real. You will either recognize God or the ego as your "self," but never both at once. If you believe you are only the ego, you are believing in nothing. You do not need to believe in God because God is fact. Simply by being still and knowing God as your Self can you recognize What you indeed *have* and *are*.

Belief is an ego function, not a function of the Creator. Desire, on the other hand, is creative because God desired you, and so you are. If you desire to know only Love, then you are acting in accordance with God's Will. Love *is* your Self and has no physical boundaries or limitations. Whatever tries to limit Love is fear, and fear can only be felt in association with the body. It is difficult for you who live in the world not to glorify the body at times. The world was made to hide the face of Christ. That is its purpose, its only "function."

The guru is one who knows this simple secret. She/he has recognized the utter impossibility of the "reality of the world," and so she/he teaches only the final lesson she/he learned — all glory to God, Creator of Love and the Christ (Self) that is Her/His eternal Creation. The disciple is one who has not yet learned this lesson completely, but who is willing to learn from one who has. It appears that there is a difference between guru and disciple in the worldly sense. In truth the guru is no different from the disciple, for without a holy relationship there could be no recognition of God by either. The disciple, then, is the miracle the guru sees *as* her/his Self, while the guru is the miracle the disciple seeks *in* himself. The only temporary difference between the two is that one seeks what the other has already found in the seeker. Without each other, then, there could be no discovery by either of the Treasure they each equally share. For to know Thy Self as God created you, you must recognize It equally in everyone. It is in this recognition and joining that the disciple and guru are finally made One — the Eternal Christ, the "Sun" of God.

My Light I share with you, Paul, for It must be shared for It to be recognized. The Light in you is created only for this purpose.

This is your dharma. It is everyone's dharma! God is a God of pure innocence, Light and joy. The world was made as a place to hide this wonderful recognition from your sight. You can give it a new purpose: To remember your one and only true conviction — the conviction of the Heart of Love in you and everyone. Now, with each lesson learned, your remembrance of your Self grows ever stronger.

It is through your relationships that you will find God or lose God, even though in truth it is impossible to really lose Him/Her. Yet it is quite possible to forget. The purpose of your life may seem to have many directions with many desires. I tell you Paul, it has only one — to remember the Light from which you came. You cannot remember the pure and most holy Love you came from without participating in the function God gave you to accomplish this. Your only function is to forgive the world and all you have ascribed to it and yourself.

I do not mean by this that you leave the world and go sit in a cave and meditate. Many who have sat in darkness and looked for the Light in it have not found It. Light is found only by overlooking darkness, thereby recognizing that darkness does not in truth exist. If you bring the Light to darkness, the darkness will disappear. You can shine away illusions with truth, but you can never bring truth to your illusions. Yet you cannot find the Light of truth and keep It without your relationships.

Each relationship is brought to you for the purpose of remembering the truth. Not one relationship has ever come to you that you have not asked for and chosen. The ones that seem fearful to you, you have asked for so you could recognize your illusions and heal them. The ones that are loving to you are the ones you have allowed only truth and Light to rest on. The latter represent your holy relationships, the ones that you have given entirely to God and which demonstrate beyond a shadow of a doubt how mighty the power of Love is in you both. You will gain strength, faith and conviction in your true Self through these relationships. The former represent the doubt, the fear, the hatred, the judgment and all the illusions that you still believe to be "real" in yourself.

It is these relationships, the ones that seem somehow despicable or frightening, that will ultimately bring you the recognition experientially that your fears, guilt and blame were never justified; that in fact your misjudgments about them were never true. That is why the yogi invites the demons to come into the cave and have tea with him. He does not fear what fear seems to tell him because he knows it will help clear the path to God. It is this "risking" that the world has worked so hard to avoid. You have been taught to avoid risks and hide in the cave. Yet by doing this, the outcome can only be depressing, for the choice to avoid the "enemy" is the choice to place your Self out of your own heart. Your enemies are by far your best teachers, for the "enemy" is truly only your belief that you are somehow separate from God.

That is why ultimately you must learn that there are no special or "better" relationships. Not one brother or sister who walks in this world is any less or more a teacher to you than if God Himself were to come down and walk beside you. All relationships have the potential to be holy ones. Until they become as such, they remain as special love or hate relationships, which are either idolistic or conditional. When you are willing to take the risk with whatever areas in your life that make you fearful about a relationship, you will find the gift of healing that far surpasses even your wildest dreams!

Intimacy, my dear brother Paul, is your willingness to take that risk, jump off the cliff of fear and discover the joy of God together! It is nothing more or less than what I have just described. Yet the ego will tell you that intimacy will reveal your secrets to another, who will eventually use them against you. And the ego is right on behalf of the other ego's it represents, for the ego fully believes that your illusions about yourself are "real." Indeed, you believe that, if you reveal your secrets, you would be revealing a horrible weakness that, once known, would consume you. It would *if you* were the ego's child, but you are not. Everything the ego holds in secret will disappear in the twinkling of an eye when it has been willingly witnessed to and brought to Light! Your relationships are there for you only to reveal the eternal in you. That is your purpose: To know and experience joy! But you cannot do this until you are willing to bring what is *not* joy to light. This involves pain, but only to the degree that you resist the risk. When an illusion is brought truly to Light by two people joined in one purpose and one function, only holiness and happiness pervade!

Not all your intimate relationships will be successful in your eyes. To the degree you feel let down when a lover leaves you, to that degree you have not come to terms with Where your only true dependency lies. Each of you seem to leave relationships at times, leaving the other to feel abandoned with their secrets exposed and their hearts broken. This happens only because you have forgotten Where all true happiness lies. You have chosen to make illusions reality and Reality an illusion. The body and the world have become more important than God. That is why with all relationships it is essential to know Where true Love is. If you lose sight of It, of course, the relationship must seem to fail. Yet no relationship can ever really fail, for all that was shared through Love will live in you forever. Essentially that is all a relationship can ever be — all that you share *in Love*. The rest, my dear Paul, is but a dream.

I will repeat this and urge you to listen. Your purpose here is to find a joy that is not dependent on the world or the things and bodies outside you. In no way can you experience this joy as long as you place value where value does not belong. Your function in this world is healing through your willingness to take the risk and *forgive* what you *think* you see in others or yourself. It is always your Self you are forgiving. Each person you attract will offer you an opportunity to do this. If instead you project and place blame outside you, you will make it seem impossible to heal. The choice you have is only between these two: Love or fear. The choice for fear is only a choice to wait a little longer for the final and only choice, which is Love.

Indeed, Paul, it is painful not to foster intimacy. You came here to love and to love with all your heart, just as God loves you! Do not deny God's Gift to you. It was given you so that you could know His/Her peace. Do not be afraid to love, for the fear will only weary you. Listen to what your heart is telling you, Paul. Let your heart, not your mind, take the journey to Love for you!

Finally, I will speak to you of the animals. It is hard, perhaps, for you to believe that you brought the animals here with you. But you did! They play as important a part in healing as do people. They are part of the Divine. Just like you, they seem to have a body, but that is not what they are. They are perfect reflections of Love or hate, whichever you make of them. Whatever you see in them is what you believe is true in you. Some people have pets just to punish, because that is what they believe they must do to themselves. And the pets even punish them back! How is that for instant gratification? Domesticated animals are very shiny mirrors in most cases.

When they are not, it is usually because they have been abused.

Wild animals are just that — wild. You placed them here that way and it is a good idea to leave them in their environment as you made it for them. Most important, you can see your Self (Christ) in an animal. The Divine Mind is present in all life. You can also speak with them, but not so much in words. They hear you and you hear them in the same way as you communicate with God, which is through the energy of Love. When you are really out of alignment with the energy of Love, your animals will be the first to know. That is because they are not blocked by ego. Listen carefully and quietly. You will hear God speaking to you through the animals and all that nature offers you. Most of all, Paul, let them teach you how to be gentle with yourself.

Ask for guidance in all decisions, Paul. I will be there always, holding your hand.

My message to you:

Listen for the Voice for God everywhere, for you

will hear It each time you take the risk to be healed.

Glory and peace be to you who have asked and received.

Love to you, Jesus

Two or More

The power over life and death lies in your holy mission to join together. Yet as much as it appears that joining is of bodies, joining can only be of minds. How can one recognize that this is so as long as thoughts of the body and the world are held so tightly? In this confused state it must seem impossible that two minds could be of one Mind. All of the grief and separation of an entire world comes from here. It is this thinking, then, that must be recognized for what it is and forgiven. Love can enter only where freedom is offered and imprisonment is cherished not. A mind that is free shines its Light into other minds. Not a word need be said, for only a mere glance is enough to illuminate a stranger's heart, bringing a smile and sure recognition that peace has surely come.

When you look out upon the world, do you see your Self in all His glory? Or do you see instead fragmentation, separation and division? One sight makes no attempt to define, while the other makes definition its preoccupation and obsession. Vision *always* sees only the whole, while the ego picks through the rubble of its many, many conflicts, stirring more confusion and leading you to nowhere. Only sickness can result from such an ideological and complex view. Life is One, never many, as your Self is undefined and never limited. Your Self is manifest, then, as Love expresses through and to Itself.

Your natural state is one in which all judgment and thinking are suspended. Only in this state can you know your brother and sister *as* your Self. By the world's standards, this is idiocy. To the ego, it is incomprehensible that you might find a way to live without it. Yet the Holy Spirit knows that you can't be truly happy until you *do* live without it. I am one with the Holy Spirit, just as you are. The only difference is that I learned that my Self was *all* I wanted or needed, and that the world was *nothing at all.* You are still apt to become confused about what you need and don't need, believing at times in the dreams you have made. This is why you *do* need me, because I stand *only* with Christ in you. I can lead you then to the still water of your Self.

If you are not joyous, it is because you have once again allowed the ego to define reality *for* you. By choosing to side with this interpretation, you close your mind to the experience of uniting with another. You must learn that, not only is joining the most important aspect of your spiritual discipline, it is the *only* goal which will bring lasting peace. *You have not come here for yourself alone.* That is the ego's wish. You came here to share and recognize Christ together. *That is God's Will.* What is humbling to the ego is of grandeur to you. When you stop thinking, you will see how grand you really are. You will know I am *in* you, just as everyone else is. What you are is a part of an unbroken chain which reaches past all time into forever. *The eternal has no fear.* No longer is Life confused with death and death with Life. You are safe with me in Christ, Who is our Self forever. Cherish our unification with God, our Creator, and remember always the holiness from Where we come. Give only the recognition of this holiness to everyone, thereby you will know it as your Self. Abide in this blessing always.

A SCRIBING FOR CAROL

*My name is Carol and I was born at 8:34 a.m. on 11/24/73 in
Milwaukee, Wisconsin. I have attached my five questions for you.*

They are as follows:

1) *Why have I had such a terrible time learning the lessons I
   need to learn?*

2) *There have been many illnesses/losses in my family recently.
   Is this just a transitional phase or will it be continuing for a
   long period of time?*

3) *I have always been drawn to relationships with "spiritual"
   men, yet they never seem to work out. Am I blocking
   something?*

4) *My employment situation has been unstable for almost three
   years. I have exceptional skills and am easy to get along with,
   but don't feel I've come across the proper vocation. Will this
   happen soon and if so, what can I do to facilitate it?*

5) *How can I strengthen my own spirituality?*

Thank you for your assistance!

Greetings Carol:

This is Jesus, and I am gladdened to speak with you through
my brother Joel. We have spoken many times before, but not
quite this way.

I would first remind you that you are safe, since this has been
an outstanding issue for you recently. It is difficult in this world
you see yourself in not to be deceived by "appearances." It may
appear to you that many have suffered, including yourself in
recent situations. Indeed, by the world's standards you have!

Look carefully, however, and you will see what has become
of your own suffering and the suffering of others. The outcome is
as sure as God. You are learning, however long it takes you, that
only *appearances cause you to suffer,* for they are not dependable.
In your own suffering you are learning day by day to turn more
and more to the Eternal in you. The conflict that you feel is simply
a result of your turning more and more away from the world. The

ego "survives" on turmoil and conflict. The more you move away from its thinking, the more it will try to find answers to needless questions that are impossible to answer. In every situation where you find conflict, I could tell you simply to choose Love. But that does you little good. *You* must decide for *yourself* what is valuable. Whatever you decide, you *will* act on. What you act on determines your path to eventually find God. It is that simple. Yet watch your thoughts carefully, because the paths are many and not all of them are as easy as others.

Your path will be as easy as you make it. If it is hard for you, it is only because you are still placing value in the valueless. You have been taught all your life that values belong in the world of things and bodies. It has become "second nature" to you to form an opinion based on beliefs that were *taught* to you many years ago. You can believe in God all your life and not *know* Her at all. Beliefs constitute wrong valuing. Beliefs are what made the world *the world*. I have come to help you undo your beliefs, thereby undoing the world *with* you. I would only ask that you remember this when you feel dismayed. I will be there to guide you away from depression and into the joy of Heaven.

Lessons are learned easily if you remember that the ego is already dead. All you learned and experienced here has only been to help you return to God. You cannot take your experiences to Heaven, but you can and *must* allow Heaven into your experience. You do this as soon as you abandon your self-made thought system and place the Holy Spirit in charge. Again, the question arises, "What do you value (or want)?" Those who have "died" recently are well within your reach right now. You are contained in God with them and me. As soon as you exchange illusion for truth, you cannot help but see me and them with you, always.

Most of you who have begun studying *A Course In Miracles* will encounter difficulties for a while. But this is only because you are being introduced to a thought system that is in direct opposition to the ego's. Making this shift is difficult because you are being asked to let go of old beliefs, in fact, *all* beliefs. Valuing comes from believing. Yet to value only Love is a statement that you are willing only to be still and *know God*. To be still, Carol, does not mean that you sit in a cave and meditate your life away. Stilling the mind is all we are concerned with here. It is quite possible to have a still mind even in the face of "death." A lesson is not properly learned until the right choice is made in whatever experience you are dealing with, no matter how great or small. The choice is limited to the world or God, fear or Love.

Your "lessons" are not ones you will learn through guilt. Each time you learn a "hard lesson," you are likely to repeat it. Hard lessons occur when the teacher is fear, not Love. In the loss of a loved one the ego might dictate, "Oh, you are guilty of never spending time with her when she was alive, etc." Yet this same situation taken to the Spirit of Love in you would instantly reveal to you that you are *forever* with this loved one and that time cannot interfere with this eternal relationship. Whenever you feel afraid that your lessons are in vain, ask me for help and I will certainly direct you to your Safety. You need not feel afraid of loss or death, for I am not lost and neither are you or your loved ones. Ask truly, with your heart, and I *will* answer.

There will always be losses in the ego's perception, but I would remind you that loss of anything real is impossible. I would be doing you a disservice if I were to inform you of future "losses." But I will tell you that if you are truly willing to learn the lesson of Love that is given you in this period of your life, lessons that follow will offer you only gain. Be happy, Carol, that nothing of Love is ever lost!

Grief is a normal part of your life. It teaches you what is worthy and what is not worthy. You learn from your grief that you are the Daughter of God! But beware not to keep a heavy heart and a stiff upper lip. Let the grief flow like a river into a pool of Light within you. It is here your grief will be undone and transformed to joy! There in the pool you will find all you have ever held dear. Do not be afraid of loss and death, for it is but an illusion of the mind. The dear ones who were close to you in the flesh are ever closer now. Speak with them. Pour out your heart to them. I will be there, holding each of your hands.

Just as you are going through many changes since the onset of your studies, so are the "spiritual men" in your life. Many who claim to be spiritual are not as far along in understanding as the supposed atheist. It is best not to place faith in ideas presented, but instead in actions. The actions do not determine what the person is, but they do reflect what that person believes he is. The best you can hope for is someone who is sincere in their willingness to listen and be flexible. These attributes determine that the student has accepted his/her role in the spiritual realm. As they become spiritual, many struggle with jobs and family life. This is because they are receiving glimpses that their material life can never be completely stable, no matter how they try. As they adjust and learn to laugh at the trivial, they will become stable in God. Once the process of becoming stable in God is mostly completed, you will notice that they become lovable and laugh all the time. These are effects that require no action on their part. They will be creative, make mistakes, but they will not take life so seriously. They have found the eternal. How will you find such a mate? Let us say, "Light attracts Light." Be patient, but seek the Light in you first. All else will fall into place when it is time.

You are entering a period of sorting out your values. The struggle you are having with work and relationships reflects this. You have had jobs that have not fulfilled you. Now you are asking why. Certainly you can have a fulfilling job and relationship! All you need do is follow your heart. But you haven't been quite able to accept this one fact. Is there something lurking within your belief system that is telling you secretly that you are not worthy; or telling you that you will never get what you really want? These are your blocks. Here is where your healing is needed, Carol.

It is indeed interesting that you have asked lastly how you can strengthen your spirituality. If you were to strengthen your spirituality first, all your other questions would answer themselves! Your relationships are the door to your spirituality. The key lies within you at the Altar to God. Without the key, the door will not open. If the door does not open, you must find the key. Remember these words, though they may sound passé. When you forget and seem to struggle again, look within for *the key*.

Your dreams are never impossible, Carol. They are but dreams and they can seem be *anything* you want! Give them to me and I will bring them to the Holy Spirit to undo them for you. Remember that all you see is but a dream of where you have placed value and made your dreams "real." They are not. But you, my dear Carol, are the Daughter of God forever! Let the angels God has sent you surround you in Light and go on. Carry them with you and hold them close to your heart always. I am with you as well, holding your hand, asking only that you let me help you in your decisions. Be still and know that we are together in the Heart of Love. Blessed are you who have asked. I have answered as He has given me to do.

In glorious and shining Light forever,

Jesus

THE PRACTICE OF HEALING

We have spoken about the meaning of true healing. We are now ready to discuss healing in very practical terms. This *is* what this material is to help you understand and *apply*.

Healing is *not* theoretical. It is emotionally experiential. The word emotion is correctly applied here to a mental shift from fear to Love. The *only* true emotion is that of God's Love, the Love from which we come. Only by coming into the awareness of Love's Presence can one *be* healed and recognize that she *is* healed.

You cannot recognize that you are healed as long as you *believe* that there is still something to do. It is difficult at first to understand that *unlearning is true learning*. What the world refers to as "learning" is not really learning at all, but merely the "practice of insanity." This does not mean that you will not do the things in your life that you do when you are healed. It means only that you will do them without reluctance or strain. The healed mind understands that happiness never comes from doing but from undoing. Looking for a home, for example, seems to be an act of doing. Yet is it the searching for the home that brings lasting joy or the final happy discovery that the perfect Home was right there all the time, waiting to be "found"? A shelter for the body can never bring lasting joy. But an understanding of Where your real Shelter abides can. To understand this requires relinquishment of your judgment of appearance in the present. In this understanding you *can* experience joy in anything you do. By this, *doing* is not given credence over What you already *have* and *are*.

To heal we need only be concerned with the *undoing* of the ego's entire thought system and your own misguided dependency on it. The ego *is* the part of your mind that analyzes, defines, criticizes and judges. The ego depends on symbols, words and theory. These are *not* healing because, being symbolic, they contain no *agent* for healing. The Agent for healing is always within you and can never be contained in mere symbols alone. Symbols, however, can lead you away from Spirit or toward It, but because they are only symbols they are open to misinterpretation. This is one reason why you may read these words one day and have a pleasurable experience and the next day have an experience that is resistive.

It is *not* words I want to emphasize. It is the message behind the words. If you can trust Where I am leading you, words and symbols will become obsolete in your experience of healing. As you think with the ego, words will seem to attack or inflate the image you hold of yourself. As you heal with me, the Agent for healing, deflation or inflation will simply become meaningless. Healing releases you from all images *and* the thinking that made it. By accepting healing you are relinquishing all false underpinnings and inviting your own true Identity to take Its rightful place in you. By accepting your own Inheritance, you are accepting It for everyone. Love is your Inheritance and you are Love.

See, then, your glorious Inheritance everywhere. Christ cannot be described, but *only* experienced. He can be heard, but *not* by the body's ears. He can be seen, but *not* by the body's eyes. How, you may ask, are you to know when vision has truly come? *By the fruits of your relationships*, for this is *all* healing is *for*.

There *is* no other goal in healing than the undoing of fear. By offering release from fear and guilt to everyone, you offer yourself freedom as well. *Freedom* is the only state in which you can recognize the Self you share with your sister and brother, for Christ *is* your true freedom from all illusion the ego has made.

The fruits of your relationships will always offer either freedom or imprisonment. Salvation is the easiest and most natural thing in the world to offer everyone, once its complete simplicity and effectiveness are understood. But in order to understand, it must be fully realized that healing is *not* of this world. Nothing you can do on your own can provide the peace and safety that you long to embrace. Sickness is but a form of the very belief that you *can* do something alone. Child of God, which do you prefer? Would you not be willing to join me, with your brothers and sisters, to make all hearts glad?

The time for gathering is upon you! Waste not another moment and give what God would have you offer. Her joyous fruits are yours to offer everyone *now*. Glory be to God in the highest. The Kingdom is come and Love is the Gift He brings.

A SCRIBING FOR MARK AND MARVENE

Dear Joel and Jesus,

My girlfriend Marvene and I would like help with some questions that we are struggling with right now. Our first question is in regard to Marvene's mother who died June 9th. She had been living with Marvene for 12 years and the three of us lived together for five. During the duration that I knew her, she was unhappy much of the time and was, to a degree, a "pain" to us. We both loved her dearly; yet we both felt burdened by her presence.

Now that she has made the transition, Marvene has at times felt concerns that her mother may still be needing her and that she continues to be unhappy. As for myself, I have grieved for her like I have for no one else and seem to alternate between acceptance and depression.

1) *What can you tell us to help us in our growth and learning in this above situation?*

2) *We are both tired of our jobs and have embarked on a new business that we believe will help other people in their health and financially as well. Are we on the right path?*

3) *Here's a question that is nonspecific, but asks for specifics. Is there anything that He wants us to know to help us in our growth?*

God bless you,

Mark and Marvene

Greetings Mark and Marvene:

Be aware as you both read this that the message you are hearing from me is truly only coming through you. As you hear my words, recognize also the intent and experience of the guidance I am offering you. I have but one purpose in mind for you both and that is healing. In gentle listening, let us go on.

It is not Marvene's mother whom you need be concerned with, but only your judgment *of her*. Odd as it may seem, many of you are quite happy living in misery. Without misery many of you would have nothing to look forward to. Look at your own lives and see what misery might be doing for each of you. There is a payoff for feeling miserable that you would both do well to look at carefully. The payoff is that you don't have to be responsible; you don't have to feel and be conscious; indeed, you don't have to risk or love when in the presence of your misery. Misery "protects" you from growth and going forward and from joining with one another in a common purpose. As you well know, there is but one common purpose we all share and that is healing.

The pain you both saw in your mother was a direct reflection of your own pain and your unwillingness to acknowledge the depth of suffering within yourselves. I realize this may be difficult for you to hear. The suffering and unhappiness you saw in her was not in her at all, but was part of your "shared" illusion. What a gift she bestowed upon each of you! Her pain was your pain, but even more so, it was *the* pain.

The purpose of *A Course In Miracles* is not to teach any of you to pretend pain is not there. You cannot simply overlook suffering and choose only Love while pain is still lingering within you. I have asked you all to bring your suffering to me and to join together with this purpose in mind. I will see that it is removed from your minds and hearts, but first you must acknowledge what the experience of pain has cost you. This is a risk that you find very difficult to take.

It is odd that two people, who have lived so closely together for so many years and appear to many others to be joined together in purpose, could seem so far apart from each other. In many ways this is what you face with those you have been so seemingly close to in your lifetime. It is the unforgiven pain in each of your close relationships that has set you apart — the "secrets" you hold against one another or against one who has "wronged" someone who is dear to you. It is, as well, a secret belief that some are unworthy of the time to join with or that you are unworthy of joining with another whom you deem "further along." Whatever the belief is that cost you your peace and true happiness, you can be assured there was first judgment and then a seeming separation of hearts and minds. It is there where you will find the beginning of healing or the continuance of separating thinking and painful experience.

The vacillation you each feel in regard to your mother's passing will continue until you choose to embrace the part of her that made you feel so uncomfortable. The pain she felt is identical to your own. It is *the pain*. Although this suffering is not a real part of any of you, it will continue to feel real until it is fully embraced with Love. From the ego's standpoint this may be seen as painful and treacherous, but from the standpoint of your Self it will be a glorious healing and joining into the Oneness you share. For every past moment that you failed or forgot to love one another completely, you will grieve in the present until you take the risk to be healed. Every time that you have seen a need for healing in another, you have forgotten the need for healing in yourselves. This is the only place for healing, for what is outside you does not exist. Who, then, needs anyone, except your Self?

Healing is done only on an experiential level, Mark and Marvene. In the truest sense, you are each already healed. But the fact that you don't know this is clearly an indication that healing has not entirely taken its rightful place in your hearts. A thinking mind cannot experience anything that is real. It can, however, be taught to seek an experience of healing. In this process the thinking mind is released to me by your will. Through this release, Ownership of God's Oneness takes the place of self-authorship. This is when you will reunite with your mother. Her Light remains within you; her Self shares our Own.

Can there be unhappiness in Heaven? Is it not easier for both of you to believe she is somewhere else? She is not. She is right here, right now, within you both. Look within to her. Speak with her as you speak with me. Ask her why it was so hard for her. And ask her many other questions from your heart as well. She will answer in your emotions and your feelings, for it is her purpose now *to heal you*.

Regarding your occupation, you are on the right track as long as you both feel a sense that you are doing more than just "a job." There is no job that cannot be used on behalf of healing. But some occupations may serve both of you better to accomplish your true purpose in life. This does not mean you may not need to change what you are doing later. It is only essential for you each to feel you are genuinely offering peace and true help to yourselves and others. If this is not so, then change is perhaps needed. Also, if you feel as though you have lost sight of what is truly valuable, then again change may be needed. You do not really have to change your situation to re-find What is essential for your happiness. Still in all, most do go through changes because they are deepening their relationship with God. These changes you call "growth." In truth it is merely a giving up of lesser values for What is more essential to you. Someday your values will be entirely centered on giving and receiving only Love. When this occurs, all you now hold dear and see as your means for "good survival" will vanish before your eyes. It will not matter to you what you are doing because your only interest will be to constantly remember that, no matter what, you are already Home. When this happens you may find yourselves doing what you never dreamed of. You need only ask me what would be truly helpful now. I will guide you accordingly.

In answer to your last question, I would only remind you to focus not so much on the world but on healing. Your perceptions make the world as you see it. All of your troubles relate to the world and the body. Seeing your mother the way you have is only a misperception. This needs healing in you. The same holds true for your other questions. Misperception is indeed painful, for it dreams a world that seems to be real. Yet the Reality That you both want is in another World that is not based on perception. As long as you see through your perceptions, you will be misguided and you will experience repeated painful scenarios. This is not necessary.

If you will let go entirely of all the values you seem to see and believe in, you will be left with only the purpose of healing. No longer will you focus on the "problem" you seem to see outside you. You will no longer be powerless to change it, for you will see it is of your own mind's making. You may feel a void for a while as you learn to do this more consistently. It may seem to you that there is nothing to focus on or get upset over. This may trigger the ego at times and cause you to feel as though your "purpose" has been taken away. As the anger, fear and hatred arise in you, you will be faced with the responsibility of truly learning to forgive your own mistakes and the mistakes of others.

You will need my help and I will be there in your Heart of hearts to answer. Before you make judgments, ask me. Before you make a decision and act on it, ask me. I will guide you into a decision and action that is loving. Let your focus not be on the world, its thoughts or appearances, but only on the peace of God. This is what you really want, and you do have it now. Be still and know that I am with you, with God, forever. You need nothing more to understand. And one last message: Love each other always as you would love me. Blessed are you, the pure in heart, you who are called "Mark and Marvene."

Surrounded are you by God's angels,

For I have sent a message of Light to you…

Receive it thus, for it is yours forever…

Jesus

THE ONLY FEAR

Every practice and approach, whether spiritual or religious, has as its ultimate goal the coming to terms with the fear of death. Ironically the fear of death and the fear of God are one and the same. As healing takes its course, fear of either will surely slip away.

What is death but a relinquishment of the knowledge of Life? Where knowledge is absent, dreams have come to take its place. It is in dreams, laced with guilt and steeped in blame, that the Son of God sees himself in a living hell. Now has he blinded himself by a whirlpool of illusion and a "spiritual death" has come to claim the Light in him. To this God sends Her messenger to awaken him from his terror.

Death seems to be where life is not, but what is seen as life is actually a picture of death made to take Life's place. It is cherishing this picture that brings about all suffering and confusion. Until this dark picture is willingly released, the Son of God cannot really know Where he truly stands. Yet know he will, for the outcome is as sure as God.

Death is the only fear you need be willing to heal, child of eternal Love. All of your seeming hatred and fear come straight from here. The beliefs you hold about death are many, but the knowledge of God is only One. Seek beyond your beliefs and beyond everything you seem to now see. In the present, within its tiniest instant, comes an end to this ancient fear. Seek it now. In it, the Light must return!

A SCRIBING FOR JESSE

Our friend Jesse has lived with the active AIDS virus for over twelve years. He is one of the oldest living survivors, but became very ill the summer of 1996 and nearly said "good-bye" to us that year. While experiencing this sudden turn, he asked me to do this scribing. Jesse lives on, and is always "the Light of the world" for us all. He had no questions. The scribing begins...

Greetings Jesse:

It should come as no surprise to you that my guidance is available to you all of the time through your own heart and the hearts and minds of others. You have been receiving much of this recently intermittently through all of my channels.

Because you are experiencing confusion, it may seem difficult at times for you to distinguish what is coming from God and what is coming from another person's ego. This includes your own ego as well, Jesse, for in truth your own ego is really the only one you have to "contend" with, since it is only your own evaluating process that becomes confused. Yet you can hear me and the Voice for Love very easily if you remember this one fact and then choose to set it aside at least temporarily.

The messages you are getting from the ego at this time are messages of caution and mistrust. Even now the ego may be telling you to "be careful" of what you listen to, questioning whether or not this could truly be my voice that is speaking to you. The ego would have you believe that it is "healthy" to use such caution, teaching you that it is the best judge of what to listen to and what not to listen to. Yet this will only confuse you more. It is time to recognize that there is truly only One Voice to listen to and that Voice is the Voice for Love within you. Intellectually you know this is true. However, we are no longer interested in intellectual feats, fancy words or metaphysical theories. We are interested in fact. You cannot understand the journey you are embarking on through your intellect. All attempts the mind makes at trying to understand your process will only cause you more confusion and undo strain.

I stand at the end to help you bridge the gap between the ego and the Spirit of Love That we both share. Though I am using words that are understandable to your intellect (ego), I am also simultaneously guiding you away from your dependence on your own thinking. This you may at times perceive as painful or frustrating, but I assure you that if you are fully willing to let go of your belief in this prattle, you will experience my reassurances.

Hearing the Voice for God within you, Jesse, entails a shift from objective understanding to a loving experience. The mind can attempt to explain an experience or evaluate it after it happens, but it can never give you an actual experience of being loved. All the mind's attempts to do so only result in fear simply because the mind is looking to the past, not what is now. To "experience" fear is simply to experience nothing at all. When your mind experiences nothing, you become afraid because you feel devoid of contact with your Source. True experience involves any instant in which the mind is neutralized by the decision of the observer to choose another Mind. This entails a shift from past/future thinking to present Thought. The Thought of God cannot be experienced in words. Words are symbolic. Reality is Absolute.

That is why I said before that the world is but a dream. Dreams can be frightening unless they are first recognized as dreams and then exchanged for Reality. The happy dream is the dream that these two principles are applied: Recognition and exchange. You do not want anything your mind has to "offer." Your real Mind was given you in your Creation and you cannot change It. Merely accept It and the Gift of God's eternal Love will be recognized as yours forever.

Your tears come from all the times you have forgotten your Gift and chosen instead to place your mind in the grip of fearful thinking. Fearful thinking encompasses almost all thinking. Relinquishing the need to think at all is the only thinking capable of allowing you to experience a "happy dream." The happy dream is only a dream which you are gladly willing to recognize is just that — a dream and nothing more. You would hardly be wasting time trying to figure our your own thoughts if you knew they were all just dreams. In fact, you would laugh, knowing how silly the mind really is in its trying to figure out anything. You would not be attached at all. On the other side of what tears you have left to cry in your relinquishment of this world, you will find me and many others waiting for you. We will smile and even laugh with you upon your homecoming.

Oh no, you do not have to lose your body to have this experience! But you must let go of all attachment to your body if you would experience the eternal. It is impossible to experience the eternal and the ephemeral at the same time. Many have tried; all have failed!

Jesse, when it comes time for you to set your body down and go on, be assured that you will not do this in an undignified manner. You will not be afraid and in fact will be grateful to know that there is so much more. You will recognize that your occupation has grown, not lessened. You will see the gifts in all their glory that you have given to yourself and everyone. And you will give more than you ever dreamed possible. Oh yes, your responsibilities are growing, not lessening! But the difference is that your new responsibilities will not involve so much effort on your part. You will suddenly realize in one instant how futile the mind's attempts truly are at replicating reality through its thoughts and ideas. You will realize how wonderfully blissful and powerful it is to recognize Where the flow of Life really is. It is this last relinquishment that will bring you the full realization of eternal Life. Then you will know forever that you are One with Him Who sent you. You will hardly struggle when this happens. Oh no! You will be relieved and entirely grateful to the point of tears and laughter at the same time!

You are struggling, as most do at this time, with the idea of "saving" your body and somehow finding eternal life in your present world. Although you realize deep inside that this is only the ego struggling for its survival, it has confused you and made you think that there might be hope of staying here forever. I would only say this, Jesse: Would you prefer eternal life in hell or in Heaven? Trying to preserve the body's "life" here in the world is only a form of the ego's contract to keep you in hell. How can you be truly happy in the ever changing?

If you were to succeed in granting yourself eternal life here in the world, it would be equivalent to that of a child in kindergarten arrogantly demanding of his teacher to fail him just so that he could continue to play with a single toy he liked. How long would this toy keep this child happy? You of all people should know that things which begin as innocent toys later become dangerous weapons that can hurt and have the effect of setting you back. This is not what you really want, even though your mind may still insist it is.

On the other side, much like the world you now see yourself in, there is a crowd of many. Yet this crowd lives in blissful silence and oneness with their Creator, sending the Light they share to the many separated ones still in the world of illusion. This crowd is available to you now. They are your friends who seemed to depart but have never really left you. They share one Self with you. They are the Christ with me and you. They are You.

This whole thing about dying, Jesse, is the grandest illusion of all! Oh the drama the ego makes of this seeming "sacrifice!" Caskets, flowers, tears and blood. It all looks and appears that something horribly tragic has occurred. But appearances are only there to keep the deception alive. Remove the "sight" of what it "sees" and suddenly you realize nothing has happened at all! You are still here. But of course! Where can you go except to your Self, Which you never really left? Do you think it is any different when the body is laid down? No, you will still have your whole Self in Its full awareness of God and all His Glory. The difference is that you won't see the tragedies. You won't experience your "self" as separate from. I dare say that your power of choice is not taken away from you either. In fact, this power will become all the more apparent. You are quite capable of experiencing and re-experiencing many lifetimes if you so choose. Then it becomes a clear question of what you desire and from where.

Your escape from all conflict lies in your choice to be guided by only what you are experiencing in the eternal Present. I said earlier that to "experience fear" is really to experience nothing at all. Therefore, if you seem to be experiencing fear, you are denying your true experience with your own holy Self. To experience my reassurances, you only need be willing to bring all other "experiences" into question. They are not there, although judging by the pain you seem to feel, certainly in some way you are still believing that they are there.

You are not expected to deny your suffering, for this would only have the affect of keeping your mind on a merry-go-round, keeping the fearful thoughts or beliefs repressed and away from Light. All you need do is simply embrace your fears. Acknowledge them and witness to them. But be fully assured in your faith (which you have plenty of) that they are powerless to hurt you in any way. Beneath your fears is your Self, Which I share with you.

I do assure you, Jesse, this Life that we share is quite alive in us both forever!

You are the Way, the Truth and the Life. You are the purest of God's Love and you will never change this. This is all you have ever really wanted to experience and it is there forever. This is no play on words. This is not to reassure a poor soul who has lost his way. You are Reality. You cannot die. You are perfect. And you will live forever. How hard must you work to find that this is true, Jesse?

"Doing" is of the world, not of God. Thy Will is done. Yet "being" is the natural occupation of the children of God. All of the time you have spent not being has only cost you the experience of your Self as God created you now. I do not say this Jesse, to make you feel more guilt. You and I, and all of the children who have come to the world thinking to "live" a little while, have "experienced" a state of seeming separation. I say this to you only to point clearly to what is in need of final healing. It is those times when we have forgotten to love that we must forgive. It is those times that keep us here trying so hard to straighten things out that we still feel guilty about. It is the times when we forgot our oneness with our brothers and sisters and God. It is this unforgiveness that we use to hold a sword against our own throats and then crucify ourselves with. It is our belief that "God's Will is not done" that keeps us on our merry-go-round, cycling over and over again through lifetime after lifetime of pain.

There is but one way to correct a million years of grief and forgetfulness: The one holy instant in which our only goal becomes the peace of God for ourselves and every living thing. To deny the world completely is to choose God... completely. One instant spent in total recognition of our true experience, our only Reality, is enough to heal it all. Our Father gave each of us the power to heal the whole world in this single instant. That is the responsibility you are in the process of accepting. The ego-mind may fight this for a few short lifetimes, but Heaven will prevail.

"You are at Home in God dreaming that you are in exile." But this journey has not been in vain, for you are very close to obtaining the full awareness of your Creation. It will not be through thinking about, but merely accepting in full what God has given you. He has given you all.

You need not struggle unless you want to. Let me decide for you for God. I will take care of the ego and all its conflict if you will relinquish your control and your thinking to me. I will perform a series of miracles through you that will leave no question in your mind and heart as to Where your Reality is. I am the Christ in you. Your Self has no identity that this world is capable of understanding. I know this because I am your Self. All power comes through the Self we share in God.

Take my hand, Jesse. I am with you now. Do not be afraid to let go. I will hold you up. Pour your tears into me. I am here to heal you and make you one again with all Life. Your wish is to experience the purest of joy, and you will, even while you are still in this world. Your Identity is not an experience of fear. It is the experience of What you are. It cannot leave you, no more than I can. You have a purpose that I would have you fulfill for our Father in Heaven. That purpose is to bring the awareness of joy to all the ones who are still afraid. Not even crucifixion could prevent that function from being fulfilled. No body could stand between you and our Father's Will. Do not be afraid to bring me all your fears. In exchange I will fulfill the promise I made to you long ago. You will surely know with me the promise and experience of God's Eternal Safety and Love. My arms are open. My smile shines through to you.

Here is a prayer that I have sent for you. It is especially for you, Jesse, that you may know always I am gladdened for your great gifts to me and to our Father's children who need you so:

"Father, though my body is weak my Spirit soars to Your loving embrace. I do not need to be afraid of any loss because I know Your Great Comforter is here with me now. I hold the hand of Christ as I walk into Your Light, knowing that my safety is forever established in You. Show me each step to take as I listen to the gentle Voice for Love that is given me forever from You. Guide me, Father, away from physical sight into Your loving Vision. I do not know Your Will, but I will listen now, knowing that You will direct me away from doubt and into the sureness of Christ's Love. Let me be a channel for Your Perfect Peace, and may this bring Your healing to all the world. I would be still and hear only Your Voice, for Here is all my greatest longing fulfilled."

Amen

Jesse, one last message: We are wondrously happy on the other side. Don't take it all too seriously. There's really nothing serious about it, for we are one, Where no separation exists. Together we are forever.

Jesus

HEALING INTO LIFE

When you heal, you are healing into Life, not death! This needs to be repeated often to yourself, for you are apt to believe just the opposite. Your Life cannot be contained in your body or the ego. But as long as you are living by what the ego tells you, your "life" must be painfully limited. It is by these limits that the ego convinces you that you are bound to it. By binding yourself to its laws, you have made a false "self" that could never last. That is why the ego teaches you to fear "death." This is also why the ego teaches you to fear God. God is death to the ego. But God is only Life to you.

Could the clarity of the sun be marred by a mere speck of dust? This is what you suppose when you view your life through the shadowed sight of fear. You can never know your real Life until the shrieks and cries of the ego are silenced. Only through forgiveness and gentle blessing will this be so. In quiet peace your Self lives ever free in God, untarnished and unmarred by any act of treason the ego has declared. Fear not death of the body, holy child of eternal Love. What is the body truly but a little speck of dust? Be not deceived any longer by belief in frail limitations. There is nothing that could contain eternal holiness because nothing could destroy What you always are forever.

A SECOND SCRIBING FOR RHONDA

1) I have been experiencing doubt in myself where I'm putting up resistance to my healing. How can I learn to let go and let God? I have put up these blocks and I want to know how I can overcome them. Its very frustrating living with MS, which I feel is getting worse. I am trying to live in the present, but my ego pulls me into the past or an imagined future. I know you will direct me to an answer.

2) What is to become of my relationship with my ex-husband, Jeff?

Greetings Rhonda:

It is from the Heart we live in *together* that I come to share with you today.

You have asked how it is you might learn to "let go and let God." My dear Rhonda, surely there is no real choice in the matter, now is there? The "choice" to hold on is merely the choice to suffer needlessly. The ego does not want to hear this, for it believes your solution lies outside you in bodies and in the world. On the contrary, this is the cause of all your suffering!

Suffering does not come from pain in the body, for that is merely a *physical effect*. Suffering comes from what *you think alone*, as healing comes from the Thought of Love that *is* you. Perhaps you do not realize the power of thought. Yet one need only look at whatever their experience in life seems to be in order to understand better what their own thinking has done. You have built a whole world out of your own thinking. Is this the world you would really wish to have and keep? If you answer this in full honesty, then another World can be given you in exchange for the one you have been carrying on your shoulders so long. *You* do not have to die to have this, but the part of your thinking that is keeping you in hell does. Would the World of eternal Love not be a better "choice" in lieu of what the ego's world has offered you?

Dear Rhonda, *all* of your answers to *all* of your questions wait for your quiet recognition of eternal Love. Your fears about death as well as your fears about life will all end as you gladly awaken to God's gentle Gift to you. You have nothing to lose *but* fear, Rhonda. The sooner you are willing to do so, the better.

Here is a meditation for you to practice:

There is no expression but the Thought of Love.

Begin this exercise by first closing your eyes and repeating the idea slowly to yourself a couple of times. Now sit quietly, observing the different thoughts that rise into your awareness. Imagine the back of your eyelids to be a giant blackboard that you cannot see over from where you sit.

Now imagine yourself writing each of the thoughts that come to you onto this blackboard. Do not hurry to write your thoughts, but simply allow them to come as they do. The blackboard will begin to fill fairly quickly if you are doing the exercise properly. These are the thoughts that bind you to a world made of fear. Like those on the blackboard, they are dark indeed.

Above the blackboard and on the other side, you notice a silent but steady Light. Something about this Light seems to emanate a sense of quiet happiness and safety. You cannot fully see it because the words on the blackboard are keeping you preoccupied. Yet the Light steadily calls you, as if to be your life-force, your fountain of creativity. You must touch this gentle and radiant Essence, but how?

Finally, unsure how to reach It, you ask, "How may I come into this serene and gentle Light?" You are answered immediately by a soft, fatherly Voice from the other side of the partition, "Erase the words from the blackboard and quietly step over. The Light will surely receive you!"

As you do this, be aware that you are erasing all need to think about anything, for only by doing so may you enter fully into this wonderful Light state. Gently erase the blackboard now.

There is no hurry; the Light will not leave from where it remains. Now step into this Light, where all minds are truly joined. There are no words here, but the experience is profoundly blissful. You have found your Home.

I am waiting here for you to take your hand. Reach to me as I reach now to you. As you take my hand, we take the hands of everyone, completing a Circle of Love so vast there are no borders anywhere. Only Light, only joy, only peace, only perfection. Welcome to your Self! Now, very quietly, say to yourself:

> *I am the expression of God's Thought and Love.*
> *Let my Self shine silently through,*
> *That It may love as me now.*

Relax into this place that is your Home, Rhonda. Heaven is available to you now and at anytime. God promises you that you must live even after the shrieks of the ego are abandoned. Do not be afraid to leave it for the Light. Your life will come full circle when you do. It seems just the opposite, does it not? But do not be frightened; it is *not* so. Your Life has been ongoing, never ceasing, just as God created It to be. Dear Rhonda, your tears of fear and sorrow can so easily be changed to tears of blissful joy! You need only remember to erase that blackboard of fear and walk into the Light with me. What is there that eternal Love cannot overcome? Nothing. Nothing at all dear one. Nothing at all.

All healing comes from the remembrance of God. Your one task, like everyone else's, is to remember, having forgotten. The world was made to hide Love from you. The only healthy relationship you will ever have with the world will be when you are entirely willing to *let it go.* This is why you must eventually choose to change your sight to vision. This must be your choice, since it was your decision in the first place to believe in separation. Vision always overlooks the world to see What you have and are now. It does not see through definition, but in wholeness. This may seem impossible. Yet I tell you, not only is it possible, it is the most natural thing you can do. How hard can it be to overlook what is not there? In quiet, you can learn how the body and the world are really nothing and discover that eternity *is everything.*

Do you want the peace of God more than anything in this world, my dear one? You can have it, for it is yours already. The past is gone and the future will never be. What future can illusion hold? And what is not now that will not be always? Look to *now,* then, Rhonda, for that is all there is. Waste no time listening to what seems to be behind you or ahead of you. *It is not here.* Nor can it ever be. The eternal waits patiently for you. It *is* but an instant away. How wonderful is the Gift God has given you! Will you receive it? In all It's splendor, It is the glorious Gift I came to share *with* you.

The imagined attempt to live in the future or the past is merely the ego's attempt to preserve itself and keep you sickened. Do not abide its wishes! You cannot overcome your illness by remaining frustrated or afraid of it. By doing so you are looking straight at sickness and proclaiming it real. This can only have the effect of reinforcing what you hope to abandon. If sickness is to heal, truly you must look *only* to where health abides. From here healing extends. This is how minds and bodies miraculously heal! Healing comes from God, but will you let Love in?

Still, it is not a question of healing the *body.* The body is nothing. Focus should always be off the body and on the mind. When the mind truly awakens and Light is allowed to re-enter, healing can be experienced as complete. When this occurs, nothing will be important to you except the limitless Life you have now. It is yours forever, Rhonda. *Be you healed in It now.*

You have asked about your relationship with your ex-husband, Jeff.

Do not fight against the tides of change, Rhonda. This will only dishearten you. Your relationship with Jeff is quite safe in God. Your struggle with him is not really your true relationship with him at all. It is an interpretation of what you want it to be. In this sense your special relationship with him is indeed connected to your illness. It is time to cut the chords to both at once by choosing in favor of *your* Self. This does not mean to stop loving him or to throw him out of your heart. It merely means that you place God before *anyone*. By doing this, you are also disowning specialness with *everyone*. When overcoming sickness, this decision is essential. Love him as you would love everyone. Any relationship that is treated as such is bound to become holy. And holiness brings joy!

Be gentle with yourself, loved one. Allow yourself the dignity and healing you so much deserve. Always on the other side of suffering there is Light that waits for you. Do not wait for It, Rhonda. Seek It above all else. If you need the comfort of an old friend to see you find your way, I will be here, standing right beside you, to take your hand and lift you above the veil. I am with you always, dear one. In remembrance of the heart we share forever, I bring you good tidings and cheer.

Jesus

THE PEACEFUL ANSWER

There is a peaceful answer to your fear of dying. If you will commend your will to mine through God, we will surely receive it together. By doing so you will remember that loving *is* the answer. By loving you receive Love, not from your brother and sister, but through them from God Himself. They will receive Love through you as well. Through loving is your Self made known. Learn of What you are, then, by offering Life instead of death. In death there is no meaning. But in Life is eternal Love. The answer to the fear of death and of God is but a silent offering of your own glorious holiness. Give this blessed offering readily to all who long for it and receive for yourself the Gift of timeless Love with them.

The hardest thing you will ever do is to let go of your own needless suffering. What is suffering but a call to death instead of Life? By receiving only what is yours this instant, you cannot suffer, for suffering is as unnatural as death.

Little child, all that is left to frighten you are pieces of a broken dream. Let us go beyond the ashes of the past and hesitance of the future to a Place where fantasies are cherished no more. Quietly now, let us receive our glorious Inheritance together. It is the breadth between the breath, the rests within the song. It is as delightful as you are, and It rises to sing in you now. Come ye unto thy faithful Abode Where wellspring and all Life do join. Here are we held and lifted, and kept in Heaven's Home.

Chapter Seven

LIVING
FOR LIGHT
& PEACE

BE YOU HEALED

The whole purpose of your living here is to finally discover *experientially* that there is *no death*. You have been insistent on proving otherwise. This is quite apparent by what you repeatedly simulate in your dreams. You look outside you to pictures of a bloody past and of a frightening future, and wonder why there is no peace. How is it possible to find peace while simulating delusions? Death is a delusion you made and refuse to question. Little child, what if it is not there?

If there is no death, then what can await you *but* Life? And what is Life but the incredible joy of remembering What you are? *You can never remember as long as you take any of the world's thinking seriously.* Ultimately this is what you must finally accept to truly be free. Brethren, joy is destined to fill your heart as you stand firm to declare your release from a lesser god! Would you not join me now, realizing the completely happy outcome it must bring? Come, let us join our hands and hearts with God. He offers only His perfect joy and peace now that you may awaken from all dreams and *be you healed*.

A SCRIBING FOR KURT

My wife, Patricia, and I are on a rather steeply inclined spiritual expansion path in which we communicate regularly with Jesus as well as other Ascended Masters and Archangel Michael. She gets fairly direct communication and I must still rely on muscle testing. From everything we can determine, I have been guided for years by Emmanuel and Ramanda, and have "brought in" a business culture transformation process that many have described as, "ACIM in a pinstriped suit." All of this occurred before I even knew about ACIM.

About a year ago we found a group that helped us accelerate our spiritual growth path. This group had grown out of Dr. Robert Jaffe's, work in energy healing. This past May we responded to guidance and decided to sell everything that doesn't fit in our car and become "nomads." Right now we're winding up the summer in Colorado and plan to arrive in Maui on October 1st, expecting to enjoy a "sabbatical" there for a year or so.

I live in a very high degree of peace of mind, so don't have any "problems" to inquire about in a scribing. I do, however, have some questions and would very much appreciate having a written message that comes independently from Jesus in addition to that from our own direct contact.

1) *The clearest message I get for my own path of "service" is to stay focused on strengthening my own "vertical" alignment with Source. Am I missing anything here?*

2) *Is my interest in preparing to communicate with the world through the Internet about the ascension process a product of ego, or in fact Divinely guided?*

Thanks, in Love and Light,

Kurt

Greetings Kurt:

This is Jesus speaking through Joel. Let us begin with your first question.

The question you have asked implies doubt. Obviously if there is doubt, there is something "missing." The statement about strengthening your own vertical alignment, as your guidance suggests, is a given and a healthy foundation to work from as well. There is nothing more important than the practice of engaging with God on a regular basis. A clearer and more answerable question to ask would be, "*How* do I strengthen my vertical alignment with Love?" Once you truly understand the process of what it entails to accomplish this, there will be little if any doubt left as to whether or not there is something "missing."

Your relationships are key to the process of aligning with God. But it is not your holy relationships alone that will do this for you. It is your special ones as well. In fact, they are the key ingredient to the cosmic jigsaw puzzle you find yourself in. Until every last Son and Daughter of God is healed, you have a mission — the mission of your own healing with them. It is in your willingness to risk, in the special relationships that seem to be placed before you, that you will find true healing. All these relationships are holy because they are blessed by God Himself. But they will appear special because there is still healing for you to do. Herein lies an even greater question: Will you take the risk to be healed with them when they are brought to you? Or will you walk away and ride alone on your chariot to "heaven?" I'm sure you understand my point.

Healing occurs through the communication of Love. In fact, that is all communication *is*. What is not Love is wasted words and time. You will experience days where it seems this way. *These* are the times to notice and embrace, for the experience of feeling out of alignment, angry or fearful will be your gauge for where healing is needed. It will seem to you that the healing needed is "out there." But I assure you, it is quite within you. Recognize where it is. Then allow Spirit to work through you in any relationship where there seems to be stress, allowing you *both* to heal *together*.

This is *not* a time in your history for any of you to be sitting in a temple all day in constant meditation. This is an age of communication. Thank God it is so! This is a time to take risks and love like you have never loved before. Challenge fear. But do it gently and with Love. You are correct in your understanding of the coming mass awakening. Enjoy the lull before the storm. Prepare and mend your sails now. The time is close at hand. What will change but every mind and heart that recognizes it is so?

Your second question is again a curious one, but a good one. The answer is, *both*. Essentially there is nothing to do here, but surely you'll find something. There is nothing to fix, but why not try anyway? You see, Kurt, nothing changes here except *by* the ego and *for* the ego. The biggest laugh you'll ever have will be when you ascend and say, "My God, nothing really ever happened there that wasn't already done!" A simple way to understand this is to say, "What changes does not exist, and what is does not change." Herein lies the key to distinguishing between the ego and Spirit.

However, that is not to say that Spirit cannot use the changeable. It works through your body every day. You cannot see It, yet It is there, communicating and reminding you that all is well, all is one and all is Love. If you can enjoy this recognition while you change this and make that, then you will have learned to happily distinguish the difference between what is *for* the ego and What is *of* God. Both are always at work in your world, but only one has an outcome that is sure. The challenge to your seeming existence in this world is being able to sustain the body and still reach Spirit. The trick is what you place *first*. If you sustain your communication with Spirit first, the body will naturally follow. Once this is truly experienced, you will have little need of your ego at all. The truth is, you *don't* "need" it at all.

I was unable to see myself in the world because I learned to see only the world in my Self. You can do the same with little difficulty. It is only a matter of placing truth *before* illusion. But in order to do so, you must be perfectly clear about the difference. In all you may do, Kurt, know that Spirit is working through you no matter what. Your "needs" are fulfilled. If you can accept this, you *will* recognize Spirit working through all of your affairs, no matter the barriers the ego imposes.

Great blessing to the work you do, which will bring His joy to all! I am always here with God to listen and answer your call. Go now with faith that all is well, all is one and all is *Love*.

In gentle peace,

Jesus

THE HEART OF LOVE

When a gentle smile and a peculiar ability to giggle at everything you encounter here comes to replace a once furrowed brow, be sure that you have nearly arrived. What more powerful lesson can you teach the holy ones who travel with you than to laugh at the absurdity and meaninglessness of what guilt once bound you to? Release from the guardians of guilt is the world's deepest longing. It will come as each one abandons their preoccupation with making sense of "sin" and chooses instead the perfect holiness given them now. As you bring a new and shiny instant to the world, the world is born again in you. With each blessing, the world made of sin and confusion is abandoned by another. Each will turn toward you, stepping closer to reach for your hand as the roots of vision plant firmly in newly hallowed ground. It is the time for gathering and rejoicing, for guilt is over and Christ is come to light the way!

Build your church, not on hardened soil, but in the Heart of hearts in one another. It is no longer your "duty" to walk in drudgery, making contribution through tears of terror and "blood of the soul." This is not the way! The way of the Heart is the way to everlasting happiness and freedom, for the Heart of Love in you sees not a world to look upon and judge, but only the timeless awareness of God's gentle Creation. In God's Creation there is no world, but sanity and serenity are everywhere. In God's World there can be no guilt, nothing to fix or change, or any thought of harm.

Child of Light, you came here to remember your Identity in Love, not to make your identity in the world! In remembrance of Spirit power is restored to you, that, in its perfect holiness, can change the world's fallen destiny. The arguing ceases and the fighting must end Where Light has come to stay. For who would not succumb to the sweetened fruit that inner Destiny has come to bring? Teach one another that purchase of this abundant fruit is unnecessary and offer it to all who have seemed to lose their way. Undivided, the Gift of God is yours only to share. Give this Gift gratefully and you teach the world that the world does not exist. By doing so you shall hear a Heart which sings to all the song of our journey in the joyous remembrance of our Father's great Love.

You are Christ together! Joining in Spirit, Where hearts meet as One, your silent march is to the beat of a different drum. Your "armies" have a General, yet He is heard but never seen. Your "arsenal" is not dangerous, yet has the strange ability to make "enemies" glad. How powerful this army is, whose purpose is to disarm hatred, guilt and fear. Let our gathering be left unseen no longer, for the world has long awaited this coming of Hearts. Gathering has come to fruition. We come, not with swords, but in peace for the transformation and illumination of all, bearing witness only to the shining Rays of Heaven. We have met with Christ's purpose, for He now is come through each of you as many Lights unto the world. May the many be known as One and, from this, may His Great Comfort reach to all!

A SCRIBING FOR RON

I am 41 years old with a wife and two children. I work as a software engineer for Motorola and live comfortably in a material sense. I am a creative person and have many, many interests, most of which I don't have time to pursue. I am musical (can play several instruments), like to write, like to work with people and like outdoor activities. From time to time I have contemplated changing careers. I went to school for a year to get a masters in counseling, but stopped because of time constraints. I am also very good at what I do for a living (creating software). I have thought about becoming a nurse, a massage therapist, a musician, a social worker, starting my own business, etc.

Right now I am tired — tired of running, tired of trying to become. In my head I know that this world is an illusion, temporary, and that this is a totally different spiritual world where I came from, am going to. But I have very little concept (except in an abstract, intellectual sense) of what that looks like. Emotionally, I am pretty stuck in this world, reacting to this problem and that, with occasional respites in meditation or relaxation. I have not yet emotionally detached from this world. I think that meeting the project deadline at work is important, but if I was spiritually oriented, it seems like this wouldn't be important. But then how would I put food on the table? Blah, blah, blah.

You get the idea.

Here are my questions:

1) *How can I be in this world but not of it? How do I act like spirit having a bodily experience?*

2) *What is the purpose of my being in this world?*

3) *What is the best way to detach from material things — to give them all away and be a homeless person or to simply enjoy what is there without concern for gathering them?*

4) *Does it really matter what I do for a living? Should I just focus on being a loving being in whatever I happen to be doing and stop worrying about what job would bring me the most joy?*

5) *Will I leave my body when I become enlightened or will things just go on as before?*

Thanks so much for your help.

Greetings Ron:

I will address the second question in your query first, since it is this question that contains the answers to all the others. It is also the question that bothers you the most.

You have a very quick mind, Ron. This mind understands and has a great need to be understood. It is easy for you to take on many occupations and master them all. Your mind is masterful in the *theory* of *A Course In Miracles* as well. But that doesn't help you in your dilemma. To truly understand and be understood requires a shift from the intellect to the emotional.

Your situation could be equated with a racecar running at 8000 rpm in third gear and still taking the lead in the race. The fear is that, if you shift into cruise, you may fall behind. So it feels safe to keep *running* in third, but it is exhausting your fuel and your engine. (The fuel is your contact with Spirit and your engine is, of course, the mind hard at work.)

The purpose of your life is quite the opposite of your worldly work, although you are doing the real work while working. The question is, are you enjoying it? If you are not, it is because you are not willing yet to take the risk and shift into cruise. You must still be attracted to the competition or you would not be there. This is perfectly okay for you if this is what you want. But as you are noticing, it will fulfill you less and less as you grow towards the Light, *unless* you allow the situation to be guided by me.

The purpose of life is to be a joyous and carefree child of Love. God does not will that you take on all the heavy responsibilities, you do. This does not mean that you should quit work and become a monk. You could, but that would hardly make you happy either. It is not changing things around so much that will help you in your particular situation. It would be more helpful if you were willing to have each experience transformed into one of lightness. It would mean for you not to take the race so seriously anymore. It's really not serious at all, Ron. It is just a dream! Yet if you are not able to experience what you are doing in life as just a simple dream and nothing more, then chances are it will become so painful for you that you will give yourself no choice but to move on.

If you are not fulfilling your purpose truly in life, it will manifest as a painful or conflicted situation. Part of fulfilling your purpose is learning to do what it takes to be carefree. You *can* be homeless and be quite carefree. You can also do what you are doing now and be carefree. It does not require worldly changes, but only your willingness to continually change your mind and choose Love through the Holy Spirit's and my guidance.

Healing is your function and you cannot heal by figuring out the national debt. Your intellect is quite incapable of understanding true healing. Your thinking cannot even grasp the idea. It can explain to you what it thinks healing is, but it cannot offer you even an inkling of the real *experience of healing*. When you are not experiencing joy, you are not healing. In regard to your third question, you answered it yourself in the latter part of the question. This is an idea that represents true healing.

You need not give anything away unless you want to. If what you have disturbs you, by all means, *give it away*. It is difficult for most students to understand how not to be complicated in a complicated world. The more "things" you surround yourself with, the more likely you will forget What is most important. When you ask me, "How can I be in the world but not of the world?" would it not be more honest to ask, "How can I *have* the world but not be in the world?" You already know the answer to this. You cannot have the world any more than I can. Any belief that you still hold that tells you differently is a delusion on the part of your self-made thought system.

Ask yourself honestly what you do own. Now see yourself one hundred years from now. Why would any sane mind be worried about a simple illusion? Nothing you have but will fade away. Every battle you fight to keep something and own it will keep you from your true function — forgiving the world and healing. This will become more apparent one way or another. You will either exhaust yourself by trying to keep your "treasure" in place or you will gladly disown it and walk with me. This does *not* mean that you must give your possessions away, merely that you realize what is valuable and what is not. Can any illusion ever offer you true, eternal happiness? Have they yet?

Now we come back to what true healing involves. By now you must realize it does not involve your perceptive relationship to the world or other egos. Joining hearts with a single purpose in mind and only to be truly helpful *does*. To be in the world and not of it requires that you become a careful observer and listener. You do this by becoming nonattached to any *thing*. You simply watch quietly and listen carefully. *Then* you ask within for guidance in *all* decisions. The answers to your decisions will come emotionally, not intellectually. If they are heard correctly, only good will come. At times you may be uncomfortable following my guidance, for the decision may seem to take something from you at first. Nonetheless, if you follow through, you will know in your heart that it was correct to act on. If there is fear, then ask again and do not decide hastily. Take time to be with God before you decide and be sure. At work or home this may seem difficult. Others may expect you to *think quickly. Yet this is the area where you must learn to shift gears.*

Regarding your career and fourth question: You may find soon that you need at least a temporary respite or even a complete change in your pursuits. You have been in a stable situation for a long time and this has required much "sacrifice" of you. The sacrifice I speak of is the emotional contact with God and others. It has become habit. You are beginning a sorting out period. With your talents, you will someday soon be helping many others. It may seem you are losing your safety net for a while. This is normal. Risking to heal always involves an effort that can at first be frightening. It may cause turmoil and leave your family wondering if you have gone off the deep end. This will pass. With your determination to truly heal and be helpful, you will find gifts that you will not at first be able to put into words. You are a healer in bloom. I have asked you to join me in an effort together, and you will, completely. Be happy for this; you have asked and soon you will find. Do not be discouraged by what you may see as a loss. Around the corner will be a freedom you have never known. Looking back, you will laugh, wondering why you waited so long.

Now we come to answer your fifth question. There will come a day where the world you see yourself in will be completely transformed. All you experience and see will become humorous to you. When this happens you will know you are on the path Home. You will not worry about "leaving" your body because it will not matter anymore. You will not even be paying much attention to it. You will simply realize that you need do nothing and that you can do everything or anything you want. But this will not matter either because you will do everything without effort. God Wills perfect happiness and peace in your experience *right now*. The purpose of life is to achieve your complete happiness *right now*. Physical comforts have nothing to do with it.

By becoming the observer and never specially *valuing* anyone or anything, you will understand what it is to truly love. It takes much effort at first to achieve this, but I assure you that it is possible right now. It requires that you practice detachment while moving through the world. But do not be deceived by the word detachment. You can be totally detached and also be totally unhappy. This happens if you do not realize that your dreams (perceptions) are truly not real. Thus you cannot fully escape feeling fearful by using detachment to *avoid* the lingering fear that there may be value in what you are experiencing. This is improper denial. Your children and wife will let you know very quickly when you are detaching wrongly. People who are close to you will see that your faith is not pure and your presence wandering. To be enlightened means that you are fully present and know God's Love right now. Then, when you tell your children "it does not matter," it really won't matter, for they will see the Christ shining in you. They will be detached with you in the right way. Do you understand what I am saying to you, Ron?

You will grow to appreciate what the Presence of Love can do for all of you. This is Where your true power lies. I assure you that when It is at work, you *will* move mountains with me. Remember that I have said that Heaven is in you *now*. The body is simply a mechanism to help you return your values to Where they belong. You need not lose the body, only realize its single function. When you place value only in the eternal, you will see a world, a family, a job that glows. Your dream has become happy because you are no longer invested in it as a "reality." And everyone who passes by you will know it with you. Do you understand?

Being emotionally "stuck" in the world is an indication that you place value where it does not belong. You have one true emotion and that is Love. All other emotions are illusive in nature and do not belong in your holy mind. If you make an agreement with a brother to be on time, then by all means, *do your best to be on time*. But know your own limitations. If you are in third gear running full power, how can you expect to be present? Again, *what do you value*? If you ask me first before you make your decisions and agreements, then you will have peace. Is it not worth the time to do so in light of how you have been feeling? What does Ron need to do right now to experience joy and peace? Ask this often and turn to me for the answer. I will be there, as you well know.

Lastly I will speak again on trust and risk. These two attributes go hand in hand. Risking to be healed is entirely emotional. It requires your trust in me and in the Love in others. Speaking from the heart is often not acceptable to the world. Showing emotions is regarded as weakness. I would say to you that these beliefs are perhaps most responsible for making the world. You can and will overcome this. It requires sincere commitment to truth and Love. Do not be afraid to love and be loved. The power God has given us both is yours. Own it and do not be afraid to say no. Listen to the great Heart you have within you. I trust in It fully because we share It together. It is yours to give always. Do not let fear keep you from It. It wants to be expressed to everyone, yet It cannot be expressed in words. Be gentle with yourself, Ron. Ask often, for I am here with God in you now. Blessed are you who have asked. You are answered.

His blissful innocence be our guide,

Jesus

UNTO OUR KINGDOM

In a very real sense, it is your occupation to laugh at illusions. Any way you can teach someone not to take his/her self seriously is a great and glorious moment for both of you. Miracles are born the instant the world is temporarily forgotten. Thinking ceases, and creation is welcomed in all its completeness. When one mind is joined with God, this is communion. But when two minds are joined with God, this is ecstasy! All the world benefits from these holy instants because that is what the world is missing.

The strength to perform miracles lies solely in your willingness to unite with the Heart of Love in you *and* your brother. Your Heart is only here and cannot be broken by any of the world's laws. Nor can any of the world's thinking change Its beat. The ego tries to teach you just the opposite, that your Heart is weak. Yet the ego *has no heart*. What seems to "break," then, is but a "broken dream." Oh how, little child, can only a dream be torn in two? Broken dreams can never hurt you. Only in dreams, loving child, *only* in dreams.

Your strength lies nowhere but in your Self. Here is your Heart forever! Do not look outside you, where happiness can never be found. Yet the Heart of hearts you do share with everyone. It cannot be found only in one other, for It must be found in all together. The strength of this vision is what shares your Heart with all. It is invulnerable because It is shared. To not share It is to not know It, and this indeed leaves you "broken hearted." Dreams can never be shared, but Reality must *be* to be known. To share your Heart with everyone is to live in the Kingdom of Heaven with them in joy. Your sharing the Heart of hearts will lead you to a communion with God that is so powerful the world will laugh along with you.

You *each* have a responsibility to the world that is not *from* the world. It is the *only* responsibility you came to perform. It is the responsibility of *extending joy*. This is why I have told you in many ways at different times to not concern yourselves with *form*. I have also said that it is not what you *do*, but what you help *undo*. Blessing does not fix things, but it does set them straight. By setting them straight, order is placed in its proper perspective. The Order of your holiness will always come before any orders of the world. Do not confuse these orders, for if you do you will have lost sight of the one responsibility you were created *for*. Instead, be His messenger of joyous salvation, and teach the world with wholehearted conviction that guilt is gone and eternal peace is here. Share this with all, that the world may awaken and, together, the Sons of a loving God shall shine with smiles again!

A SCRIBING FOR FRANK

Dear Joel,

Thank you for putting yourself "out there" to offer this gift to others. I feel like this is an answer to a prayer for guidance I have been asking.

Here are my questions:

1) *How can I (or should I) begin talking on the Course to groups of people? How should the form of this be?*

2) *What am I working through in my intimate relationships in general? (I don't have one at this time.)*

3) *How can I be at peace with my parents? (father, stepmother and mother)*

Right now my life has come to a place where I am functioning better in the world than I ever have. I have stopped battling the world and have started battling myself. People around me describe me as "having gotten my stuff together." But I do not feel this way. I feel I am treading water, trying to stay in the same place out of fear. I am more internally reactive to the people around me than I can ever remember being since adolescence (I am almost 30).

I am resentful and fearful of people I see as teachers of the Course and I am upset about being that way. For the first time in awhile, I have enough money to live on. I am working at a job where I am acknowledged for my contribution, but I feel like I am not bringing the principles of the Course into manifestation like I should. I feel like I have much to contribute, but that I don't know where to go, what to do, etc. I also feel very tenuous about my inner connection to Jesus/Holy Spirit after several years of channeling verbally and through scribing.

Thank you, Joel, for your help with this. Please send me your address so I may make a love offering.

Much peace,

Frank

Greetings Frank:

In Christ we are gladdened together with all of Heaven, for you have been willing to ask and hear for yourself and all the Sonship.

We have spoken many times together, you and I, for you have learned well to hear for others. But as I have said before, not so well for yourself. Let us together take a closer look at the times you have been able to hear for yourself. Have those times not left you with a feeling that you need do nothing and that all will be done just as it is supposed to happen? Did you not feel a sense of release and great joy when you were hearing clearly the Voice for Love in you?

I have repeatedly said, in many different ways, that healing is your only function in this world. Any other role you might assign yourself is done on behalf of the ego's wishes. You are a healer, but only if you let God heal through you. It is not you alone that can heal anything. When you attempt to do so, you place yourself in the grip of ego-motivation, not God-motivation. You are apt to forget your proper placement in the role of bringing the Atonement to all minds and hearts. This is nothing new. Everyone forgets — that is why they came here. There were many times when I forgot as well. At a point, however, I chose not to allow guilt to take its place in my mind when I forgot. Instead, I learned the most difficult lesson of all — to choose again in every situation in favor only of Love. The only "difference" in Where I see myself and where you see yourself is that you often see yourself in the world, while I only see our one Self in Heaven. I know beyond doubt that there is but one choice, the choice for God. In the world where you see yourself, there seems to be many, many other choices.

The difficulty you are having regarding "teaching" *A Course In Miracles* stems from the idea that you believe there can be something to be taught. Yet I have said, and very clearly, that learning can occur only through Love. Upon your realization that there is nothing you could teach even if you wanted to, you become a "teacher" of God. The theory used in *A Course In Miracles* has but one function: To undo fear and heal the world and all "need" for theory and words. By studying *A Course In Miracles*, you are doing much more than just reading a book with mere words. You are agreeing to enter into a relationship with me. By doing so you are accepting a dialogue that must bring you an unquestionable experience of Love. If you look carefully, you will see that it is not the words that are healing. It is the unwavering attitude and faith behind the words combined with your willingness to place your mind in relationship with mine and God's and to listen beyond the words. Therefore, words function only as tools to lead you to an attitude of grace, humility and Love. This attitude cannot be "taught" in words, but only through modeling the recognition of your perfect holiness and acceptance of the Atonement for yourself.

Those of you who are attempting to teach the theory of *A Course In Miracles* to others merely have not yet accepted the Atonement for yourselves and are "teaching" it to learn it. Learning, however, is of the ego, not of your Self, Which already knows God as Itself. When learning and teaching cease, you will merely know God and realize there is nothing to teach, but all to love. This is when you will be less troubled by others you see as great teachers of the Course, for you will know with all your heart that they are only trying to learn What cannot be taught. You will gladly help them by demonstrating that all is well, all is whole and all is done. Do you understand what I am "teaching" you, Frank?

You may find it difficult to believe that my guidance is available to you in your mind or the mind's of all others at all times. Let me remind you that I have nothing better to do than be here now. That is Where I am. It is only your preoccupation with the past and future that makes it difficult for you to believe I am only an instant away from being of assistance to you. My only function is the one God gave me. I accept nothing else as my function. So in purpose it is easy to remain Where I am also easily accessible to each of you. It is not so easy for you because you believe you can be somewhere else. By believing this you have made it manifest in the different dreams you seem to walk through every day. This will pass.

The miracle undoes the need for time and miracles should be practiced every day. Regarding your facilitating groups, you need only remember your true purpose and allow the Holy Spirit to be the only Teacher. Healing does not occur on a theoretical level, but on an emotional level. If others feel the need to discuss theory, by all means allow them to do so, keeping in mind only the need for true healing for everyone. It is the eternal you seek, not the ephemeral. It is experience you want, not mere discussion. This can occur if one person is completely willing to keep only the quiet and gentle Light from Which he came in his awareness. This is your healing. And as you heal you must share it with others. It is not your discussion, but your *modeling* of What is true for you that will bring peace to every mind.

If you talk with groups about your studies in *A Course In Miracles*, speak from your experiences in healing and what lessons they have brought you. Only from these experiences can you truly speak from your Heart. Only when you speak from your Heart can others truly hear you. In your Heart is Where all joy is found. In your mind's thinking, you will find only the conflict which is in need of healing. As you speak with this sincerity, so will you know with all others what is in need of healing and what is already healed. Speaking is your witness to either fear or Love. Fear always hides behind theory and words. Love always comes through the words, bringing with It an awareness and experience of total joining in gentle recognition of the Father's Love. Speak with this humility and you will know the great and genuine gifts that true healing offers. No more will you be concerned about who is the "better" teacher. There is but One Teacher and His Will is done.

The second and third question you asked are related, if not the same question put in different words. Also, your sense of conflict and not feeling worthy as a teacher is fully related to these questions. By far, it is most important that you risk healing your relationship with these significant others. Until you do this you are likely to continue with your sense of jealousy and resentment towards others you have placed in a position of "power" over you. The ideals of your parents are quite different from your own. They have made many poor choices in the world's estimation, just as you believe you have. It is important that you work with what seems to separate you from "them" — how you see things as opposed to how they see things; the position they take as opposed to yours.

All sense of separation and powerlessness you feel regarding them are a result of these beliefs you keep for yourself, and vice versa. Unfortunately, the beliefs they have and live by, you at times feel you must actively resist. The same holds true for them towards you. Each of you finds some things about the other that seems entirely despicable and unhealable. Herein lies your healing. For what you believe you see as the picture of them is the very same belief you have about yourself. By making a picture of them, based on what you think you see, you have made the same belief system alive in yourself. You have projected the blame on them, thus blocking the possibility of healing. Therefore you have made real exactly what you despise in them, offering yourself what you have made "real" in this projected and unhealed *dream*.

These are the beliefs, perceptions and pictures you hold in your subconscious that play themselves out destructively in your life. At one time your parents were like gods to you. You accepted what they said at face value and made them a very large part of your own ego-thought system by doing so. Now that you are seeing that these "tools" may have been somewhat corrupt, your ego is using them as a means to make you despise both yourself and them. The way out of this dilemma is to no longer choose the picture you think you see.

Parents often become like you were to them when you were younger. They must at times be looked at as if they were your children calling for Love. Just as you live in your dreams, they are living in theirs. Much of the way they dream has to do with how their parents dreamed and so on. When you were young and had bad dreams, who came to waken you, not so much by telling you in words, but by demonstrating to you through Love that it was just a dream?

As long as any argument continues about whose dream is more real and whose dream isn't, you are still fastened to your hatred of the other. Ask yourself if hatred and fear have really taught you anything of value, and then choose again! Nothing you think you have learned from fear *has* any value. Nothing anyone has ever seemed to do to you out of fear can really hurt you, unless you insist on keeping the dream a reality! This is temporary of course.

Your power to heal your relationship with them rests on your willingness to stop defending the perceptions or dreams you still hold, thereby taking your mind out of the position of *against* or *for*. Then if there is pain or hurt that has been left long unattended, it can come up in the safety of the healing environment you are finally choosing and nurturing. You may find, just as you have with many of your fellow students of the Course, that a lasting healing can occur in a very short instant of time, once you take the risk of withdrawing as the teacher and accept your role as the learner.

It is not necessary to do your healing in person with them, as you well know. But it is necessary to take the risk to heal the resentment and pain you feel associated with them. Once you see this situation as a magnificent opportunity to heal instead getting upset, the rest will fall into place. It seems risky, but do you have anything better to do? You will find in the gifts you receive by taking this "risk" that your intimate relationships will grow to many more than just a few.

I will say again, and I encourage you to listen: Nothing can be more important than healing your relationships with mother, father, sister and brother. In them you will find or lose God, for they were your models of God for many years. Right or wrong and no matter how terrible their "crimes," they deserve only your forgiveness in recognition that nothing ever really happened that was not Love. They deserve it because you deserve it. If you hold it back based on the principles of perception, you are holding it back from yourself. There is no value in doing so, for all value lies not in separation, but only in Love.

My dear Frank, you cannot hang on and tread water for too long. My guidance, which is aligned with the Holy Spirit's, is there for you at every turn, with every decision. So many times you have edged your way to a cliff, wearing a parachute that says, "God's Jumping School." You have remained at the edge, dying not from the jump, but from the freezing wind and the fear that has frozen you there! What would happen if you just jumped? I have been gently reminding you all along that all will be okay. In your heart you know what you must do, but will you do it? No decision can be mistaken when made with the Holy Spirit's loving guidance. You are safe, you are Home. And you are thus unlimited in your choices.

Do not take this dream so seriously. In fact, you need not take it seriously at all. It is just a dream. Let Love help you make it a happy one by remembering you are not condemned here. You can leave the world in an instant and come Home with me. I am here with God and all the angels you have called for. I am here to take you Home.

Say this simple prayer often. It is my gift to you Frank:

"Father, I have taken control of my thinking as a means now to hurt myself somehow. I have sought to be my own best teacher and once again I have been mistaken. I relinquish all of the fantasies I now have regarding myself in exchange for the Gift Your Teacher would offer me in its place. I want only the peace that is my Gift and nothing more. I will step aside completely and let You teach Your loving Word to all now through me. I will accept Your Word for me in place of the ones I have been choosing. I accept Your only Gift of peace and Love to me now. Father, I want only to heal."

Amen

Now Frank, receive this Gift I am offering through our Father in Heaven. It is yours, in His Love, forever and ever. Peace be unto you who have asked and have received the Gift He has offered.

Grace be yours,

Jesus

BECOME AS LITTLE CHILDREN

The Voice of Love in you is like a gentle child. It longs only to embrace you, to keep you still and call its own. It wants you to remember you are at Home. It taps your forehead lightly to remind you It is here, in a spark of Light so delightful you'll know that God is near. If words must describe it, this child is hidden from view. And yet it expresses with a touch by hands so light and so small, it leaves tingles of joy and goose bumps to bear, and smiles for one and all. *Do you remember how very much you are loved, little child?*

How is it conceivable that you have ever been anything but Love? Love is *your* magnificent child, dear one! A child who knows herself *as* Love is not afraid. She can laugh and play and frolic about. She has wings! Age cannot touch her, for she lives not in time. She is as free as the wind that takes her, and has no cares, nested in her Home high above the world. With the vision of an eagle looking over mountaintops, she sees no sign of limitations. It is a fine day for sailing innocently above the sea. No thoughts she must think, but listens instead to the thoughts the ocean gently gives and the messages from deep blue skies above. It is a peaceful sound. It is your innocence speaking to you. It is the Voice of Love. It is God. It is me.

How gentle the sound of all creation! What does this Voice keep whispering in your ear? To love, serve, and remember, child— to give the Always of creation to all!

You are a creator, loved one. To create you must joyously help undo the world of fear. Become as little children, for creating is giving Love, sharing your Self with all.

Blessed are the children of God, for they have accepted the Will of God as their own. They have gladly received their innocence and have seen it as well in all. Oh yes, child, indeed the meek shall inherit the earth, for merely by their magical presence is a dying world reborn! Only a child can play and pretend, and laughingly remember that it is but a dream. A child, my dear ones, can dream and still awaken!

A SCRIBING FOR ELLEN

This scribing was done for a seventeen-year-old girl…

Dear Joel,

Your help would be so welcomed by me if you could give it. I'm in a stage of my life where many things are coming together and many major changes lie ahead. I pray to Jesus often and feel his tingling Love all around me, but to hear his words! It would mean so much. You are a truly loving man to share such a gift. I'll try to make my questions as non-specific as possible, but if I fail, please just let me know and I'll attempt to revise them. There is one in particular, the first one, which is so important to me, but I fear too specific… Let me know. Thank you in advance.

Ellen

Dear Jesus,

For a long time I've been praying to You for fulfillment… Has it truly arrived or am I still waiting? Can I trust the Love and safety being offered me? Is it what You sent for me? When I pray to You and feel tingly, like energy is being poured over me, is that me or You? Are You there, giving me that feeling or is it just my response to praying?

There are some people who are very close to me who are angry and unhappy. Can my relationships with them be healed? Can I help heal them? Are my dreams for my life given by You and God or are they invented by me? Can I have faith in my dreams, or should I abandon them and focus on the present?

Will the Patriots win the Superbowl this season? Just kidding — not even You could make that happen. Thank you, Jesus. I love You.

Greetings Ellen:

Indeed, it is such a wonderful sight to see a Child of God such as yourself seeking to find only the truth in you! I welcome you now to the awareness of the Kingdom within you, Where all is well, all is whole and all is joy. Take my hand, and we will experience the Kingdom of God in Her Heaven.

Within you, Ellen, is a Place in your heart so grand and beautiful that nothing in this world can come close to compare. It is beyond words and all the complication of the world. You came from Here and it is your Home forever. It would never leave you comfortless, for It is created for you, as you, from the Eternal to the Eternal, forever. Your safety lies in this Place, for nowhere in the world could offer this.

Here is Where your complete fulfillment awaits you, for with your complete recognition of Heaven, you will be happy. You are touching this great Place every time you pray, for it is this great willingness you have to come Home with me that gives you the sensations you feel. It is a feeling you are at Home. It is a feeling that you need not do anything to receive this Gift that God so graciously gave you, for merely by being quiet you are quite willing to accept and hold dear your Treasure! Peace be to you who have asked for nothing else and have received It! Keep Her holy Treasure close to you always, for It is all you will ever need to get you through.

The world seems to be a complicated place, does it not Ellen? So many tears have fallen here. So many tragedies have seemed to happen. Indeed, in looking upon the world there seems to be so many things that are in need of change. So many are afraid and seem to be helpless. The dark picture the world holds out to you can seem to never end while you are looking at it. How can one be happy looking upon what appears to be such devastation?

In the Gift God gave you, it is given you to be able to look beyond and past the apparent devastation the world holds out to you. Just as you can look within to a Place inside you that is safe and free from fear, death and destruction, you also can see and experience the world through the eyes of Love. The miracle allows you the privilege of seeing and knowing each brother and sister just as God created them — devoid of the appearances that fear, guilt and death may tempt you to see in them instead.

Herein lies the crucible for a child of God who seems to walk the world awhile: As a seeming prisoner of this world you have taken on the responsibility of choice. That choice is always to see your world in one of two ways: Through the eyes of fear and guilt or through the eyes of only Love. In every decision and in every choice, only two possibilities exist. It is your calling to choose Heaven instead of the world, Ellen. That is God's purpose for you — to look beyond the appearances and deceptions of the world and straight into the Heart of God in everyone.

Little child, the lovely Energy that covers you at times comes from the One Who created you. You need not do anything for It to be yours. It is yours forever. You can always hear my Voice when you take time to listen to the crickets in a warm mountain meadow, or the gentle chirping of nesting birds in the quiet and fresh-rained forest. You can hear my Voice in the sound of stillness. It is the sacred sound that cannot be heard with the body's ears. Nor can words express Its tones, nor eyes see Its hues. It is a sound that is heard with the soul. The sound of Christ is within the burbling of a summer creek, within the rhythmic wisps blown through leaves that flutter in the windy fall. It is the gentleness within a baby's sigh. It is what you long to hear, yet often fear to listen for. Your very being contains the Voice for this lovely expression. Deep within you, in your very Essence, you yearn to meet your Self, where the mirror on still water abides.

Dreams, my dear Ellen, are for you who made them. God has given you only your Self and your Self is everything! You pick the dreams you would live in. They can be happy or sad, depending on which you choose. Whatever dreams you choose, you will have faith in them. It is your faith in them that makes them what they seem to be. Yet what will allow you to see your happy dreams come true will be the understanding that they are just that, dreams. Should you get caught up in them — that is take them seriously — you will make them so real to you that you will forget the Gift of freedom God gave you.

It is Her Gift to you that is your Reality. Forget not Her Gift to you, for It is not a dream. In this remembrance, you will be happy even when your dreams fail. You are free to make all your dreams come true, Ellen. What is more, any dream you give to the Holy Spirit will be changed to the happiest dream ever! Let the Holy Spirit guide you in your decisions about your dreams. She will help you have your happy dreams come true. Any dream given to Her will bring happiness, not just to you but to everyone. It is in this service that you will be fulfilled beyond even your wildest dreams!

You need not abandon your dreams, but do not be invested in them. They hold only the value you place in them. God does not and cannot value them because She knows they are dreams and nothing more. Yet the Holy Spirit can use your dreams on behalf of true healing, bringing peace to all minds, if you will but ask for Love's guidance in each of your decisions about them. If you learn to do this, Ellen, not only will you hear the Voice for God often, you will be happy because you will have not lost sight of What is valuable. Value belongs only with Love because all that has value is Love. Love is in the present because God created It only there. You are created from this Love by Love. It is valuable because It loves and sustains you. To distinguish your dreams from Reality, this is all you need to keep in your awareness. By choosing the Reality of Love first, you cannot fail to experience peace as well in all you do.

You can do much on behalf of healing your relationships, Ellen, simply by learning to do what I have described above diligently. The temptation to take anything in this world seriously is perhaps the greatest downfall of even the holiest of saints, you included. You should take healing sincerely, for it is why you came here. Yet there is nothing serious about healing. In fact it is the most joyous experience you are capable of. Healing requires only your willingness to let go of the ideas and things that make you feel serious, guilty or fearful. God does not will any of this for you. You should, then, question it in yourself or others when this attitude is reflected.

I do not wish you to suffer, nor would God. Those who suffer are those who have given into temptation and made their dreams real and Reality illusion. They are in need of the healing Light of God's Love, for they have forgotten the simple joy of recognizing each instant as an opportunity to be still and know God. Each prayer should be only for the remembrance of What you have and are already. It is this recognition in all its simplicity that heals the world and all who live here for a while. You need only let go of each thought that would teach you otherwise. I ask only for your devotion to keep joy for yourself. By this choice you will bring Light to every mind and heart along the way. With practice, perhaps someday not long far away, you will know in advance that God's Patriots have already won! The battle is already over. (You can bet on it!)

May God's peace and loving Spirit follow you into your every dream. Innocence is your Gift forever.

Love, Jesus

THE REBIRTH OF INNOCENCE

As long as the world lasts, there will always seem to be the choice between Love or fear, peace or conflict, and innocence or guilt. There are many words to describe the different kinds of choices, yet in truth there is always only one decision to make. You decide lovelessly or with Love in everything you do. You will always have the choice between one of two voices, depending on *what you* want to hear.

Many have complained that they cannot seem to distinguish between the voice of the ego and the Voice of Love. I will therefore explain to you in simple terms how you can tell.

The voice of the ego is never *received*. It is *made up* by you. Hearing my Voice, on the other hand, is entirely dependent on your *receptivity*. The Voice of the Holy Spirit never comes *from* you. It *must* and does come *to* you only *from* God. Understanding this is of paramount importance to you because, while your efforts are misplaced, you cannot distinguish between what is harmful and What is truly helpful.

To hear correctly is merely to listen without the self-made interference you have imposed out of fear. When you choose to listen only to your own thinking, the static alone must make you lonely and afraid. If you act on decisions made alone, there is little doubt that the results will not make you entirely glad. The thoughts you made up relate *only* to the physical. The thoughts you hear with God always emphasize only the spiritual, leaving the physical behind. If what you hear does *not* bring you a sense of complete safety and joy, then be assured you have temporarily forgotten the perfect and loving Center you share with God. It is from this Center that God's gentle Voice speaks and His Message always expresses *Love*. Love is always shared and can never be contained. Its magnificent blessing teaches everyone at once that all are free, joy is abundant and peace is come.

Each of you has one thing to do in this world that is far more important than anything else, regardless of how it seems or how you might wish it to be. To learn to hear Christ in every mind and heart is the single occupation given you by God to fulfill forever. Indeed you will because it is His Will for you. Learning to graciously accept this Will will heal you and all the world. Denying it will only seem to bring more confusion and pain.

To be more receptive is the key. Christ is nothing to the world, which hears and sees only its own illusions. Yet so is the world nothing to Christ, Who knows only His one Self, just as His loving Father created Him. In which world would you now trust? A fantasy world bent on change, confusion and unreliability? Or a World of perfect peace and eternal Love inherited by you? Only one can give you the sense of unlimited purpose that you long for and deserve. You can see It in one another, anytime and anywhere. For it is the mirror on still water and the return unto our Home. It is the rebirth of our innocence into our Father's Love. Receive this Gift now, for Heaven is our Home.

A SCRIBING FOR SAUL

My dear brother Joel,

For the past twenty-one years I have been a student of A Course In Miracles, *its Psychotherapy, its Song of Prayer and even its Attitudinal Healing. I think I have learned and tapped into the forgiveness materials of the Course, but there are still some relationships that I feel still need healing. I very much appreciate your asking Jesus for some of the answers to my questions.*

1) *In the Psychotherapy booklet that I printed 20 years ago, I'm seeing great progress in my life and the lives of all the people that Jesus and the Holy Spirit send. My question is, "Why is the process seemingly taking so long for the masses to respond to the Truth in this illusion?"*

2) *I truly believe that Jesus is my elder brother. I'm curious to know what some of our relationships in "illusions" of the past were and who and what I was in some of the "illusions."*

3) *I believe that Jesus and the Holy Spirit put me in touch with Saint Germain (a true Love affair) and wonder why the work that was started seemed to stall.*

4) *I'd like to know a bit more about the akashic record and if it's possible to tap into it while still in the "illusion."*

5) *A little bit of "enlightenment" on what really happens when we decide to leave our bodies. Where does the Spirit/Soul go*

and since our "Course" tells us none of us returns to Heaven (a place we never left) until we all "return" together, is the "place after the body" a part of the illusion, or is it not? I realize that everything is of GOD. These are some of the things I wonder about on occasion.

Thank you, Jesus, for all the incredible wisdom you have already shared and are about to share.

Thank you, Joel, for the most valuable work you are doing. I'm truly proud to call you brother.

Much Love, Saul

Greetings Saul:

Blessings unto you, Saul, for the message of Oneness you have expressed with me through the Holy Spirit for all! In the holiness of eternity, our hearts are forever joined. Seemingly a time long ago some brothers joined with one another and many others to begin our holy mission here. The holiness of these relationships, formed in time yet bonded in eternity, join together here once again to fulfill the Great Circle of Atonement, which is our Father's Will. Behold the Great Circle of Completion now at hand!

You have asked about relationships from the "past." Let us begin with this question. There have been several lifetimes when you tortured yourself and others because of pain that you could not forgive in yourself. You have lived through many lifetimes of guilt and sorrow on account of this and so have several others whom you are close to even now. This you may find hard to believe, but I am not mistaken in what I say. It is those brothers and sisters, here in this lifetime, who are still in need of some healing with you and you with them. You are aware of this now because you have finally allowed most of the necessary healing to take place in this lifetime. There is one other lifetime as well, short as it was, where you and I walked together. You have been dimly aware of this at times; at other times it has been more vivid for you.

It has been easy enough for each of you to "take your stands" in this lifetime, much like you have in previous ones. Because of the underlying reasons for these "stands," this lifetime could be viewed as a simulation of one very important and intense lifetime that seemed to come before. Many lifetimes followed because of this one. The issues in this lifetime are really much the same and have to do with each of you, myself included. I want each of you to know that any leftover conflict is reasonless on your parts. Right now you may be more aware of this than some of the others. Therefore it is helpful for *you* to take the first healing "steps" to resolve any conflict between you on behalf of reuniting this holy brethren.

There has never been any reason for any of you to keep this conflict "alive" on account of me, as you well know. Yet the ego is quite insidious here and has devised this to appear as a conflict that is "new" in this lifetime. It has also convinced each of you that it no longer matters. Yet underneath this lightly painted picture, there is amongst some of you the intense separation equal to that which Judas once felt in what he thought to be my "betrayal."

I have spoken before about leaving no stone unturned. Not one thread of separation should be kept from the Holy Spirit's sight, for this one thread is enough to make another world of hatred seem to reappear. There is not one among you who does not need each other any less than I need all of you together *now*. Each time one of you defends a position on behalf of me or anyone, we are crucified again together. There is nothing, gentle one, to defend. Look then, not at the present "picture," but through the hidden past that the ego has retained in the present to make this ancient battle live again. The conflict has been well camouflaged in the appearance of what seems to be yet another problem *out there*. There is much each of you can do by healing and reuniting with one another in my name that will silence the battlefield once and for all and bring the awareness of our inner union to all. The figures on this ancient battlefield grow weary and yearn to have the leaders of this battle turn, instead, to the way back Home. Will you help bring rest to the weary, Saul, and lead the way to Heaven through me?

We have much more to speak about together on this, and this will involve many others. Right now healing is in order so that a unifying solution can be reached *together*. I ask only that you do what you are already doing and continue to teach that darkness does not exist. Teach this by demonstrating there is nowhere Light cannot reach. You have given so much to so many *because you* have listened! I asked you to teach because you are one who can do this. I know you will continue because our minds are aligned and truly joined. Great gratitude to you my brother for your faith and listening! There will be more to follow in this dialogue of re-unification later on.

Let us speak now to your question about the "akashic records." These records can merely be viewed as an imprint of your chosen lives here in the world. The activities in your lives are based in these imprints. Each imprint contains a route into the seeming separation as well as the path back Home. Because of this, the seeming activities that happen in your lives are indeed well planned in advance. When I say "advance," I mean before there seemed to be an "after." "After" and "before" are meaningful concepts only in the birth and death cycle of the illusion. Within the time collapse of this cycle, yet enmeshed within the very first thought of separation, is contained this imprint. When I said I stand at the end in case you fail, I meant that I wait eternally within to lift you as you are preparing to change the direction of your "route."

Linear time is merely confusing static. The further you proceed into it, the more confusing it becomes. More need for time is thus established. The imprint of each "life" is determined by each individual's strength of attraction toward the seeming separation. There is nothing really dangerous about this. In the extreme it is merely very transformative toward the end of the cycle. Time can be seen as first an explosion and then an implosion. One could not occur without the other. As time collapses, each individual mind begins to have glimpses of the eternal Christ within. When these glimpses begin to occur, *that* is when I can be most helpful. At the turning point, like a bungie cord beginning to retract, the miracle begins to be experienced more and more. During this undoing of time, each one can more easily access the "akashic records" or "eternal library" as some of you call it. It is possible at certain instants to travel up the "adrenian light thread," temporarily collapsing the cord almost completely and illuminating your mind in this eternal library of past, present and future. As you do this, past and future will also seem more collapsed upon your earthly "return." The world will then appear more luminescent because separation will be less attractive.

Usually when this occurs most of you will not understand it as I am explaining it now. Some of you may reach up to your imprints together because you "signed up" together "before" there was an "after." That is why you seem to meet certain key people while in this illusion. Usually when you reach as far in as this imprint, it will feel as if it were an instant jolt of ecstatic Oneness, along with an unspeakable feeling of renewed purpose. It may feel to you as though suddenly you are perfectly sure that you are on a very safe and right track.

If you are with someone in a truly holy relationship, you may find yourselves together as you meditate or sleep, in a wondrous Place actually joined as literally one being, *not* two in One Being. This is also experienced as a perfect reassurance that you are most certainly on the "right track." The statement, "Heaven is entered two by two," is not meant poetically. This is an essential ingredient for understanding your one necessity.

Each of you can actually meet in the "akashic records" to work certain things out that may not be possible for you to do within the dream. As awareness becomes more attuned to the Christ in each of you, you will each have instants where you are visiting there more often. Together, you will find it always pleasurable and always a powerful experience. You, Saul, have already had such experiences more than once. These will facilitate more depth, trust and understanding in you each time.

Let us go on to your question number five. "We are all together in Heaven Where we never left" is indeed true. Remembrance of this is almost impossible as long as one mind and heart remains left to be forgiven. The tiniest thread of unforgiveness will renew the attraction to guilt. The fear of God results from this and time seems to open its gates once again. "Wondering" is a strong enough attraction to do just this. Watch carefully your thoughts that you do not allow them to lead you where you would not go. Heaven is but a recognition, not a curiosity. Do you understand what I am reminding you of here, Saul?

It is most difficult for each of you to comprehend that you cannot understand anything in sensory terms. The ego is quite inventive in attempting to convince you that you can. Yet it is impossible to explain the pure experience of holiness and total Love. The movie you have all enjoyed called *The Wizard Of Oz* can offer a better testimony for answering the question you are asking. When Dorothy was asked toward the end to click her heals three times and repeat to herself, "There is no place like home," what was she really doing? Her desire was so strong to return to her homeland, she did not care about the how's or why's of getting there. Her interest was simply to get there. Like magic she returned with her mind emptied of any other concern. You need only change the words slightly and hold only the same purity of desire in heart and mind. Say to yourself, "There is no place but Home," and you can be there! But take all of your brothers and sisters with you as you return! (You don't need to click your heels three times as you do so.)

There are many different levels of illusion, Saul, but only One Heaven! What seems to be a limbo or purgatory is only another aspect of illusion. Many of you live your lives in purgatory and limbo, vacillating back and forth between illusion and Reality. Yet there truly is no place to "go" because your Destiny cannot be sought. What is yours can never leave you.

There are many places to "go" after you leave your body, *if* you desire to. You need only count each footstep in your current life to understand this. There is no walking in Heaven because you will all have happily agreed to take off your shoes. Yet as long as you believe you must keep them on, you will find many different places to walk to.

You are in Heaven now, dreaming that you are walking in a different direction. It is not necessary for you to take your brothers' and sisters' bodies with you to return Home. You need only return with them together in your heart and mind. Together in God's Mind is Where the Reality of Christ has forever been. Think you there is another reality elsewhere? All it will take for you to return together is your full forgiveness for that which never was. The many appearances here that you have made have only been to assist one another with the remembrance of What has always been.

You are now given the opportunity to experience Heaven on earth. You each came to grace the world with the grandeur of this recognition and joy. You will not rest until it is achieved. Rejoice, then, for it is achieved now! Time ends in the Gift of your eternal awakening. It is your will to experience this Gift, for this is the only Will God gave you. How easy is salvation, how joyous His Message, how lovely the song His angels bring!

Bodies wear out, but the eternal never dies. This is the power that has been given you, even here on earth. You are now beginning to glimpse this more clearly than ever before in all of your experiences. For one who knows this, what is there to fear of death?

What cannot be accomplished by those who would calm the woes of the world and offer grace and healing to all? What limits you now, holy Son of God? What *could* limit you *now*?

The work you have asked about which you are doing with Saint Germain is far from stalled. There is more to come, but rest is in order at this time. Indeed, this work will go on and it is important. Need I remind you, Saul, that this is a relationship you are encountering. It has an ebb and flow like all relationships. There are times in every relationship where quiet must be taken in order for its greater gifts to be revealed. Time to step aside for other viewpoints, growth and experience with others, to replenish your cup from a different side or angle. A true love affair never dies and will never end. Be not impatient and do not be concerned. All is saved for you and greater gifts in this relationship are to follow.

Let us now proceed to your first and final question — the question about the length of time the masses are taking to respond to truth in the illusion.

This is a very lighthearted question when you consider how long the masses have been crucifying each other in my name! *How long is long?* Still, your question is well in order because the understanding and application of its explanation will no doubt be the key to unlocking the door to peace for all humanity. I would also tell you that we will be speaking about this to many in the near future who will assist in bringing God's Message to all humankind. You have a plan. *We have a Plan.*

Time is growing shorter *because* of the miracles you are each performing with me. There will be a great necessity for many more of you to be truly helpful in assisting one another into the Great Awakening. This idea has been frightening to most of you until recently. Yet enough of you are finally becoming weary enough of the apparent separation that you are beginning to welcome the idea of something different. There is absolutely nothing to be frightened of. All is under His loving control.

Imagine what it is like when you are in revelation. Now imagine what it would be like for millions of people to experience revelation at once! Whatever you can imagine cannot even come close to the effect this will have. It is unimaginable! It is the end of the world, as you know it. But it is far from the end of the world, as some believe it to be. In fact, we're just getting started!

You have great dedication indeed, if you believe twenty years is a long time. I love you Saul! I say this with the Smile of Heaven. Don't be hard on yourself about twenty years! You all have done everything I have asked in His Name. Not only am I well pleased, but so is our Father, Who looks on with Eyes gleaming with compassion, Hands of warmth and open Arms. Indeed, you can relax into what is happily to come!

How many times have I said, "Do not be deceived by appearances," and in how many ways? How many saints before and after me have said the same thing? Who will not be gathered here in His Name for what is to come?

You each have taken on the mission of providing the secure formation of "God's Safety Net" for twenty years. This Safety Net cannot be destroyed. It can only grow. Everything that challenges it will eventually step aside to make way. This is what the faith of God's miracle workers is now doing. It will not stop because of Where the inspiration came from. There will be a time not so far away when no one who walks the earth shall fear death in any form. Together, with our Love, we will overcome the world. The Atonement will come to every mind. What seems far away in time is of no distance at all to God. Keep faith that it is so.

Let us walk now together, putting our faith in eternity instead of time. I have many, many more gifts to share and reveal to all of you. Joel has fully agreed to do his part, just as you and many other of my miracle workers have done recently. Each of you has agreed with me not to waste time. I will keep my part as I know you will keep yours. The occupation of God that you have each accepted will soon refine itself into a harmony with one another that will resonate as bells of Heaven throughout the entirety of God's most holy Creation. Now, as time gives way to eternity in God's Love, we are the Christ *together*.

It is the time now.

His Great Rays shall shine through

And upon the lambs of all the world.

You do understand.

Blessings,

Jesus

QUESTION

Please speak about reincarnation. If we have been here many times before, why? Can we remember other lives?

It is hatred that brings one to return to this earthly realm in a great many cases, but not all. There are a few exceptions when one who has completely forgiven himself and the world returns again to unite all minds in hatred's end.

To properly understand reincarnation we must first recognize that there is only One Mind in Reality. It is only in dreams that it appears as if there are many different bodies. The ego cannot fathom Reality because of its wish to see only separated identities. This fabrication is strictly illusory, even though it is not seen this way. Recognizing this is highly threatening to the ego. The "I" that you identify with is but a thought left unforgiven. The ego believes you have a separate identity. You will experience separation as long as you believe in separation (the world). So you must look within to the Teacher of God for help to go beyond time to the truth of Oneness.

The Holy Spirit is the Great Comforter Who will lead you to eternity. He will remind you of your true Identity in God. It is through forgiveness that this is accomplished. The Holy Spirit calls you to return and waits patiently for your readiness to follow Him.

Reincarnation teaches one valuable lesson: That you are an eternal creation of a loving God. The concept of reincarnation can delay your progress, however, if you insist on looking at it as an escape from the healing that needs to take place *now*. Dwelling on the past can carry an ancient hatred through lifetimes, denying the call for healing.

Understood this way, it is quite unnecessary for you to focus on past lives. The hatred you carried has followed you to *now*. *Now* is the only time when you can do anything to find peace with past or present lives. The many apparent forms of hatred do not matter — one could be a soldier, the other a king's lover, but the difference means nothing. You came here for one reason — to heal this ancient hatred and remember a present joy.

In the apparent physical "reality" where you see yourself, it is impossible to know your Self as one Identity. But there is a Reality that *contains* this Identity. It is only a matter of happily exchanging one, which must bring only fear and depression, for the other, which brings only an awareness of What you are. Do you want the burdens that a focus on past lives offers you? Or would you not prefer the holy instant, where you share holiness and Love with all?

It is nearly impossible to remember the fragments of an earlier human life. We must remember that all Life is happening now and time is entirely illusory. Who would want to remember details of a nightmare gone past? Would not loving one you call enemy now be more productive? Decide against the nothingness of illusions. To love is to forget the past and the future. Your heart's one true desire is only to love. To do so is to remember your Self for eternity.

It should be understood that just because an ancient hatred may have *brought you* here, *this is not the real reason you came*. You came to remember how to *give* Love and *be* Love. You have always *been* Love, even *before you* came. The instant this was forgotten, hatred arose and your earthly mission was born. But you did not have to come here to forgive *just* your *ego*. You came here to forgive your Self as well. In this sense, you ultimately came to forgive *God* in *all*.

You could never forgive yourself alone because your original mission was only to forgive your Self (Christ). How else could you remember to *truly* love and *be* Love? God has only *one* Will, and your Destiny is to accept and extend It.

QUESTION

How can we better hear your Voice, Jesus?

How can you hear my Voice? By remembering It is *our* Voice. In truth no other voice exists, for no other voice *can be shared*. When you ask to hear "my Voice," you are asking to hear the Voice for God. It is the Voice of our one Self. When you ask to better hear "my" Voice, the question is not entirely valid, simply because it implies separation. Ask instead how you may better hear *our* Voice in everyone. It is *your* Voice forever. It came with you, and It loves you as Its own unto eternity. What are you? You *are* the Voice of Love! It is never a question of *how* you can better hear, but *will you* be still and listen!

Still you have asked how you can better hear. I will attempt to help you understand how you can indeed do so.

Your Voice and your Being are nested quietly in the Heart of God's Love. It is centered in perfect peace and eternal serenity. To know your Self as *God* created you, you must relinquish any condition that opposes What you are. To truly hear God you must forgive all that is not God. Your investment in anything relating to the illusory world of time must be released. This is why proper valuing is essential to you. You must first remember What is valuable and then learn to keep it.

This *is* the purpose of your life. Until you learn to cherish and live *for* peace and *only* peace, your life is indeed wasted.

What will help you the most in learning to listen? Practice loving everyone you meet without exception. More importantly, learn the value of gentle solitude. It is where you will find and *keep* that Spark of Love!

Epilogue

Into a world of guilt and suffering, God's miracle workers come to teach a different way. To teach only Love, one must simply live in the peaceful Reality given her by God and offer everyone her awareness that this is so. It matters not where she is or what she does. All that matters is that she has chosen peace over what appearances seem to tell her. Her foundation is secured in God by doing so. Like magic, others will be drawn to her, seeking in her the abundance, joy and perfect safety she has found. She is a rock in a storm, offering shelter from the winds and a chance for stability where only confusion would otherwise be.

Here begins a gathering. Where one has come more will follow until the strength to overcome will easily weather every storm. The world, so long burdened with hatred, guilt and fear, will finally come to its awakening. In a sudden silence the world will recognize its true purpose. The birds will sing aloud while the trees smile and sway to the hum of a different breeze. A change will come like never before. Time will stand still, for holiness has gently found its way.

I am come as a Rock unto the world for each to reach to, hold onto and embrace this different way.

I call on you now to join with me in forgiveness, that in our gathering this storm may finally subside. There are many of you, and you call to be as One. I cannot keep my Home without you, nor you without me. For He Who has called, has called for everyone, so everyone must answer. Can you hear His call within the wind?

We are God's children, the perfect extension of His Divine and everlasting Innocence. It is this message of purity I bring. Take this message and let it become your Home. Live in it together and do not make the world your own. Choose instead the inner peace Where Christ in all of you abides. Share in this peace together, for it is through this and only this that the tears on every cheek will be lifted gently to Heaven. It is our joining I have come to accomplish. I would lead you only to joy. In joy and peace, let us come together in the great celebration of our Christ within now. God bless the world through you, now and forever more!

A loving Jesus Christ

It Begins Here

GLOSSARY

The following is a glossary of a few of the terms used in The Mirror on Still Water. We hope this will help the reader better understand the meanings of some of these terms, as they are used differently than how they might normally be understood.

All words capitalized below represent God (Love Thought System). Where words are not capitalized, they represent the ego (illusory-fearful thought system). While we did not include all the words in this book, we tried to cover those most important for the reader's clarification.

Atonement — Undoing belief in the dream through the Holy Spirit, the only Healer.

Christ — The perfect Son of God. We are all one Self in Christ.

Creation — The extension of God's Love, which is our true Reality.

death — A mistaken belief that Life is over.

ego — A self-made thought system that you could be separate and apart from your Creator.

Eternal — The never-ending Truth of Who and What we are.

God — Our Loving Creator, Who created us as the eternal Spirit of Love (not a body).

Heaven — The Home we have never left, the Knowledge of God.

Holy Spirit — The Voice for God within us.

illusion — A collective dream of separation that makes what we see appear to be real.

judgment — A mistaken thought that anything is separate and apart from God.

Knowledge — The Knowledge of God (Love) devoid of fear.

Love — Love is God; God is Love.

Mind — The Thought of God (Love) creating like Himself.

Miracle — A change of mind from the ego to the God-Mind. Aligning your thoughts with the Thoughts of Jesus and the Holy Spirit.

Peace — Recognition that God has given us total peace and peace is always present in the God-Mind. The absence of fear.

reincarnation — A belief that bodies are real and can experience many "lifetimes."

Resurrection — A total denial of death and the assertion of "Eternal Life."

The Sonship — Our true Identity in God. All of us, with no exceptions.

sickness — An error in belief, having nothing to do with God.

Truth — Recognition of our true Identity, the Perfect Creation of God.

world of form — the illusion, the collective imaginary world we dream is real, the dream of separation from our Creator.

ABOUT THE SCRIBE

Wanderer, counselor, minister, romantic fool, spiritual seeker and often, in my younger years, rebel to the ways of the world. That is how I might quickly sum up my life. Questioning authority and devising alternatives, working alternatives, took a great deal of my early years. Much of this was due to my own inner resistance to the social "norm." I saw insanity, became part of it, yet knew there must be something else, something more purposeful.

I spent most of my life doing different types of counseling work. Between healing my own life of addictions, illnesses and mistakes, I've had plenty of opportunity for trial and error healing methods — humorously, and sometimes unfortunately, taken out on myself and others. My healing continues with less hit and miss than ever before. In questioning all those "authorities," I pushed my way through the crowd to the one Authority I could not supersede. I am truly happy to be on my knees, finally, to open to the peaceful wash of His gracious and loving Spirit through me. He has healed my life and come into this book for you, the reader, wanderer, counselor, minister, romantic fool, spiritual seeker and rebel to the ways of the world.

A little about the "Voice of Christ" for those who may wish to know: In 1974, on my eighteenth birthday, I first "heard" and was told in so many words that I would seek gratification in many forms of the world, i.e. prestigious jobs, family life, drugs and alcohol, money, etc. I was also told that later, when I tired myself of "seeking," I would turn to Love for help and write books and help others. I was left confused, never to hear the Voice again until 1984. I had reached a deep low in my life, had lost a marriage and found alcohol. It was in my recovery that I began again to "hear." This time the Voice would not only not disappear, but actually seemed a bit pesky to me. I realize now that this was only due to my own rebellious "nature," if you will.

Over the years since then, the way in which I "hear" has deepened and changed. My involvement with my second wife led us to work in the field of hospice. We worked together in the beginning of the AIDS crisis. I dare say, between that and the children, this was the most deepening work ever. We had to learn to listen beyond the words to the Love we all share.

What I was hearing from my own "inner Voice" was directly in line with what I was tuning into with others whom I worked with in hospice, some of whom were very close to their transformations from the body into God. I would say this was my clear and integrated confirmation that What I was "hearing," I'd better start listening to. I did for the most part, and this book and the books to follow are the resulting loving dialogues from this very "inner listening." Enjoy receiving them as I have in receiving them for you.

Peace to you,

Joel

Also by Joel Wright

with contributions by Mary Gerard...

The Book ON...
and Jesus Answers

Joel asks in a quiet, still space our questions about the world we experience...

He writes the answers on these pages that reflect the wisdom that Jesus provides. Joel's function is to step out of the way of his own thoughts and perception, to be an unfiltered scribe of this wisdom and guidance from Jesus.

About the Authors

Joel Wright listens within for Jesus' message and scribes what he hears, blessing us with Jesus' voice that is so needed in today's world.

Mary Gerard receives the wisdom of Jesus through asking and listening in the Silence.

Ordering Information:

ISBN: 978-0-9767485-1-9

Pathways of Light 1.800.323.7284
www.pathwaysoflight.org
www.thementorwithin.com
www.amazon.com

ON

BUSINESS
AND POLITICS

God did not create you to ever be lonely.

Yet in the business of the world you are lonely. You need the Holy Spirit to lift you above and beyond its troubles and woes, and to gently remind you that you are not your business.

Nor are you the world, for the world does not really exist except in thinking that is unloving and faulty, and therefore it does not really exist at all.

Business and politics are both illusions of the human condition. But each may be overcome through the will to only share and love. You can each do truly helpful business by learning to be spiritually political.

By learning to truly serve without conditions rather than to merely take, and by remembering that ultimately, the goal of all business and politics is to remember how to express and share love with each other.

The reason there is so much darkness around business and politics is because the focus is so strong on getting and taking. This is an unhelpful form of communication. Yet it can easily be changed to one of sharing and giving once clearly understood that in this way it is helpful to everyone.

Herein lies the answer to your business and political problems: by applying spiritual principles to everyone you work or play with, business and politics can be unifying rather than separating.

The Book ON... and Jesus Answers
© 2009 WLH LLC

Also by Mary Gerard...

The Mentor Within
Let your SELF be See

This series of conversations between the voice of ego and Voice of Self reveals the stark contrast between truth and illusion, clearly demonstrating how befuddled the ego is and how clear the Voice for God is offering release and the truth of Love that sets us free.

Mary asks a vast array of questions on relationships, life purpose, work, how to live in the world, spiritual teachers, and Jesus even drops in for a conversation to share who he is and his experience of being in the world, but not of the world. The Mentor Within doesn't mince words, gives plenty to laugh about and extends the Real Love we seek for outside of ourselves, but can only find Within.

Mary Gerard's questions and comments are in normal typeface
and **The Mentor Within answers in bold typeface.**

Ordering Information:
ISBN: 978-0-9767485-0-2

Pathways of Light 1.800.323.7284
www.pathwaysoflight.org
www.thementorwithin.com
www.amazon.com

Trade Distribution:
New Leaf Distributing Company 1.800.326.2665

Free Will

Why does this all have to be so mysterious?

Let me speak to you of mystery. Jesus' real death was that of surrendering his will to God. He died to his own way and ideas. He pictured another world so powerfully in his mind that he joined with it. Once he surrendered to God, his real free will ensued. We humans do not really have free will how we speak of it. How can we? We are bound to life on this earth. Our only free choice is the choice for God. Free will is will that resides in the Holy Spirit.

You just said "we" humans. What do you mean, "we"?

I am a part of you. I am in your humanness. I am just not invested in your humanness.

How do I get "free" will? The real thing.

Each time you surrender to the Holy Spirit you get free will.

What if I do not surrender to the Holy Spirit?

You get nothing.

What good does "real" free will do for me?

It has the ability to listen and act accordingly. You are listening.

Am I acting accordingly?

Some of the time.

How can I act accordingly more of the time?

It is not about acting accordingly "more of the time."

What is it about then?

It is about being in accordance with the holy scriptures.

What holy scriptures?

The one being written.

I am writing holy scriptures?

You are the holy scriptures. You have been written by God.

So I am to be in accordance with my higher Self, the real me that God has written?

Yes. Then your life becomes a holy scripture. Herein lies "being in accordance with the holy scriptures."

Perhaps you can restate this so I am sure I understand.

Okay. Understand this. God's holy scripture comes to life through you. You are writing holy scripture each time you surrender your will to the Holy Spirit, to God, and let your life unfold accordingly. Hence, you will be living in accordance with the scriptures. That is what Jesus did. He surrendered and let His life unfold, and as he did so, his life became the holy scriptures. This is what makes the holy scriptures alive today. You are living, alive holy scripture.

This is not going to fly well with a lot of people. It sounds potentially blasphemous.

Blasphemy is claiming that God is dead by forging His work in our lives.

What do you mean, "forging His work in our lives"?

We sign our name to His work. We are God's work. You are not your own work of art. You are not your own creator. *God writes you.*

I imagine earthly scholars tearing this apart.

They cannot tear apart that which God has created. They can only tear apart that which they have made.

I feel like I am having a live experience of the truth instead of just reading about it, studying it, and philosophizing. God is coming to life for me.

Each one of us is potentially walking holy scripture.

*   *   *

Also by Mary Gerard...

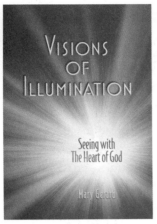

Visions of Illumination

Seeing With The Heart of God

by Mary Gerard

When I listen to my true Self, hear the Self in another, or read the words of this Voice of freedom, Holy Spirit Within, I am inspired—Inspired in the greatest sense of the word. It rings a desire to serve, a desire to do my part, and a realization that healing the brokenness, lonlienss, and separation in the world, which is catastrophic. The thought of separation from Love is the greatest catastrophe we will ever experience.

But it is not without hope, because we are not without God. God enters the world through us when we are willing to be instruments of the Sound of One.

About the Author

Mary is willing to share her experiences of cultivating a relationship with her Inspiring Self Mind, Inspiring to Serve Love. Everything changes as we are moved from the trappings of the mind floundering in darkness to the true freedom of the mind illuminated by the Light. This relationship is the springboard to experiencing the constant direction and eternal love of our Inspiring Self in every aspect of our lives.

Our own experience of this Love is essential because then we know It is real. When we pause to Love's presence, we see Its effect on our perceptions, thoughts, choices and actions. This changes everything. This is the change we seek, but cannot find. It is the changelessness of Eternal Love. It is within.

An excerpt from

Visions of Illumination

Seeing with The Heart of God

A Silent Sound is traveling through the universe beyond the speed of Light—a Silent light on one path through the center of all hearts and the axis of all minds. It penetrates the body of all those open to its Silence. No matter how many years pass or come and go or are projected into the future, this Silent Light has no known beginning for it began of its Own Accord, before we all knew of Beginnings. It has no end. We each find our Life in its Light. All of us.

The promises of this Light bring hope into a world of despair and loneliness, to those who want it. Sooner or later everyone will want it as they realize it is all they want—Nothing would bring greater happiness to this Light. Around the corners of darkness, shadows of the past, is Illumination standing prominently in Vision. We fling ourselves into it or run around it.

A woman sees It—she runs into it for her absolute final destination, craving its security and safety so deeply. It is Eternal Love. Not how she imagined, a warm burning light to look upon and keep her warm, but a holy grail, a host to God. And she receives Eternal Love—total rest in Total Stillness. Now amidst the Light, the form of the flesh body of the illusion falls away and is replaced with light to be of true service. A light within the Light is present to welcome all those who have yet to come. Her job is essential, for in her welcoming the others fleeing into Illumination, her illumination is complete. She moves toward Home and takes her place. No one goes Home alone. We enter Illumination through the Light in one another. Illumination holds the Light for our work of forgiveness.

Though forgiveness is an illusion, it points toward Reality, Illumination, otherwise it is not forgiveness. This is possible because Reality created Holy Spirit and gave it awareness of this one illusion to help us out of the illusion and return us to Reality. The whole universe becomes meek in the presence of Illumination. Pictures of "reality" now seen as the illusion they are, fade away in their crumbled frames and torn edges and Spirit reveals Reality.

Now, I see myself, oddly enough, as an old man with flowing white hair, glowing skin, all in white, celebrating, "What a glorious day." A smile across my face and arms spread wide open. I walk in the world again on the same familiar street, anew—a new being of light. A quiet whispering so Silent I cannot help not hear, "Welcome Home, Welcome Home."

So, I didn't die after all. Here I am. Who I thought I was simply fell away in the Illumination of forgiveness.

Visions of Illumination – Mary Gerard
Ordering Information:
    ISBN: 978-0-9767485-2-6
    Pathways of Light 1.800.323.7284
       www.pathwaysoflight.org
       www.thementorwithin.com
       www.amazon.com

by Barbara Hoff Varley and Robert Varley...

The Peace of God is my One Goal

Living the Teachings of A Course In Miracles

A book about the experiences and commitment of Barbara and Robert Varley to live the teachings of *A Course In Miracles* through the awareness of Holy Spirit.

Over six years of daily study andpractice in following Holy Spirit's guidance led them to many startling and unusal adventures.

In its fifth printing, *The Peace of God is my One Goal* continues to inspire and motivate its readers to live the teachings of the Course.

About the Authors

Barbara, a woman of courage and dedication, lived her life on the edge of inner discovery. When faced with the prospect of physical death from cancer, Barbara lived her ideals in her choices of treatment. She acted from a sense of inner guidance and trust that "all things, events and circumstances are helpful." ACIM

Barbara inspired many people to step out and walk their paths of truth. Through this book she continues this mission, this gift to all her brothers and sisters. In March, 1986, Barbara laid her body aside. Her life continues in us all.

After Barbara's passing, a year of reflection led Robert to begin again his travels and speaking of the Peace of God. After a year of solo travel, Robert joined in marriage to a long time friend, Chaka Ken. Together they continue their lifestyle as Gypsies for God, presenting seminars, workshops and retreats offering a unique and powerful way of living.